WATER AND WASTE WATER
ISSUES AND MANAGEMENT

ENV BOOKS SERIES

WATER AND WASTE WATER

ISSUES AND MANAGEMENT

Editor

Dr. Pawan Kumar 'Bharti'

Society for Environment, Health Awareness of Nutrition & Toxicology (SEHAT)
B-225/5D, Top Floor, Subhash Gali, Road No. 7, Block B
Ashok Nagar, Shahdara, Delhi - 110 093
(India)

DPH

DISCOVERY PUBLISHING HOUSE PVT. LTD.
INDIA

Published by:
Namit Wasan

DISCOVERY PUBLISHING HOUSE PVT. LTD.
4383/4B, Ansari Road, Darya Ganj
New Delhi-110 002 (India)
Phone : +91-11-23279245; 23253475; 43596065
E-mail : discoverybooksindia@gmail.com
discoverypublishinghouse@gmail.com
namitwasan9@gmail.com
web : www.discoverypublishinggroup.com

***First Edition:* 2019**

ISBN: 978-93-88854-15-3

Water and Waste Water: *Issues and Management*

Printed at:
Infinity Imaging Systems
Delhi

Preface

Water is a valuable resource that is critical for the health, vitality, and long-term sustainability of all natural ecosystems. For humans, water plays an essential role in food and energy production, transportation, and recreation. Worldwide, however, water resources are at a risk. Unsustainable population growth, land-use changes, pollution, and global climate change all threaten the distribution, quantity, and quality of the water on which all life depends.

Water covers 71% of the Earth's surface, mostly in seas and oceans. Small portions of water occur as groundwater (1.7%), in the glaciers and the ice caps of Antarctica and Greenland, and in the air as vapor, clouds (formed of ice and liquid water suspended in air), and precipitation (0.001%). Water plays an important role in the world economy. Large quantities of water, ice, and steam are used for cooling and heating, in industry and homes. Water is an excellent solvent for a wide variety of chemical substances; as such it is widely used in industrial processes, and in cooking and washing.

Wastewater (or waste water) is any water that has been affected by human use. Wastewater is "used water from any combination of domestic, industrial, commercial or agricultural activities, surface runoff or stormwater, and any sewer inflow or sewer infiltration". Therefore, wastewater is a byproduct of domestic, industrial, commercial or agricultural activities. The characteristics of wastewater vary depending on the source. Types of wastewater include: domestic wastewater from households, municipal wastewater from communities (also called sewage) or industrial wastewater from industrial activities. Wastewater can contain physical, chemical and biological pollutants.

The present book updates the subject content of water quality monitoring, water management, lake water assessment, wastewater management, toxic pollutants, tank based irrigation system, nanocomposite for leachate degradation and bioremediation technology for wastewater treatment.

Thanks are due to publisher and contributors from various institutions and universities.

The book will be helpful for the researchers, academia working in the field of water quality monitoring, water management, lake water assessment, wastewater management, toxic pollutants, tank based irrigation system, nanocomposite for leachate degradation and bioremediation for wastewater treatment.

–Editors

(envbooks@gmail.com)

Contents

Pages: 1-3

Water and Waste Water: ***Issues and Management***
Edited by: **Dr. Pawan Kumar 'Bharti'**
ISBN: 978-93-88854-15-3
Edition: **2019**
Published by: **Discovery Publishing House Pvt. Ltd., New Delhi (India)**

1

Introduction

Water occurs as a liquid on the surface of Earth under normal conditions, which makes it invaluable for transportation, for recreation, and as a habitat for a myriad of plants and animals. The fact that water is readily changed to a vapour allows it to be transported through the atmosphere from the oceans to inland areas where it condenses and, as rain, nourishes plant and animal life.

Water is a valuable resource that is critical for the health, vitality, and long-term sustainability of all natural ecosystems. For humans, water plays an essential role in food and energy production, transportation, and recreation. Worldwide, however, water resources are at a risk. Unsustainable population growth, land-use changes, pollution, and global climate change all threaten the distribution, quantity, and quality of the water on which all life depends. Protecting and preserving our water resources requires that we take a "big picture" approach that addresses where water comes from, where it goes, how it travels, how it is used by living things, what's in it, and how to remediate problems and develop policies to protect water.

The interdisciplinary study in Water Science & Policy educates people to address the complex challenges that we face today; to develop solutions that are socially acceptable, economically viable, and environmentally sustainable; and to be true stewards of our environment.

The water on the surface of Earth is found mainly in its oceans (97.25 percent) and polar ice caps and glaciers (2.05 percent), with the balance in freshwater lakes, rivers, and groundwater. As Earth's population grows and the demand for fresh water increases, water purification and recycling become increasingly important. Interestingly, the purity requirements of water for industrial use often exceed those for human consumption. For example, the water used in high-pressure boilers must be at least 99.999998 percent pure. Because seawater contains large quantities of dissolved salts, it must be desalinated for most uses, including human consumption.

Water is the transparent, tasteless, odorless, and nearly colorless chemical substance that is the main constituent of Earth's streams, lakes, and oceans, and the fluids of most living organisms, and that is vital for all known forms of life, even though it provides no calories or organic nutrients. Its chemical formula is H2O, meaning that each of its molecules contains one oxygen and two hydrogen atoms connected by covalent bonds. Water is the name of the liquid state of H2O at standard ambient temperature and pressure. It forms precipitation in the form of rain and aerosols in the form of fog. Clouds are formed from suspended droplets of water and ice, its solid state. When finely divided, crystalline ice may precipitate in the form of snow. The gaseous state of water is steam or water vapor. Water moves continually through the water cycle of evaporation, transpiration (evapo-transpiration), condensation, precipitation, and runoff, usually reaching the sea.

Water covers 71% of the Earth's surface, mostly in seas and oceans. Small portions of water occur as groundwater (1.7%), in the glaciers and the ice caps of Antarctica and Greenland (1.7%), and in the air as vapor, clouds (formed of ice and liquid water suspended in air), and precipitation (0.001%). Water plays an important role in the world economy. Approximately 70% of the freshwater used by humans goes to agriculture. Fishing in salt and fresh water bodies is a major source of food for many parts of the world. Much of long-distance trade of commodities (such as oil and natural gas) and manufactured products is transported by boats through seas, rivers, lakes, and canals. Large quantities of water, ice, and steam are used for cooling and heating, in industry and homes. Water is an excellent solvent for a wide variety of chemical substances; as such it is widely used in industrial processes, and in cooking and washing. Water is also central to many sports and other forms of entertainment, such as swimming, pleasure boating, boat racing, surfing, sport fishing, and diving.

The water cycle (known scientifically as the hydrologic cycle) refers to the continuous exchange of water within the hydrosphere, between the atmosphere, soil water, surface water, groundwater, and plants.

Wastewater (or waste water) is any water that has been affected by human use. Wastewater is "used water from any combination of domestic, industrial, commercial or agricultural activities, surface runoff or stormwater, and any sewer inflow or sewer infiltration". Therefore, wastewater is a byproduct of domestic, industrial, commercial or agricultural activities. The characteristics of wastewater vary depending on the source. Types of wastewater include: domestic wastewater from households, municipal wastewater from communities (also called sewage) or industrial wastewater from industrial activities. Wastewater can contain physical, chemical and biological pollutants.

Households may produce wastewater from flush toilets, sinks, dishwashers, washing machines, bath tubs, and showers. Households that use dry toilets produce less wastewater than those that use flush toilets.

Wastewater may be conveyed in a sanitary sewer which conveys only sewage. Alternatively, it can be transported in a combined sewer which includes stormwater runoff and industrial wastewater. After treatment at a wastewater treatment plant, the treated wastewater (also called effluent) is discharged to a receiving water body. The terms "wastewater reuse" or "water reclamation" apply if the treated waste is used for another purpose. Wastewater that is discharged to the environment without suitable treatment causes water pollution.

In developing countries and in rural areas with low population densities, wastewater is often treated by various on-site sanitation systems and not conveyed in sewers. These systems include septic tanks connected to drain fields, on-site sewage systems, vermifilter systems and many more.

At a global level, around 80% of wastewater produced is discharged into the environment untreated, causing widespread water pollution.

There are numerous processes that can be used to clean up wastewaters depending on the type and extent of contamination. Wastewater can be treated in wastewater treatment plants which include physical, chemical and biological treatment processes. Municipal wastewater is treated in sewage treatment plants (which may also be referred to as wastewater treatment plants). Agricultural wastewater may be treated in agricultural wastewater treatment processes, whereas industrial wastewater is treated in industrial wastewater treatment processes.

For municipal wastewater the use of septic tanks and other On-Site Sewage Facilities (OSSF) is widespread in some rural areas, for example serving up to 20 percent of the homes in the U.S.

One type of aerobic treatment system is the activated sludge process, based on the maintenance and recirculation of a complex biomass composed of micro-organisms able to absorb and adsorb the organic matter carried in the wastewater. Anaerobic wastewater treatment processes (UASB, EGSB) are also widely applied in the treatment of industrial wastewaters and biological sludge. Some wastewater may be highly treated and reused as reclaimed water. Constructed wetlands are also being used in wastewater treatment.

REFERENCES

http://www1.udel.edu/watersciencepolicy/
https://en.wikipedia.org/wiki/Water
https://www.britannica.com/science/water
https://en.wikipedia.org/wiki/Wastewater

Pages: 4-18

Water and Waste Water: ***Issues and Management***
Edited by: **Dr. Pawan Kumar 'Bharti'**
ISBN: 978-93-88854-15-3
Edition: **2019**
Published by: **Discovery Publishing House Pvt. Ltd., New Delhi (India)**

2

Impact of Toxic Pollutants on Aquatic Fauna and Flora of Yamuna River and its Implication on Human Health

Pawan Kumar 'Bharti'

ABSTRACT

The aquatic environment of a river is continuously being contaminated with toxic chemicals having heavy metals and pesticides. The use of pesticides in agriculture may lead to contamination of surface and ground waters by drift, runoff, drainage and leaching.

Heavy metals pollution in aquatic environment has become a worldwide problem during past few decades. This fact is mainly attributed to their persistent stability and toxic effect to aquatic as well as terrestrial creatures. Heavy metal concentrations in aquatic ecosystems are usually monitored by measuring their concentrations in water and biota.

Identifying indicators which can be used to diagnose causal agents of adverse change in ecological systems is a major challenge in environmental risk assessment. Traditionally, biomonitoring of freshwaters has been based on measures of community structure, focusing on assemblages of benthic macroinvertebrates and calculating biotic indices. Although such diagnostic measures have been described for communities impacted by organic pollution, acidification, flow modification or habitat degradation, there are no reliable indicators of impairment caused by contaminants.

Yamuna river is lifeline for the entire Delhi state and its ecosystem can influence the health of residents of Delhi. Increasing pollution in Yamuna can cause many effects on aquatic and terrestrial biota of the region. Water samples will be collected from Yamuna river for physico-chemical

Shriram Institute for Industrial Research, 19, University Road, Delhi - 110007 (India)

parameters as well as heavy metals and pesticide content. Major aquatic faunal species (Fish) and flora (algae) of the river will be captured to execute the toxicological studies. A control site will be selected for comparative evaluation of pollutants in Yamuna river.

Keywords: Aquatic biodiversity, Yamuna river, Flora and fauna, Aquatic Toxicology, Bioassay, Freshwater ecosystem

INTRODUCTION

Due to increasing industrialization, urbanization, agricultural activities and other developmental activities, most of our water bodies such as ponds, lakes, rivers and estuaries have been polluted extensively. Rivers are vital and vulnerable freshwater systems that are critical for the sustenance of all life. However, the declining quality of the water in these systems threatens their sustainability and is therefore a cause for concern. Rivers are waterways of strategic importance across the world, providing main water resources for domestic, industrial, and agricultural purposes. The maintenance of healthy aquatic ecosystem is depended on the physico-chemical properties and biological diversity. A regular monitoring of water bodies with required number of parameters with reference to the quality of water not only prevents the outbreak of diseases and occurrence of hazards but checks the water from further deterioration.

Due to pressure on land, water and bioresources, there is continuous impact of various types of human activities on our environment in different forms. One of the major impacts of human activities that have a strong bearing on the environment is the use of pesticides in agriculture. During monsoon as well as runoff, flooding etc.. Soil is washed out towards the aquatic environment and the pesticides used in agriculture end up in the water and also in sediments thereby affecting the biota. Pesticides stay in the environment very long since they are mostly non-biodegradable.

It is well known that the chemical pollutants present in water may induce severe ecological consequences, generating reorganizations of the biocenosis, changing it and consequently affecting the aquatic ecosystem integrity. The pollution of rivers, streams and larger water bodies like lakes with chemical contamination in the form of industrial effluents and pesticides has become one of the most critical environmental problems of the century. There is growing concern worldwide over the indiscriminate use of such chemicals resulting in environmental pollution and toxicity risks to aquatic organisms.

The aquatic environment of a river is continuously being contaminated with toxic chemicals having heavy metals and pesticides. The use of pesticides in agriculture may lead to contamination of surface and ground waters by drift, runoff, drainage and leaching. Pesticides are one of the major xenobiotic substances that have been used in India for longer period for management of pests in agricultural fields. Most of the insecticides are so hydrophobic that they can easily be adsorbed by soil particles and can migrate to water bodies through the run off causing severe aquatic pollution. Consequently, these xenobiotic molecules are found in water bodies that have the greatest impact on the environmental quality. They become accumulated in aquatic organisms and can enter the food chain.

In the present fast developing world, man has synthesized a number of chemicals and then tested their effects in agriculture. In spite of knowing the side effects, due to lack of necessary facilities for effective collection, treatment and disposal of effluents in developing country like India, they are released directly either into water bodies or are disposed off on land. This causes gross pollution of aquatic bodies, resulting in biomagnifications of pollutants. Pesticide toxicity in aquatic environment depends on the species, water quality and the formulation ingredients. Various chemicals, which have been used as pesticides, are grouped as organochlorines, organophosphorus compounds, carbamates, organo-thiocynates, *etc.*

Chlorinated hydrocarbons are perhaps the most toxic to fish. Many of them are stable compounds and not easy to metabolize or excrete. Some also remain stored in fish tissues. Organophosphates are generally less toxic to fish but adversely affect other aquatic biota.

Heavy metals pollution in aquatic environment has become a worldwide problem during past few decades. This fact is mainly attributed to their persistent stability and toxic effect to aquatic as well as terrestrial creatures. Among environmental pollutants, metals are of particular concern, due to their potential toxic effect and ability to bioaccumulate in aquatic ecosystems. Heavy metal concentrations in aquatic ecosystems are usually monitored by measuring their concentrations in water, sediments and biota.

Algae can cause toxicity to aquatic (and terrestrial) animals because of the accumulation of pollutants inside algal cells. In consequence, animals may be directly exposed to pollutants by absorbing pollutants from water or ingesting algal cells via feeding activity. Because pollutants can be bioaccumulated, biotransferred and biomagnified through food chains and food webs, aquatic and terrestrial animals (e.g., carnivorous fishes, dolphins, seals, birds, and humans) may also be indirectly exposed when they consume algae or other animals containing pollutants.

In India, aquatic toxicology has gained an outstanding importance, due to total dependence of human beings on the quality of the natural resources. Therefore environmental scientists are giving high priority to investigate the causes of aquatic pollution, evaluate its impact on aquatic ecosystems and also to study the self purifying processes of the freshwater resources.

Yamuna River at Delhi

The river Yamuna is a major Himalayan river originating from Yamunotri glacier (20,000 ft above sea level) descending from Mount Kalindi and forming into a regular river from Yamunotri onwards. It is the largest tributary of the Ganga, one of the three main rivers originating from the Himalayas. During its 1,376 km journey from Yamunotri to its confluence with the river Ganga in the gangetic plains at Allahabad, it sustains millions of people. The river can be divided into five segments based largely on geographical and quality of water parameters.

Table 2.1: The length and course of the river Yamuna

Segment	Course Covered	Length in km
Himalayan Segment	Yamunotri – Tajewala	172
Upper segment	Tajewala – Wazirabad	224
Delhi Segment	Wazirabad – Okhla	22
Eutriphicated Segment	Okhla to Chambal Confluence	490
Diluted Segment	Chambal Confluence to Ganga Confluence	468
Total		**1,376**

The main sources of raw water in Delhi are the Yamuna (surface water and Western Yamuna Canal WYC), the Ganga (Upper Ganga Canal), Bhakara-Beas Storage, and ground water through tube wells and ranney wells. The estimated water availability of NCT (National Capital Territory) of Delhi from surface water sources, viz. the Yamuna, the Ganga and the WYC is about 1150.2 million cubic metre (mcm). The river Yamuna contributes 724 mcm, a substantial part of the surface water requirements of Delhi.

Table 2.2: Production Capacity of DJB based on Yamuna river (DJB, 2007)

Water Treatment Plant	Source	Capacity in MGD	Capacity in MLD
Wazirabad	Yamuna	120	543.60
Hyderpur II	Yamuna (WYC)	100	453.00
Chandrawal	Yamuna	90	407.70

In the case of the river Yamuna three main sources of pollution are untreated domestic wastewater; untreated industrial effluents and agricultural run offs. Undetected and untreated pesticide residues leave a toxic mark all across the river.

Untreated domestic wastewater falling into the river causes bacterial contamination. Other sources of bacterial contamination are open defecation near banks, dead body dumping and cattle washing. Untreated industrial effluents can be toxic and contain harmful heavy metals such as cadmium, aluminium and mercury. Agricultural run-off to river carries chemical fertilizers and deadly pesticides including DDT, hexa chloro-hydrocarbons, and cyclodiene.

The Delhi stretch of Yamuna is largely defined as its 22 km course from Wazirabad to Okhla barrages. The health of Yamuna in Delhi is aptly summaried by (CSE 2007): "Yamuna in Delhi is barely 2 per cent of its entire length but according to CPCB it contributes over 70 per cent of total pollution load. It means that Delhi plays a very significant role to pollute the river Yamuna. In 2001-02, CPCB reported that the Delhi segment (of the Yamuna) was the most polluted.

DETAILED LITERATURE SURVEY

International Status

River water quality from various sources has been studied all over world. Many workers explain and share their findings through various publications.

McKim (1977) made a study for the evaluation of tests with early life stages of fish for predicting long-term toxicity. Ewell *et al.*, (1986) carried out a simultaneous evaluation of the acute effects of various chemicals on seven species in aquatic ecosystem. Williams *et al.*, (1986) made some studies on the acute toxicity of pollutants to freshwater macroinvertebrates with special reference to Ammonia. Schmitt and Finger (1987) highlighted the effects of sample preparation on measured concentrations of eight elements in edible tissues of fish from streams contaminated by lead mining. Nriagu and Pacyna (1988) estimated and carried out a quantitative assessment of worldwide contamination of air, water and soils by trace metals. Clarkson (1988) explained the biological monitoring of toxic metals in various components of aquatic and terrestrial environment. Coogan *et al.*, (1989) evaluated the toxicity and carcinogenicity of various nickel compounds against few target biological agents. De Flora *et al.*, (1993) emphasized on multiple genotoxicity biomarkers in fish exposed in situ to polluted river water. Hendriks *et al.*, (1998) pointed out the accumulation of metals, polycyclic (halogenated) aromatic hydrocarbons and biocides in zebra mussel and eel from the Rhine and Meuse River. Cope *et al.*, (1999) carried out a biological assessment of mercury, cadmium, polychlorinated biphenyls and pesticides in the Upper Mississippi River with zebra mussels (Dreissena polymorpha).

Birge *et al.*, (2000) studied on comparative toxicology and risk assessment of amphibians in an aquatic ecosystem. Barata and Baird (2000) explained the determining the ecotoxicological mode of action of toxicants from measurements on individuals and showed the results from short duration chronic tests with *Daphnia magna* Straus. Cataldo *et al.*, (2001) carried out environmental toxicity assessment in the Parana river delta

(Argentina) and made simultaneous evaluation of selected pollutants and mortality rates of Corbicula Fluminea (Bivalvia) early juveniles. Mc William and Baird (2002) highlighted the application of post-exposure feeding depression bioassays with *Daphnia magna* for assessment of toxic effluents in rivers. Alonso and Camargo (2003) presented findings on short-term toxicity of ammonia, nitrite, and nitrate to the aquatic snail Potamopyrgus antipodarum (Hydrobiidae, Mollusca). Alonso and Camargo (2004) also explained the toxic effects of unionized ammonia on survival and feeding activity of the freshwater amphipod Eulimnogammarus toletanus (Gammaridae, Crustacea). Koukal *et al.*, (2004) made an assessment of water quality and toxicity of polluted rivers Fez and Sebou in the region of Fez (Morocco). Barata *et al.*, (2004): highlighted the role of â-esterases in assessing toxicity of organophosphorous (chlorpyrifos, malathion) and carbamate (carbofuran) pesticides to *Daphnia magna*.

Liess and Von der Ohe (2005) concluded the analyzing effects of pesticides on invertebrate communities in streams. Camargo and Alonso (2006) made a global assessment on some ecological and toxicological effects of inorganic nitrogen pollution in aquatic ecosystems. Yacoub (2007) studied on some heavy metals accumulated in some organs of three River Nile fishes from Cairo and Kalubia governorates. Ogunlaja and Ogunlaja (2007) carried out a physico-chemical analysis of water sources in Ubeji community and their histological impact on organs of albino mice. Barata *et al.*, (2007) pointed out a combined use of biomarkers and in situ bioassays in *Daphnia magna* to monitor environmental hazards of pesticides in the field. Duong *et al.*, (2008) highlighted the seasonal effects of cadmium accumulation in periphytic diatom communities of freshwater biofilms. Damasio *et al.*, (2008) explained the combined use of *Daphnia magna* in situ bioassays, biomarkers and biological indices to diagnose and identify environmental pressures on invertebrate communities in two Mediterranean urbanized and industrialized rivers in NE Spain. Palma *et al.* (2008) demonstrated the acute toxicity of Atrazine, Endosulfan Sulphate and Chlorpyrifos to Vibrio fischeri, Thamnocephalus platyurus and Daphnia magna, relative to their concentrations in surface waters from the Alentejo region of Portugal. El-Naggar *et al.*, (2009) find out the bioaccumulation of some heavy metals and Histopathological alterations in Liver of Oreochromis niloticus in relation to water quality at different localities along the River Nile, Egypt. Ashauer *et al.* (2011) find out the environmental risk assessment of fluctuating diazinon concentrations in an urban and agricultural catchment using Toxicokinetic-Toxicodynamic modeling.Rimet (2012) highlighted the recent views on river pollution and the role of diatoms to assess the pollution level. Lasheen *et al.*, (2012) utilized the fish as bio-indicators in aquatic environmental pollution assessment and explained in a case study of Abu-Rawash area in Egypt. Nyman *et al.* (2013) declared that the insecticide Imidacloprid causes mortality of the freshwater amphipod gammarus pulex by interfering with feeding behavior. Ashauer *et al.* (2013) explained a method to predict and understand fish survival under dynamic chemical stress using standard ecotoxicity data.

National

Several research studies had been carried out at River Yamuna between 1947-1976 by various organizations. However, these studies were irregular, unsystematic and limited in the scope.

CPCB (2006), CPCB (2009) and CSE (2009) carried out a large scale monitoring work related to Yamuna river and demonstrated main aspects of water quality, i.e. physico-chemical parameters, bacteriological parameters, etc.

The Central Pollution Control Board (CPCB) has established National Water Quality Monitoring Network comprising 1429 monitoring stations in 27 states and 6 in Union Territories on various water bodies across the country. The monitoring is undertaken on monthly or quarterly basis in surface waters and on half yearly basis in case of ground water. The monitoring network covers 293 Rivers, 94 Lakes, 9 Tanks, 41 Ponds, 8 Creeks, 23 Canals, 18 Drains and 411 Wells. A few new monitoring stations were also added during the year 2008 – 2009. Among the 1429 stations 810 are on rivers, 102 on lakes, 18 on drains, 23 on canals, 9 on tank, 15 on creeks/ seawater, 41 on pond, while 411 are groundwater stations (CPCB, 2009).

The entire stretch of river Yamuna (1376 km) is being regularly monitored by Central Pollution Control Board on yearly frequency at 20 locations, quarterly frequency at three locations, while on monthly frequency at other locations. The water quality trend of the river during the last five years (2004-2008) in terms of Dissolved Oxygen (DO) Bio chemical Oxygen demand (BOD), Total Coliform (TC) and Faecal Coliform (FC) was presented (CPCB, 2009).

Many other researchers have made studies on toxicological effects of heavy metals and different pesticides on aquatic ecosystem. Few of them have observed the quantity of various pollutants in the water of river Yamuna. Ajmal *et al.* (1985) pointed out the distribution of heavy metals in plants and fish of Yamuna river. Saikia *et al.* (1988) observed heavy metals in water of upper Ganga. Jha *et al.* (1990) find out some heavy metals in water of the Yamuna river. Gupta and Chandra (1994) highlighted the lead accumulation and its toxicity in aquatic plants Vallisneria spirallis (L.) and Hydrilla verticillata (F.). Only quantification of selected heavy metals was conducted in the study. Hans *et al.* (1999) emphasized on agricultural produce in the dry bed of the River Ganga in Kanpur, India and explained a new source of pesticide contamination in human diets. Singh (2001) observed heavy metal pollution in freshly deposited sediments of the

Yamuna river and presented a case study from Delhi and Agra urban centres. Rashed (2001) stated the monitoring of environmental heavy metals in fish from a lake.

Vinodhini and Narayanan (2008) pointed out the bioaccumulation of heavy metals in organs of fresh water fish *Cyprinus carpio* (Common carp). Aktar *et al.* (2010) performed an assessment and occurrence of various heavy metals in surface water of Ganga river around Kolkata and highlighted a study for toxicity and ecological impact. Venkatesharaju *et al.* (2010) studied on physico-chemical and bacteriological investigation on the river Cauvery of Kollegal stretch in Karnataka. Lokhande *et al.* (2011) performed a toxicity study of heavy metals pollutants in waste water effluent samples collected from Taloja industrial estate of Mumbai, India. Sen *et al.* (2011) conducted a study for determination of heavy metals in Fish species of the river Yamuna (Delhi) by Inductively Coupled Plasma-Optical Emission Spectroscopy. The fish samples Rahu (Labeo rohita), Tilapia (Tilapia zilli) and Catfish (Chrysichthys nigrodigatatus) were collected from Yamuna River in Delhi. In this study, Inductively Coupled Plasma-Optical Emission Spectroscopy (ICP-OES) technique was used for determination of Al (Aluminum), B (Boron), Ba (Barium), Cd (Cadmium), Co (Cobalt), Cr (Chromium), Cu (Copper), Fe (Iron), K (Potassium), Mg (Magnesium), Mn (Manganese), Na (Sodium), Ni (Nickel), Pb (Lead), Sb (Antimony), Sn (Tin), Si (Silicon), P (Phosphorus) and Zn (Zinc) in fish tissues. The concentrations of Ca, K, Mg, Na and P are too high as compared with other metals as these metals were not in the maximum permissible level set by World Health Organization.

Christopher *et al.* (2012) emphasized on water quality status of river Yamuna in Delhi with reference to presence of heavy metals. Fatima and Usmani (2013) made a study for toxicity and ecological impacts of heavy metals on fish species and emphasized on histopathology and bioaccumulation of heavy metals (Cr, Ni and Pb) in fish (*Channa striatus* and *Heteropneustes fossilis*) tissue. The bioaccumulation of these metals was estimated in different body parts (Liver, Kidney, Gill & Muscle). It was found that Cr accumulated the most in these organs (gill being most influenced) in both species. Heavy damage was observed in Liver and kidney of both species.

OBJECTIVES:

- To assess the physico-chemical characteristics of water quality of Yamuna river at selected sites
- To detect the level of heavy metals and pesticides in Yamuna water at selected sites
- To detect the level of heavy metals and pesticides in the body tissues of aquatic biota

- To compare the experimental site data with control site data
- To draw influences, based on findings, for possible implications on human health residing in Delhi region
- To make a strategy to conserve the Yamuna ecosystem on the basis of findings

DETAILED METHODOLOGY

Toxicity bioassay constitutes one of the most commonly used biological study methods in the aquatic environmental studies in the world. Bioassay is a "tests" in which the quantity or strength of pollutant material is determined by the reaction of living organism to it. In other words, bioassay tests is the "estimation of the amount of biologically active substances by the levels of their effects on the test organisms". The laboratory determination of toxicity may be divided into short-term acute toxicity tests and long-term chronic toxicity tests.

Since last three decades, acute toxicity bioassays in general are useful in measuring the toxicity of different pollutants to aquatic organisms. Since then, many workers have directed the studies towards the toxicity evaluation. Chronic toxicity tests are an important tool to assess the effect of pollutants on physiology, biochemistry, growth, reproduction and behaviour of animals.

The effect of pesticides on the aquatic organism depends on physico-chemical parameters of water such as salinity, temperature, dissolved oxygen, pH and hardness. Accumulation of chemicals pollutants is known to adversely affect the liver, kidney, muscles and other tissues of the fish, which can be visualized through histopathology. Fish muscle is commonly analyzed to determine contaminant concentrations and to assess the health risks because it is the main part consumed by humans. Fish can be considered as one of the most significant indicators in freshwater systems for the impact of metal pollution.

The sampling site lies in Delhi in north India, at an altitude of 216 m above sea level. The downstream received water from 17 major drains of Delhi and also from western Yamuna canal and upper Ganga canal via Najafgarh drain and Hindon cut canal. Yamuna river has a polluted stretch of about 22 Km from Wazirabad to Okhla within City. Najafgarh Drain is the major polluting drain of Yamuna River in Delhi contributing about 40.3% of total pollution to river followed by Shahdara drain. The categories of industries discharging wastewater into Yamuna river includes pulp and paper, sugar, distilleries, textiles, leather, chemical, pharmaceuticals, oil refineries, thermal power plants, food processing industries, etc. Yamuna in Delhi is barely 2 per cent of its entire length but according to CPCB it contributes over 70 per cent of total pollution load (CSE, 2007; Jain, 2009).

River water samples were collected using acid washed, distilled water rinsed Polyethylene bottles. Water samples will be collected from Yamuna river for physico-chemical parameters as well as heavy metals and pesticide content. Few major aquatic faunal species and flora of the river will be captured to execute the toxicological studies. Morphological and histopathological studies will be carried out to know the impact of toxic pollutants on aquatic biota. A control site will be selected for comparative evaluation of pollutants in Yamuna river.

Water sampling and analysis will be carried out as per standard methods described in APHA (2012) and IS: 3025 (various parts). Heavy metals will be analysed using AAS/ICP-OES. Pesticide content will be analyzed using GC/HPLC.

Toxicological studies will be carried out as per standard methods like IS/ISO/OECD/OPPTS, Singer *et al.* (2010), Wittmer *et al.* (2010), etc.

PRACTICAL RELEVANCE/UTILITY OF THE WORK

Rivers are vital and vulnerable freshwater systems that are critical for the sustenance of all life. However, the declining quality of the water in these systems threatens their sustainability and is therefore a cause for concern. Rivers are waterways of strategic importance across the world, providing main water resources for domestic, industrial, and agricultural purposes.

The maintenance of healthy aquatic ecosystem is depended on the physico-chemical properties and biological diversity. A regular monitoring of water bodies with required number of parameters with reference to the quality of water not only prevents the outbreak of diseases and occurrence of hazards but checks the water from further deterioration.

The proposed work will help to assess the current status of water quality of river Yamuna as well as the toxicological effects of heavy metals and pesticides on aquatic biota. It will further help to determine the health of Yamuna ecosystem and to prepare few plans for the conservation of its biological diversity. Point sources of pollutants can be identified and can be minimize after this study. On the basis of results of work, we can identify the main problems and apply some remedial measure for the prevention of pollution in Yamuna river.

EXPECTED AND OTHER PHYSICAL OUTCOMES OF THE WORK

- Current status of Yamuna water quality
- Toxicity behavior of pollutants in Yamuna river
- Impact of pollutants on major aquatic biota and their control measures
- Data will help to make a policy for the conservation of aquatic ecosystem of river Yamuna

Yamuna river is very important for all aquatic organisms living in its ecosystem. Other organisms including human beings livings in the catchment area of Yamuna river may also be affected by the pollutants load of river water. Toxic pollutants can create a lot of problems not only to aquatic biodiversity of the river but also to riparian biota including human beings through accumulation and biomagnifications of pollutants in food chain. As environmental health is primary concern, so it is very essential to conserve the aquatic ecosystem and biodiversity of Yamuna river.

The research work will help to assess the current status of water quality of river Yamuna as well as the toxicological effects of heavy metals and pesticides on aquatic biota. It will further help to determine the health of Yamuna ecosystem and to prepare few plans for the conservation of its biological diversity. Point sources of pollutants can be identified and can be minimize on the basis of this study. On the basis of results of this work, we can identify the main problems and apply some remedial measure for the prevention of pollution in Yamuna river. The experiments for the remedial measures for the pollutants in Yamuna water may be proposed as second phase of the work. Various governmental as well as NGOs working in the field of water pollution and aquatic biodiversity conservation can utilize the results of the proposed work. The results can serve as reference data for further studies on Yamuna.

Pollutants from agriculture fields, industries and household activities, reach to Yamuna river ultimately. The level of toxic pollutants in Yamuna water is increasing day by day. If the condition will remain same, the entire aquatic ecosystem may be collapse. Yamuna water is being used in various purposes including industries, agriculture and drinking utilities. The polluted water and affected organisms can cause ill effects to human beings. Outbreak of any epidemic in adjoining human colonies can cause a lot of harm to society. Secondly, environmental health will be degraded in the absence of conservation strategies and remedial measures. The study is equally important for human beings as well as for environmental health.

REFERENCES

Ajmal, M.; Khan, M.A. and Nomani, A.A. (1985): Distribution of Heavy Metals in Plants and Fish of Yamuna River (India), *Environmental Monitoring and Assessment*, 5: 361-367.

Aktar MW, Paramasivam M, Ganguly M, Purkait S. and Sengupta D (2010): Assessment and Occurrence of Various Heavy Metals in Surface Water of Ganga River Around Kolkata: A Study for Toxicity and Ecol. impact. *Environ. Monit. Assess.* 160: 207-213.

Alonso A. and Camargo JA. (2003): Short-term Toxicity of Ammonia, Nitrite, and Nitrate to the Aquatic Snail Potamopyrgus Antipodarum (Hydrobiidae, Mollusca). *Bull Env Contam Toxicol*; 70: 1006-12.

Alonso A. and Camargo JA. (2004): Toxic Effects of Unionized Ammonia on Survival and Feeding Activity of the Freshwater Amphipod Eulimnogammarus toletanus (Gammaridae, Crustacea). *Bull Environ Contam Toxicol*, 72: 1052-58.

Ashauer Roman, Irene Wittmer, Christian Stamm and Beate I. Escher (2011): Environmental Risk Assessment of Fluctuating Diazinon Concentrations in an Urban and Agricultural Catchment Using Toxicokinetic-Toxicodynamic Modeling, *Environ. Sci. Technol.*, 45: 9783-9792.

Ashauer Roman, Pernille Thorbek, Jacqui S. Warinton, James R. Wheeler and Steve Maund (2013): A method to Predict and understand Fish Survival under Dynamic Chemical Stress using Standard Ecotoxicity Data, *Environmental Toxicology and Chemistry*, 32(4): 954-965.

Barata, C. and Baird, D.J. (2000): Determining the Ecotoxicological mode of Action of Toxicants from Measurements on individuals: Results from Short duration Chronic Tests with *Daphnia magna* Straus. *Aquat. Toxicol.* 48: 195-209.

Barata, C., Damasio, J.B., Lopez, M.A., Kuster, M., Lopez de Alda, M., Barcelo, D., Riva, M.C., Raldua and D. (2007): Combined use of Biomarkers and *in situ* Bioassays in *Daphnia magna* to Monitor Environmental Hazards of Pesticides in the Field. *Environ. Toxicol. Chem.* 26: 370-379.

Barata, C., Solayan, A. and Porte, C. (2004): Role of β-esterases in Assessing Toxicity of Organophosphorous (chlorpyrifos, malathion) and carbamate (carbofuran) Pesticides to *Daphnia magna*. *Aquat. Toxicol.* 66: 125-139.

Bharti, P.K. (2007b): Why are Indian Standards not so strict?, *Current Science*, 93(9): 1202.

Bharti, P.K. and Kaoud, H.A.H. (2013): Aquatic Toxicology and Pollution, *Ancient Publishing House*, Delhi, pp: 194 (ISBN: 9789381385920).

Bharti, P.K. and Kaoud, H.A.H. (2013): Biodiversity of Aquatic Ecosystem: Significance, Threat and Conservation, *Discovery Publishing House*, Delhi, pp: 230 (ISBN: 9350562979).

Bharti, P.K.; Zaki, M. and Chauhan, A. (2013): Freshwater Ecosystem and Xenobiotics, *Discovery Publishing House*, Delhi, pp: 202 (ISBN: 93-5056-299-5).

Bharti, P.K.; Malik, D.S. and Yadav, R. (2008): Influence of Heavy Metals on Abundance of Cyanophyceae Members in Three Spring-fed Lake in Kempty, Dehradun, *Journal of Ecology and Fisheries*, 1(1): 35-38.

Bharti, Pawan K. (2007a): Where is Environmental Science going in India?, *Current Science*, 92 (4): 414.

Bharti, Pawan K. (2012): Heavy Metals in Environment, *Lambert Academic Publishing GmbH & Co. KG, Saarbrucken*, Germany, pp: 70 (ISBN: 978-3-659-15133-0).

Bharti, Pawan K. (2012): Solid Waste and River Ecology, *Lambert Academic Publishing GmbH & Co. KG, Saarbrucken*, Germany, pp: 65 (ISBN: 978-3-659-12852-3).

Bharti, Pawan K. (2013): Aquatic Environment and Toxicology, *Discovery Publishing House*, Delhi, pp: 284 (ISBN: 93-5056-236-7).

Birge WJ, Westerman AG, Spromberg JA. (2000): Comparative Toxicology and Risk Assessment of Amphibians. In: Sparling DW, Linder G, Bishop CA, Editors. Ecotoxicology of Amphibians and Reptiles. *Pensacola (USA): SETAC*; pp: 727-92.

Camargo, Julio A. and Álvaro Alonso (2006): Ecological and Toxicological Effects of Inorganic Nitrogen Pollution in Aquatic Ecosystems: A Global Assessment, *Environ. International*, 32: 831-849.

Cataldo, D., Colombo, J. C., Boltovskoy, D., Bilos, C., and Landoni,P. (2001): Environmental Toxicity Assessment in the Parana River Delta (Argentina): Simultaneous Evaluation of Selected Pollutants and Mortality Rates of Corbicula Fluminea (Bivalvia) Early Juveniles, *Environ. Poll.*, 112 (3): 379-389.

Clarkson, T.W. (1988): Biological Monitoring of Toxic Metals; *Plenum Press: New York*, pp: 265-282.

Coogan, T.P., Latta, D.M., Snow, E.T., Costa, M., and Lawrence, A. (1989): Toxicity and Carcinogenicity of Nickel Compounds, *Crit. Rev. Toxicol.*, 19 (4): 341-384.

Cope, W.G., Bartsch, M.R., Rada, R.G., Balogh, S.J., Ruppert, J.E., Young, R.D., Johnson, D.K. (1999): Bioassessment of Mercury, Cadmium, Polychlorinated Biphenyls and Pesticides in the Upper Mississippi River with zebra mussels (Dreissena polymorpha). *Environ. Sci. Technol.* 33: 4385-4390.

CPCB (2006): Water Quality Status Of Yamuna River (1999 – 2005), Central Pollution Control Board, Ministry of Environment & Forests, Assessment and Development of River Basin Series: ADSORBS/41/2006-07.

CPCB (2009): Annual Report 2008-09, Central Pollution Control Board, Ministry of Environment & Forests, Govt. of India, pp: 288.

CSE (2007): Sewage Canal: How to Clean the Yamuna, (By-Suresh Babu, S.V. *et al*), Centre for Science and Environment, New Delhi, India.

CSE (2009): State of Pollution in Yamuna, Centre for Science and Environment, Delhi, India.

Damasio Joana, Roma Tauler, Elisabeth Teixido, Maria Rieradevall, Narcis Prat, Maria Carmen Riva, Amadeu M.V.M. Soares and Carlos Barata (2008): Combined use of *Daphnia magna in situ* Bioassays, Biomarkers and Biological indices to Diagnose and Identify Environmental Pressures on Invertebrate Communities in Two Mediterranean Urbanized and Industrialized Rivers (NE Spain). *Aquatic Toxicology*, 87: 310-320.

De Flora, S., D. Vigano, D. D'Agostini, A. Camoirano, C. Bennicelli and A. Arillo (1993): Multiple Genotoxicity Biomarkers in Fish Exposed *in situ* to Polluted River Water. *Mutat. Res.*, 319: 162-177

Divya Christopher, Simarpreet Kaur and Rachana Singh (2012): Water Quality Status of River Yamuna in Delhi With Reference to Presence of Heavy Metals: A Review, *Int. J. Pharm. Med. & Bio. Sc.* 1(2): 266-271.

Duong, T. T., S. Morin, O. Herlory, A. Feurtet-Mazel, M. Coste and A. Boudou (2008): Seasonal Effects of Cadmium Accumulation in periphytic diatom Communities of Freshwater Biofilms. *Aquatic Toxicology*, 90: 19-28.

El-Naggar, A.M., S.A. Mahmoud and S.I. Tayel (2009): Bioaccumulation of Some Heavy Metals and Histopathological Alterations in Liver of Oreochromis Niloticus in Relation to Water Quality at Different Localities along the River Nile, Egypt. *World J. Fish Marine Sci.*, 1: 105-114.

Ewell WS, Gorsuch JW, Kringle RO, Robillard KA, Spiegel RC. (1986): Simultaneous Evaluation of the Acute Effects of Chemicals on Seven Aquatic Species. *Environ Toxicol Chem*, 5: 831-40.

Fatima, Mahino and Nazura Usmani (2013): Histopathology and Bioaccumulation of Heavy Metals (Cr, Ni and Pb) in fish (*Channa striatus* and *Heteropneustes fossilis*) tissue: A Study for Toxicity and Ecological Impacts, *Pakistani Journal of Biological Sciences*, 16(9): 412-420.

Gupta, M. and Chandra, P. (1994): Lead Accumulation and Toxicity in Vallisneria spirallis (L.) and Hydrilla verticillata(F.) *J. Environ. Sci. Health A*, 29: 504-516.

Hans, R.K., M. Farooq, G. Suresh Babu, S.P. Srivastava, P.C. Joshi and P.N. Viswanathan (1999): Agricultural Produce in the Dry bed of the River Ganga in Kanpur, India-A New Source of Pesticide Contamination in Human Diets. *Food and Chem. Toxicology*. 37: 847-852.

Hendriks, A.J., Pieters, H., de Boer, J. (1998): Accumulation of Metals, Polycyclic (halogenated) Aromatic Hydrocarbons and Biocides in Zebra Mussel and eel from the Rhine and Meuse River. *Environ. Toxicol. Chem.* 17: 1885-1898.

Jain, Pushp (2009): Sick Yamuna, Sick Delhi - Searching a Correlation. *PEACE Institute Charitable Trust, Delhi*, India, pp: 68.

Jha, P.K., V. Subramanian, R. Sitasawad and R. Van Grieken (1990): Heavy Metals in Water and Sediments of the Yamuna River (a Tributary of the Ganga). *Sci Total Environ.* 95: 7-27.

Koukal, B., Dominik, J., Vignati, D., Arpagaus, P., Santiago, S., Ouddane, B., and Benaabidate, L. (2004): Assessment of Water Quality and Toxicity of Polluted Rivers Fez and Sebou in the Region of Fez (Morocco), *Environ. Poll.*, 131 (1): 163-172.

Kumar, P. and Bharti, Pawan K. (2012): Effluent Quality Assessment of Different Drains in SIDCUL Industrial Area at Haridwar (Uttarakhand). *Environ. Conserv. J.* 13(1-2): 115-118.

Lasheen Mohamed R., Fagr Kh. Abdel-Gawad, Aly A. Alaneny and Hassan M.H. Abd El bary (2012): Fish as Bio Indicators in Aquatic Environmental Pollution Assessment: A Case Study in Abu-Rawash Area, Egypt. *World Applied Sciences Journal*, 19 (2): 265-275.

Liess, M., and Von der Ohe, C. (2005): Analyzing Effects of Pesticides on Invertebrate Communities in Streams. *Environ. Toxicol. Chem.* 24: 954-965.

Lokhande, R.S., Singare, P.U. and Pimple, D.S. (2011): Toxicity Study of Heavy Metals Pollutants in Waste Water Effluent Samples Collected From Taloja Industrial Estate of Mumbai, India, *Resources and Environment*, 1(1): 13-19.

Malik, D.S. and Bharti, P.K. (2005a): Nutrient Dynamics in Rhithron Zone of Shivalik Himalayan Stream Sahastradhara, Dehradun (Uttaranchal), *Env. Cons. J.* 6 (2): 63-68.

Malik, D.S. and Bharti, P.K. (2007b): Macro-zoobanthos as Pollution Indicator in River Saung at Dehradun (Uttaranchal), *J. Exp. Zool. India,* 10 (1): 221-222.

Malik, D.S.; Bharti, P.K. and Grover, S. (2006): Alteration in Surface Water Quality near Textile Industries at Panipat (Haryana), *Environment Conservation J.*, 7(2): 65-68.

Malik, D.S.; Bharti, P.K. and Yadav, R. (2006): Role of *Eichhornia crassipes* (Water hyacinth) in Remediation of Sewage Water Pollutants, *Exp. J. Zool.* 9(1): 117-124.

Malik, D.S.; Bharti, P.K. and Yadav, R.; Kumar, P. and Chauhan, P. (2008): Dispersion of Heavy Metals in Textile Effluent and Pond Environment in Panipat Industrial Area, *Env. Cons. J.* 9 (3): 77-81.

Mc William, R.A., Baird, D.J. (2002): Application of Post-exposure Feeding Depression Bioassays with *Daphnia magna* for Assessment of Toxic Effluents in Rivers. *Env. Toxicol. Chem.* 21: 1462-68.

McKim JM. (1977): Evaluation of Tests with Early Life Stages of Fish for Predicting Long-term Toxicity. J Fish Res Board Can 34: 1148-1154.

Nriagu, J.O., and Pacyna, J.M. (1988): Quantitative Assessment of Worldwide Contamination of Air, Water and Soils by Trace Metals. *Nature* 333(6169): 134-139.

Nyman A-M, Hintermeister A, Schirmer K, Ashauer R (2013): The Insecticide Imidacloprid Causes Mortality of the Freshwater Amphipod Gammarus pulex by Interfering with Feeding Behavior. PLoS ONE 8(5): e62472. doi:10.1371/journal.pone.0062472

OECD (1992): OECD Guidelines for Testing Chemicals 210: Fish, Early-life Stage Toxicity Test. Organisation for Economic Co-operation and Development, Paris, France.

Ogunlaja A and Ogunlaja OO (2007): Physico-chemical Analysis of Water Sources in Ubeji Community and their Histological Impact on Organs of Albino Mice. *J. Appl. Sci. Env. Mgt.* 11: 91-94.

Palma P, V.L. Palma, R.M. Fernandes, A.M.V.M. Soares and I.R. Barbosa (2008): Acute Toxicity of Atrazine, Endosulfan Sulphate and Chlorpyrifos to Vibrio fischeri, Thamnocephalus platyurus and Daphnia magna, Relative to Their Concentrations in Surface Waters from the Alentejo Region of Portugal, *Bull Environ Contam Toxicol*, 81: 485-48.

Rashed, M.N. (2001): Monitoring of Environmental Heavy Metals in Fish from Nasser Lake. *Environ. Int.*, 27: 27-33.

Rimet, Frederic (2012): Recent Views on River Pollution and Diatoms, *Hydrobiologia*, 683: 1-24.

Saikia, D.K., R.P. Mathur and S.K. Srivastava (1988): Heavy Metals in Water and Sediments of Upper Ganga. *Indian J. Environ. Health.* 31(1): 11-17.

Schmitt, C.J., and Finger, S.E. (1987): The Effects of Sample Preparation on measured Concentrations of Eight Elements in Edible Tissues of Fish from Streams Contaminated by Lead Mining, *Arch. Environ. Contam. Toxicol.*, 16(2): 185-207.

Sen, Indrajit, Ajay Shandil and V.S. Shrivastava (2011): Study for Determination of Heavy Metals in Fish Species of the River Yamuna (Delhi) by Inductively Coupled Plasma-Optical Emission Spectroscopy (ICPOES), *Advances in Applied Science Research*, Vol. 2, No. 2, pp. 161-166.

Singer, H.; Jaus, S.; Hanke, I.; Luck, A.; Hollender, J.; Alder, A.C. (2010): Determination of Biocides and Pesticides by on-line Solid Phase Extraction Coupled with Mass Spectrometry and their Behaviour in Wastewater and Surface Water. *Environ. Pollut.*, 158 (10): 3054-3064.

Singh, M. (2001): Heavy Metal Pollution in Freshly Deposited Sediments of the Yamuna River (the Ganga River Tributary): A Case Study from Delhi and Agra Urban Centres, *India Environ. Geol.* 40: 664-671.

Venkatesharaju K., Ravikumar. P., Somashekar. R. K. and Prakash. K. L. (2010): Physico-Chemical and Bacteriological Investigation on the River Cauvery of Kollegal Stretch in Karnataka, *Kathmandu University Journal of Science, Engineering and Technology*, 6 (1): 50-59.

Vinodhini, R. and Narayanan, M. (2008): Bioaccumulation of Heavy Metals in Organs of Fresh Water Fish *Cyprinus carpio* (Common carp). *Int. J. Environ. Sci. Technol.* 5: 179-182.

Williams KAW, Green DWJ, Pascoe D. (1986): Studies on the Acute Toxicity of Pollutants to Freshwater Macroinvertebrates. 3. Ammonia. *Arch. Hydrobiol.*, 106: 61-70.

Wittmer, I.K.; Bader, H.P.; Scheidegger, R.; Singer, H.; Luck, A.; Hanke, I.; Carlsson, C.; Stamm, C. (2010): Significance of Urban and Agricultural Land use for Biocide and Pesticide Dynamics in Surface Waters. *Water Res.*, 44 (9): 2850-2862.

Yacoub, A.M. (2007): Study on some Heavy Metals Accumulated in some Organs of Three River Nile fishes from Cairo and Kalubia governorates. *African J. Biol. Sci.*, 3: 9-21.

Pages: 19-51

Water and Waste Water: ***Issues and Management***
Edited by: **Dr. Pawan Kumar 'Bharti'**
ISBN: 978-93-88854-15-3
Edition: **2019**
Published by: **Discovery Publishing House Pvt. Ltd., New Delhi (India)**

3

Community based Tank Irrigation Management Systems in Tamilnadu, India

Lawrence Prabu C[1]
Muthiah Manoharan P[2]
Esakkimuthu M[3*]

ABSTRACT

There is growing water crisis in India and this is becoming increasingly a serious issue. The management of water distribution across the vast areas of the country and among the millions of multiple users in a sustainable manner is becoming a major challenge. There is a serious problem in managing both surface water and ground water. Irrigation system in India is categorized as major, medium and minor irrigation works for administrative purpose. Major irrigation works are generally built on perennial rivers and constitute large dams and canals that irrigate areas of many thousand hectares. Medium irrigation works constitute reservoirs of run-off water or large tanks. Minor irrigation works include all surface and ground water sources. Each of these three types of irrigation sources evolved at different times in history to meet changing requirement of human beings. However irrigation from tank is comparatively old technology and it was common in Indian landscape but the recent trend shows a decline in tank irrigation system. There are variety of factors associated with the decline of tank irrigation systems viz., development of large-scale gravity irrigation systems, rapid spread of tube well technology and decline in traditions of community management.

Index terms: Community management, development, ground water, irrigation system, management systems, Tamilnadu and tank irrigation.

[1,2] Tamil Nadu Agricultural University, Coimbatore, Tamil Nadu, (India)
[3] Kerala Agricultural University, RARS, Pilicode, Kerala, (India)

INTRODUCTION

Water is prosperity, water is joy, water is festival, water is ritual and finally to say water is life. Today's life, the looming crisis of water convey, water is struggle, water is politics, water is problem and water can only be the solution too and in this way water flow into human life with the various transformations. Since independence, India has made significant progress in developing its water resources and the post-independence years also have witnessed large-scale investments in water storage structures which have contributed considerably in making India self-sustaining economy. India constitutes 16 per cent of the world's population but has access to only 4.00 per cent of the total available fresh water and it also has the largest irrigated area in the world, accounting for 22 per cent of global irrigated area but the prevailing uncertainty over access to and the availability of water resource may be reaching crisis level in India. The growing population, diversity of needs, competing demands for this limited resource coming from households, industry, and agriculture have wide-ranging implications for the country's future. The contemporary issues of water crisis alert us to become more vibrant and active in conservation and judicial utilization of water resource for irrigation as well as for household needs. It is not new challenge for Indians to conserve and store the water because, these practices were practiced in India from ancient days. India has many historical evidences on irrigation structures, systems and management, almost from 8th century onwards and they captured India's long history of human interventions in the management of traditional water bodies for agriculture, one of such intervention is an irrigation tank. Tank irrigation systems involve a great deal of collective action and organized community labourers for maintenance and other critical water management tasks (Janakaran, 1993). In this context the present study was conducted to explore the socio psychological characteristics of farmers which influence their attitude and their participation in community based tank irrigation management system.

HISTORICAL PERSPECTIVE OF TANK IRRIGATION IN INDIA

An irrigation tank is a reservoir constructed across the slope of a valley to harvest rainwater in rainy season and to use it for irrigation and other purposes. The tank irrigation is an old established practice in most of the semi-arid tropical parts of India, where the monsoon rains disperse erratically during few months of the year then the irrigation tanks serve to store and regulate the flow of water for agriculture use. In ancient days, tanks were a part of the political process in which rulers extended and maintained domains of control. Right to control the tanks or to control the flow of water were frequently the objects of royal donation and largesse. Many of the tanks in South India are century old and have been historically managed by autonomous local bodies and its importance can be gauged from the fact that even as late as 1990-91 tanks irrigated 8 million hectares of land in semi-arid region of south India (Meenu Singh, 2000). In such a way tanks are having historical features in the cultural landscape of peninsular India.

TANK IRRIGATION IN TAMIL NADU

Tank irrigation can be traced back two millennia in Tamil Nadu and have been central to socio-ecology and irrigated agriculture in the states of Tamil Nadu (Amarnath and Karthik, 2006). During the 1950s, nearly 40% of the irrigated area in Tamil Nadu was irrigated by tanks and there are more than 39 thousand tanks at present in Tamil Nadu, many of which were built in the 18th and 19th centuries by kings and *zamindars* and even under British rule (Palanisami and Ester 2009). Tanks are one of the most important and oldest sources of irrigation in South India and it is classified as systems tanks and non-system tanks based on the source of water supply. System tanks receive water mainly from assured source like a canal and may or may not have their own catchments. On the other hand, non-system tanks rely only on the runoff from their own catchment. In Tamil Nadu about 90 per cent of the tanks are non-system types (Palaniswamy and Easter, 1986) and the contribution of tank irrigation declined from 40 per cent in 1955 to less than 25 per cent in 2000 (Balasubramanian,and Selvaraj, 2004).

IMPORTANCE OF COMMUNITY BASED TANK IRRIGATION MANAGEMENT SYSTEM

Traditionally, in Tamil Nadu the tank irrigation management was done through the informal water user association headed by village elder or President of village Panchayat.

But the recent trend shows that there is marked decline in such a management system which resulted in poor maintenance of tank structure and low productivity in agriculture. In this context, the governmental interventions and its assistance are imperative for the conservation and development of the resources but the government has less practical possibility to have direct involvement in managing all the tank irrigation system and meeting the diverse need of the people who depend on tank irrigation system therefore it is perceived that it is the right time to take massive steps to organise the community groups for the collective management of tank irrigation system for the effective and efficient utilization of water resources since the past experiences of community approach in tank irrigation management discloses the positive note that transfer of irrigation management responsibilities from government agencies to farmers is now an important policy in many countries (Kei Kajisa, *et al.* 2006) and the experience of irrigation management transfer programmes around the world shows that farmers' involvement in water management has indeed led to a better and smoother performance of the systems (Kolavalli and Brewer, 1999; Thiruchelvam, 2004). It also reported that self-governing institutions can manage the systems more effectively than the government (Tang, 1992; Ostrom, 2000). The available common water resources are meant 'for the people' therefore it would be better served its purpose if it is managed 'by the people' and if it is so, the feeling of 'our asset' and it is 'our responsibility to protect it' will be felt by the people which ultimately lead to sustainable management of water resources.

FUTURISTIC VIEW

Irrigation sources play a key role in enhancing agricultural productivity and food security. In this way, tank irrigation in Tamil Nadu is one of the oldest sources of irrigation system and played vital role in augmenting agricultural productivity. However, the contribution of tank irrigation system shows declining trend over a period. In this context, an attempt was made to explore the existing state of community managed tank irrigation system through analysing extent of participation of farmers and their attitude with community based tank irrigation management system. Further, the study has been designed to focus on the group dynamics of farmers and their socio-psychological characteristics contribution with tank irrigation management activities. Finally, it helps us to identify the existing constraints and formulate appropriate strategies to promote community based tank irrigation management system. The research findings of the study would help extension agencies, scientists, policy makers and administrators to have an insight into the rationale behind the farmers towards tank irrigation system. It would also enlighten them to initiate suitable modifications and policy formulations for involving higher level of people's participation in planning and implementation in community based tank irrigation tank management system for its great success.

PEOPLE'S PARTICIPATION IN TANK IRRIGATION MANAGEMENT

The studies on common pool resource management have established that self-governing institutions can manage the systems more effectively than the government. But success of these institutions depends largely on the effective design and enforcement of self-created working rules which are more relevant to local circumstances and based on the farmers' own experience and knowledge of the resource (Tang, 1992; Lam, 1996 and Ostrom, 2000). Janakaran (1993) concluded that tank irrigation systems involve a great deal of collective action and organized community labourers for maintenance and critical water management tasks. Arumugam *et al.* (1997) in his study on sustainable development and management of tank irrigation system reiterated that farmer participation in the operation and management of tank irrigation system should be encouraged and the effective farmer participation and cooperation would result in equity among different reaches, minimum social conflicts and increase productivity. Tekynel *et al.* (1997) studied Turkish experiences on participatory irrigation management. This study highlighted the achievements in the process of transfer of irrigation systems to the users and reported that participatory irrigation showed remarkable success and the government encouraged participatory approach through establishing Irrigation Groups or Water User Groups. Ul-Haq and Shahid (1997) recommended pursuing comprehensive and integrated strategies for improved irrigation management which needed to be done in conjunction with the institutional framework of the local society. Yasin and Ahmad (1997) studied modernization of irrigation schemes in Pakistan and in this context the study described the system's major constraints and outlined the rationale for introducing participatory irrigation management for reduced governmental costs, improved system performance, better response to external pressures and improved environmental sustainability of system.

According to Chandran *et al.* (2001) reported that about 30 per cent of participatory activities envisaged for water user's association are being undertaken by farmers and hence participation is low and also stated that size of their landholding was found to influence extent of participation in irrigation activities. Sharma (2001) reported that the success of the watershed development programme implemented by an NGO in Rajasthan was due to effective participation of beneficiaries in the programme. The NGO formed water work force who work together to make community participation in watershed development programme. The management of water distribution across the vast areas of the country, and amongst millions of users in a sustainable manner is becoming a major challenge.

The experience over the last decades shows that if the farmer actively participates in tank irrigation management there is marked improvement in the water utilization efficiency (Gandhi and Namboodhiri, 2002). Mohan (2002) stated that the effective involvement of water user's associations can be expected when they were entrusted with meaningful role with sufficient empowerment in terms of financial resources and decision-making abilities. Reddy (2002) opined that informal bodies are more effective than formal Water User's Association as it evolves the cohesion. Sakthivadivel *et al.* (2004) reported that study of 41 irrigation tanks in 22 districts of 8 Indian states was conducted under the IWMI-Tata Programme to identify the characteristics of high-performing local-managed tank institutions. This paper discusses some best management practices used by high-performing tank institutions with respect to the following key functions: water acquisition; water allocation and distribution; decision making; enforcement of rules and punishment of violators; and mobilizing financial resources.

Research evidenced that, Anandan (2007) stated that the success of tank rehabilitation project Puducherry was due to people's participation by adopting "Participatory Approach Technique" in all activities of the project right from planning to implementation and also suggested this type of people participation project shall be implemented in other parts of our country for the upliftment and development of the farmers as a whole and for conserving water for a sustainable growth. Bhavsar and Bhagale (2007) opined that community management of water resources had proven over time as very successful and sustainable. This approach ensures its optimum utilization, conservation and maximizes the benefits. The people's participation in construction of water harvesting structures and irrigation water management shows that the community can bring revolution in the water management sector. Suresh and Ramesh (2008) conducted a study on extent of participation of farmers in watershed project in Tumkur district of Karnataka. They reported that, majority of the respondents had medium extent of participation (64.77%) followed by high (28.33%) and low (7.5%) extent of participation. Umamaheshwara (2009) in his study on community participation in irrigation tank management reported that majority of the respondents (54.17%) expressed medium participation, while 24.17 per cent of them had high participation. Low extent of participation was expressed by 21.67 per cent of the respondents. Regarding extent of participation in various activities was observed viz., collection of facts about tanks (52.50%), identification of encroachment area (55.00%), decision regarding required irrigation water (57.50%), avoiding the damages to sluice structure (52.50%), carrying out desilting activity (56.67%), repairing sluice structures (60.83%), strengthening of tank bunds (61.67%), resectioning of bunds (50.00%), deciding the crops based on critical stages of crops (51.67%) and in deciding number of irrigation (50.83%). Nanthakumaran and Palanisami (2010) stated that farmer participation was found to be a solution to arrest the deterioration of the tank irrigation system in Tamil Nadu. Further, the water users association in the tank irrigated systems should be strengthened for water management which leads to better performance of the tanks. Goudappa, *et al.* (2012) observed in their study on participation of farmers in community based tank management, majority of the respondents (58.33%) had medium extent of participation in irrigation tank management practices. An approximately two-third of the respondents participated regularly in the activities viz., identification of encroachment of tank area (75%), identification of leakages and their repairs (65%), decision on required irrigation for crops (80%), carrying out of desilting activity (73.33%), repair of sluice structures (65%), strengthening of tank bunds regularly (76.67%) and afforestration of foreshore area of the tank (71.67%).

CONTRIBUTIONS OF TANK IRRIGATION SYSTEM IN SUPPORTING THE LIVELIHOOD OF RURAL PEOPLE

According to Jodha (1986) found that common pool resources (CPR) contributed significantly to the rural poor by increasing employment and income generation and dependence of richer households on CPRs is much less. Palanisami and Easter (1986) found that most of the Tanks (>90%) in both south Indian, north India and east Thailand were non-system tanks which serve as a means to provide supplementary irrigation for rice crop in the wet season as well as to meet the domestic and livestock water needs to the villages. Tanks are eco-friendly – they serve as flood moderators in times of heavy rainfall and as drought mitigating mechanisms during long dry spells (Vasimalai, *et al.*, 1996). Thinagaran (1997) stated in his study on tanks and social forestry, apart from traditional uses of tanks for irrigation, washing, bathing, fishing, grazing and brick kilns, the raising of tree in the tank bed has come to stay in a big way of its multi various benefits. Tank systems, developed ingeniously and maintained over the centuries, have provided insulation from recurring droughts, floods, vagaries of the monsoon and offered the much needed livelihood security to the poor living in fragile semi-arid regions (Mahendrarajah *et al.* 1999). According to Narayanamoorthy (2004) reported that the farmers belonging to the marginal and small size group are mostly poor, they couldn't afford for cost intensive irrigation sources like groundwater as in the case of medium and large farmers and tank irrigation continues to play a crucial role among small and marginal farmers even today. Balasubramanian and Selvaraj (2003) in their study on poverty, private property and common pool resource management of irrigation tanks observed that tank based agricultural income make up to close to one-third of total household income for poor households. Poor households use tanks much more than non-poor for other livelihood option such as fuel wood and fodder collection and water for livestock.

According to Balasubramanian and Selvaraj (2004) conducted study on tank degradation and poverty reduction and they stated that tanks are one of the oldest sources of irrigation in India and the mainstay for the livelihood of many poor households. Tanks are providing several ecological benefits from recharging ground water and moderating floods to serving as habitat for wildlife. Sakthivadivel *et al.* (2004) stated that tanks in the Indian context inextricably linked to the sociocultural aspects of rural life and have historically been an indispensable part of the village habitat, sustaining its socio-ecological balance and conserving the tank eco-systems for multiple uses such as irrigation, domestic and livestock use and groundwater recharge is a way to provide a safety net to protect the livelihood of millions in a semi-arid India. Asian Development Bank (2006) study concluded that in tank rehabilitation works, augmenting tank water and increasing tank storage had greater impact on the livelihood options of the land less and marginal farmers. It also suggested that tanks are likely to be more sustainable when all the villagers become members of tank user group. Sakthivadivel and Gomathinayagam (2006) reported in their study on rehabilitation and management of tanks, the local landless and the poor are employed to work on the tank rehabilitation project and earn wages. They also observed that the tank silt application in dryland increased dryland productivity to more than 100% from 3 quintals of *ragi* (finger millet) to 8 quintals per year in Chunchadenahalli, Karnataka and this method of land reclamation brought additional areas under crop and provided employment opportunities and livelihood. In Keelakuilkudi in Tamil Nadu, two SHGs in the village were given 9.5 acres of wasteland by the panchayat, where the tank silt was used to improve soil fertility and the SHGs cultivated horticultural plants on this land for their livelihood. Sakthivadivel and Gomathinayagam (2006) opined that rehabilitation and management of tanks increased water availability in the tank for more number of days which in turn increased the intensity of agriculture, changes in crops and cropping pattern, agricultural production and livestock population. Palanisami *et al.* (2006) stated that tanks 39,000 exist in Tamil Nadu State as natural surface water harvesting structures and the purpose of irrigation and other water usage.

In support of Viswanathan and Khandge (2006) studied the economics of Tank modernisation project in Karnataka reported that indirect benefits of modernisation of tanks like recharge of groundwater in the area, facilitation of allied activities like animal husbandry, fisheries, contribution to the ecology, etc., would be much more than the direct benefits quantified. Sekar (2008) analysed economic performance and promotion of tank modernisation programme for sustaining rainfed agriculture. The result showed that the adjusted tank performance, paddy crop yield, net revenues and irrigation efficiency in tank command increased after modernisation. The study results are of potential use for water policy planners and watershed development planners as irrigation tanks are one of the components of watershed development programmes. Goswami (2011) observed that tanks are very important source of water in villages in India, particularly its support in terms of irrigation and are very old way of conserving water. As south Indian states do not have any perennial source of water therefore, they heavily rely upon these tanks for fulfilling their irrigation needs.

CONCEPT OF GROUP DYNAMICS

According to Kurt (1951) defined group dynamics as a field of enquiry dedicated to the advancing knowledge about the nature of groups, the laws of their development and their interrelations with individuals, other groups and larger institutions. Based on the feelings and emotions members of a group form a common perception. The interactive psychological relationship in which members of a group form this common perception is actually group dynamics. Dahama and Bhatnagar (1985) reported that no two groups are going to be completely identical in all the different aspects like size, composition, goals, programmes, activities and cohesion. For either of these reasons, the functioning of groups is considered as 'dynamic' and not 'static'. Harris and Harris (1996) found that team performance is highest when the dynamics of group process can occur and this is more likely to happen when the number of participants is limited for maximum interchange. He suggested that internal group dynamics could be the mediating variable that enables the influence of team characteristics on team effectiveness. The term "group dynamics" refers to the interactions between people who are talking together in a group setting. Group dynamics can be studied in business settings, in volunteer settings, in classroom settings and in social settings (Ann-Marie and Strazzabosco, 2009). The concept of group dynamics was first evolved by Kurt Levin in 1930s, who viewed the concept from the perspective of internal nature of group, why they form, how they form, the structure of group, how they function and its effect on other group members, other groups and the organization.

DIMENSION OF GROUP DYNAMICS

Cooperation: Accordingly, Festinger (1954) stated that the group cooperation is the resultant of all forces acting on members to remain in the group and these forces are determined jointly by certain properties of the group and by certain characteristics of the members which in conjunction and can be conceived as the immediate determinants of cohesiveness. These forces, in turn, have various effects that constitute the consequences of group cohesiveness. Balasubramanian and Ramu (1991) in his study on ranking irrigation tanks for modernization, suggested that the co-operation among the beneficiaries of the water user's organization is one of the important factors for influencing the performance of tank irrigation system. Balasubramanian and Selvaraj (2003) reported income inequality among tank users as one of the factor affecting cooperation among village communities.

Group climate: Accordingly, Parker *et al.* (2003) stated that climate is very important as it is provides a link between the organizational characteristics and individual outcomes. Organizational Climate has a profound influence on the outlook, well-being and attitudes of organizational members and ultimately on their total performance affecting their behaviour that confronts the individual's freedom of choice and providing source of reward and punishment (Arun, 2013).

Group cohesiveness: Cohesiveness is generally defined as "the resultant of all forces acting on all the members to remain in the group" (Cartwright, 1968). Group cohesiveness is one of the essential concepts for understanding group dynamics (Zander, 1979). The group's cohesion depends on the extent that the individuals in the group want to accomplish the group's common goals and group identity. The cohesion of a group is an important factor that could help to explain the group's behaviour and its inter-group relations. The elements of cohesion are the members attraction to the group, normative influence, informational influence and outside sources in the world (McCauley, 1989). The group dynamics can cause difficulties with inter-group relationships. For instance, some research stated that if a group has high cohesion based on a strong common identity for the in-group, there can most likely become a strong hatred for the out-group (Naimark, 2001; Bauman, 1989 and Kressel, 1996). Kondalkar (2007) defines cohesiveness as the degree of closeness that the members feel with the group. Cohesiveness identifies the strength of the members desires to remain in the group and degree of commitment to the group and it is reflected to the extent of unity displayed by the group members and adherence to the group norms. It is we feeling displayed by the members of the group. Cohesion can be achieved when there is a feeling of attraction and adherence to group norms. Cohesiveness of a group can produce miracles in the organization if group objectives. But if they differ then the group cohesiveness can be disastrous for the organization. According to Sekaran (2010) cohesion refers to the state of how closely the members in the group stick together and is reflected in their conformity to the norms of the group, feelings of attraction for one another and desire to be co-members of the group. Attraction, cohesion and conforming to norms are all intertwined. The more the members feel attracted to the group, the greater will be group cohesion. The greater the cohesion, the greater the influence of group members to persuade one another to conform to the group norms. The greater the conformity, the greater the identification of the members with the group which in turn increases group cohesion.

Communication: Accordingly, Rogers and Rogers (1976) argue that the behaviour of individuals in organizations is best understood from a communication point of view." Myers and Myers (1982) define communication as the central binding force that permits coordination among people and thus allows for organized behaviour. Koontz *et al.* (2008) defined communication is the transfer of information from a sender to a receiver for the information being understood by the receiver. Samuel *et al.* (2008) defined communication is the process of sharing information with other individuals. Information is any thought or idea that managers want to share with others. Communication involves one person's projecting a message to one or more other people that results in everyone's arriving at a common understanding of the message.

Decision making: Accordingly, Sakthivadivel *et al.* (2004) stated in his study on rejuvenating irrigation tanks through local institutions, functioning of successful traditional institutions indicated a decision-making process which involved all the stakeholders and where the decisions made were accepted by all as fair. Further, he reported that, In Kongudi in Pudukkottai district of Tamil Nadu, all major decisions are taken in a meeting where representatives of all the families are present whereas in Arumugamangalam tank in Thoothukudi district of Tamil Nadu, all important decisions are taken by the general body as a consensus decision. It is inferred that decision through general body as a consensus decision and meeting with representatives of all families were the main decision making process of tank users.

Leadership: Accordingly, Gibb (1947) reported that leadership is both a function of the social situation and a function of personality but it is a function of these two interactions. Hudson and Seekler (1974) reported that superior strength, superior fact, superior intelligence, superior knowledge, superior will power are may be the means to the attainment of leadership. Dahama and Bhatnagar (1985) stated that leadership is the process of influencing the behaviour of the individual in a given situations. Mosse (1999) reported that during colonial government of the time needed 'traditional' autonomous village tank institutions for its public works administration and village headmen was given leadership for the organization of its revenue system.

Motivation: According to McFarland *et al.* (1993) motivation is a form of tension occurring within individual with resulting behaviour aimed at reducing, eliminating or diverting the tension. Understanding the needs and drives and their resulting tensions helps to explain and predict human behaviour ultimately providing a sound basis for managerial decision and action. Thus, motivation is the term, which applies to the entire class of urges, drives, desires, needs and similar forces. James *et al.* (2006) defined motivation is a psychological characteristic that contributes a person's degree of commitment and it includes the factors that cause, channel and sustain human behaviour in a particular committed direction. Kondalkar (2007) defines motivation as inner burning passion caused by needs, wants and desires that propels an individual to exert physical and mental energy to achieve desired objective. Koontz *et al.* (2008) defined motivation is a general term applying to the entire class of drives, desires, needs, wishes and similar forces. The managers motivate their subordinates is to say that they do things which they hope will satisfy these drives and desires and induce the subordinates to act in a desired manner. Lauren *et al.* (2008) opined that motivations for engaging in collective action are shaped by the preferences and interests of individuals as well as by their perceptions of their chances of succeeding through collective action. Robbins (2009) defined motivation as the processes that account for an individual's intensity, direction, and persistence of effort toward attaining a goal. Intensity is concerned with how hard a person tries. Motivation refers to degree of readiness or an organism to pursue some designated goals and implies the determination of the nature and locus of the forces including the degree of readiness.

Definition of conflict: Accordingly, Stoner *et al.* (1996) defined conflict as disagreement about the allocation of scarce resources or clashes regarding goals, values and so on and it can occur on the interpersonal or organizational level. Darling and Walker (2001) defined conflict as a situation in which two or more individuals operating within a unit appear to be incompatible. They advocate when such conflict is recognized, acknowledged and managed in a proper manner, personal and organizational benefits will accrue. Robbins (2009) defined conflict as a process that begins when one party perceives that another party has negatively affected or is about to negatively affects something that the first party cares about. He also stated that a conflict process has five stages: potential opposition or incompatibility, cognition, intensions, behaviour, and outcomes. Potential sources of conflict are personal variables which include personality, emotions, and values. Further, he opined that conflict management is the use of resolution and stimulation techniques to achieve the desired level of conflict. The conflict management techniques are classified into conflict-resolution techniques and conflict-stimulation techniques. Conflict-resolution techniques include problem solving, subordinate goals, and expansion of resources, avoidance, smoothing, and compromise, authoritative command, altering the human variable and altering the structural variables. Conflict-stimulation techniques include communication, bringing in outsiders, restructuring the organization and appointing a devil's advocate.

Causes of conflict: Conflicts in natural resource management arise due to disagreement over access to and control and use of natural resources (Matiru, 2000). Jennifer and Keremane (2006) reported that around 20 per cent of the farmers perceived that conflicts were common within the Water User Association (WUA) while most of them remained neutral (65%). Further, around 21 per cent perceived that head-reach farmers took more water and again around 41 per cent were neutral. Therefore, it is clear that there were conflicts between members of the WUA regarding water distribution. Communication is an important process in the group but the poor communication, passing of incomplete information to the members may cause conflict because this may have far reaching consequences in attainment of group goals. Some of the reasons for poor communication are as under, inadequate communication, filtration effect, when information is not received on time, barriers of culture, language, inadequate training of sender and receiver and noise problems (Kondalkar, 2007). Karthikeyan (2010) reported in his study on conflicts among multiple users of tank irrigation systems that the conflicts among and between head end and tail end farmers for the use of water was found to be the most popular type of conflict prevailed among farmers in more than half of the tanks studied.

***Conflict management*:** Accordingly, Blake and Mouton (1985) listed eight activities that constitute conflict management are, definition of the problem, review of the problem, development of the range of alternatives, debate of alternatives, reaching of solutions, explanation and evaluation of solutions, weighing alternative solutions and selection of the appropriate solution. Deetz and Stevenson (1986) proposed five basic strategies for dealing with conflict. The first strategy is avoidance which is based on blocking any discussion in connection with the conflict. While avoidance may be regarded as a negative strategy, in some cases it can be viewed as valuable. The second strategy is pacification, is also based on blocking discussion of the conflict. Rather than avoid conflict, pacification seeks to undermine the conflict by minimizing or maximizing it. The result is to subvert that conflict discussion. The third strategy, competition, is based on accepting the conflict context. Competition evolves when individuals in a conflict decide to get what each one wants. Competition has the potential for growth as well as for destruction whereas compromise causes everyone involved to be more satisfied but seldom satisfies anyone fully. Finally, creative integration is a strategy which aims to break the perceived conflict context by finding options outside that context. Creative integration requires much effort, but offers the greatest opportunity for the good, long-term health of a relationship. Kolavalli (1995) found that the local organizations play a key role in conflict resolution regarding the disputes based on distribution and allocation of water. Jennifer and Keremane (2006) reported that around 30 per cent of the respondents were satisfied as they perceived the conflict resolution mechanisms to be clear and explicit. Further stated that, the conflict resolution mechanisms followed are:

(i) subjecting the accused to 'social pressure' (which we took to mean social isolation) and intervention of an external agency viz., Non-Governmental Organization or Irrigation Department (NGO/ID). Robbins (2009) opined that conflict management is the use of resolution and stimulation techniques to achieve the desired level of conflict. The conflict management techniques are classified into conflict-resolution techniques and conflict-stimulation techniques. Conflict-resolution techniques include problem solving, subordinate goals, and expansion of resources, avoidance, smoothing, and compromise, authoritative command, altering the human variable and altering the structural variables. Conflict-stimulation techniques include communication, bringing in outsiders, restructuring the organization and appointing a devil's advocate.

CONFLICT RESOLUTION MODEL

Accordingly, Robbins (1974) concentrates on strategies specifically labelled as resolution techniques. That is problem solving, superordinate goals, avoidance, smoothing, and compromise, authoritative command, altering the human variable and altering structural variables. Thomas (1976) developed a two-dimensional model that illustrates five conflict management styles: competing, collaborating, compromising, avoiding and accommodating. Conflict between parties can be resolved by five different modes. With regard to enforcement of rules and conflict resolution, it was reported that farmers have been successfully devised and effectively enforced the rules for water distribution, fee collection and conflict resolution (Kolavalli and Brewer, 1999; Brewer and Sakthivadivel, 1999).

Avoidance: One or both the parties could avoid facing the conflict. The situation pertains to un-cooperative and unassertive behaviour on the part of parties involved. The 'A' Party may avoid facing 'B' Party. When situation reaches a point of negligence by 'A' Party 'B' Party may take advantage of the situation. By avoiding, the individual might take side step, postpone or even withdraw from the conflict situation. This strategy is useful when issues involved in conflict are very minor nature or when more important issues deserve attention.

Competing: This strategy is useful in emergencies where quick decisions are required. In this strategy power must be used unilaterally as a weapon when unpopular decisions like termination, pay cuts, layoffs, cost cutting and enforcing discipline are required to be taken. This strategy is based on win-lose principle of managing conflicts. The managers who are high on powerbase have an added advantage in using competing strategy because people from opposite side would not dare confront a person who is so powerful.

Collaborating: Strategy of collaboration involves attempt of one party to work with the other party in co-operative manner and find solutions to the problem for mutual benefits. The strategy involves identification of areas of disagreement, examining the issue in greater detail and a workable solution arrived at, which is for mutual benefits. This strategy signifies joint efforts, gain for both the parties and integrated solutions arrived at by consensual decisions. Sekaran (2010) concluded that when people are high on collaborating, they have to be concerned about how they spend their time and other organizational resources. Collaboration is time and energy consuming.

***Accommodating*:** In accommodating mode, a person scarifies his own interest for accommodating other person's interest. It is a form of selfless generosity, obeying other person's point of view. This mode is usually adopted when other person's view is stronger, we want to achieve goodwill and indicate that you are reasonable. This strategy of conflict resolution is important when we want other person to give at a later date when it favours you. Sekaran (2010) concluded that when people are high on accommodating score they might be differing too much to the wishes of others and pay very little attention to their own ideas and concern even though they may realize that they are not getting the attention they deserve.

Compromising: In conflict situation, compromising is a mode when both parties try to find out some expedient, mutually acceptable solution that sacrifices both the parties partially. In compromising, there is no clear winner or loser. None of the party is fully satisfied as they ration the object of conflict and accept the solution which is not complete to either of the parties. From perusal of literature reviewed conflict management is summarized from the meaning of conflict, causes of conflict, types of conflict and conflict management styles. Conflict is a process that begins when one party perceives that another party has negatively affected something that the first party cares about. Conflict can be considered as an expression of hostility, negative attitude, aggression and gross misunderstanding. Intra-personal conflict occurs when there is a conflict of values, which may relate to roles that an individual is required to play and decisions he has to take in the organization. Inter-personal conflict occurs due to dis-agreement over the goals of the organization. These are further aggravated due to difference of opinion. Intra-organizational conflicts relates to horizontal, vertical and line and staff conflicts. Conflicts can be resolved by displaying high co-operative behaviour. It can take various forms like avoiding, accommodating, collaborating and compromising on various issues between individuals, groups and organizations. Minimum level of conflict can keep groups vibrant, cohesive and creative.

ATTITUDE OF FARMERS TOWARDS TANK IRRIGATION MANAGEMENT

Accordingly, Thurstone and Chave (1929) defined attitude as the degree of positive or negative effect associated with some psychological object towards which people can differ in varying degrees. Hema (2003) reported that more than half (61.67%) of the respondents had more favourable attitude towards group activity, followed by less favourable attitude 31.66 per cent. Favourable attitude towards group activity was found with 6.67 per cent of the respondents only. Sakthivadivel and Gomathinayagam (2006) reported that as the project moved on, persuasion and clearing farmers doubts by the Centre for Water Resources (CWR) staff helped to change their attitudes. Jennifer and Keremane (2006) reported that most of the farmers perceived that process of forming a Water User Association (WUA) was driven by several factors. The important among them as perceived by the farmers are water shortage, inefficiency of the Irrigation Department (ID), government policies, encouragement by a key person, and influence of other farmers. Around 71 per cent of the farmers indicated water shortage was the main reason for forming a WUA. Seven per cent indicated inefficiency of ID as the most important reason. The view of above authors indicated that the attitude of human beings towards an object, programme etc., varied with situation. It can be concluded from the above studies that favourable attitude towards development programme, new ideas, technology or innovation, is prime requirement for the participation and success of the programme.

SOCIO-ECONOMIC AND COMMUNICATION CHARACTERISTICS OF FARMERS

Age: Age was operationalized as the number of completed years of the respondent at the time of enquiry and the chronological age was taken as a measure. Accordingly, Shankara (2010) observed that 50.84 per cent of the respondents were middle aged category followed by old (32.50 per cent) and young (16.66 per cent). Sasikala (2011) reported in her study on vulnerability and adaptation to rainfall variability in rain-fed tank irrigated agriculture, 61.00 per cent of the tank user farmers in below normal rainfall blocks were above 45 years old and 31.00 per cent were middle aged and 8.00 per cent were in the young aged. Mohan and Rameshkumar (2012) reported in his study on profile characteristics of farmers under tank irrigation command, majority (60.56%) of the farmers were in the middle age group and in the district wise also the majority of Chittoor (63.33%), Vizainagaram (53.34%) and Warangal (65%) of the respondents were belonged to middle age group. Periyar (2012) observed that 64.50 per cent of the farmers were found to belong to old age group followed by 24.50 per cent in the middle age group and 11.00 per cent were seen in the young age group.

Education: Educational status of a respondent was operationalised as the level of literacy possessed by the respondent at the time of interview. Elamurugannan (2001) found that 84.17 per cent of the rainfed farmers were literates, while about 15.83 per cent of the farmers were illiterates. Senthilvadivoo (2003) inferred that 31.67 per cent of the respondents were educated up to middle school level followed by high school level (18.33%), primary education (16.67%) and functionally literates (15.00%). Umamaheshwara (2009) reported in his study on community participation in irrigation tank management, nearly 27.50 per cent of the respondents had education up to high school, followed by middle school (26.67%) and primary school (24.17%) while 11.67 per cent of them were illiterates and only 5.83 and 4.17 per cent of respondents had education up to college and degree programme level. Sasikala (2011) observed that in below normal rainfall blocks 28 per cent of the tank farmers were illiterate and 24 per cent of the farmers had only primary level education followed by 23 per cent of the farmers had middle school education. With regard to level of education Mohan and Rameshkumar (2012) reported that, 32.78 per cent respondent farmers had middle school education followed by illiterate group (26.11%). In case of Chittoor (38.33%) and Vizainagaram (31.67%) districts majority of the farmers had middle school level education. Periyar (2012) observed four-fifth (81.50%) of respondents were educated primary and above level. Considerable per cent of the farmers.

Occupation: It has been operationalised as the profession in which an individual spends much of his time, money and resources to gain better livelihood to maintain himself and his family. Kavitha (2001) reported in her study on Integrated Water Management, 68.33 per cent of paddy farmers had agriculture as their main occupation. Karpagam (2004) revealed in her study on encroachment in tank irrigation system, nearly half of the encroachers (47.90%) had their main occupation as agriculture whereas 22.9 per cent of them were wage earners, 10.4 per cent of encroachers were doing business and earning wages along with farming, 6.30 per cent encroachers were found to be self-employed and 2.10 per cent were government employees. Thirumoorthy (2009) revealed that 77.50 per cent of the tank user farmers had agriculture as their main occupation and 22.50 per cent of the farmers had non-agriculture as their main occupation. Suresh (2011) found that in garden land majority (66.70%) of the respondents had farming alone as their profession while 20.00 per cent of the respondents were farming + business and 8.90 accounted for farming + allied enterprises and the rest (4.40%) of them were found to engage in farming + services activities. Periyar (2012) observed that more than half of the tank user farmers (55.00%) were engaged in farming and often worked as wage earners followed by 32.00 per cent of respondents involved in agriculture alone. Exactly eight per cent of the respondents had farming and business as their occupation and five per cent of the respondents had farming and government or private service.

Land holding: It refers to the number of acres of land possessed by the farmer. Jennifer and Keremane (2006) reported in their study on farmers' perception on self-created water management, more than 70 per cent of the respondents were marginal and small farmers category. Reddy and Bhagirath (2009) found out that tanks restoration had a positive impact on small and marginal farmers in the drought prone areas. It also had a positive effect and influence on poverty. Umamaheshwara (2009) reported that 30.83 per cent of the respondents belonged to semi-medium category, followed by 25.83 percent in small category and 25.00 per cent in medium category whereas 11.67 per cent of them had marginal land holding and a meagre 6.67 per cent of them belonged to big landholding category.

Farming experience: It refers to total number of years of experience in cultivating crops by the farmers. The experience of the farmer in completed years at the time of investigation was considered. Suresh (2001) report in his study on farmers adoption of agricultural technologies in tank fed area, 56.67 per cent of the respondents possessed high level of farming experience followed by medium (37.50%) and low (5.83%) levels respectively. Senthilvadivoo (2003) revealed that majority (66.67%) of the respondents were found to possess more than ten years of farming experience followed by 20.83 per cent who had attained five to ten years of experience and only 12.50 per cent of the respondents possessed less than five years of experience. Umamaheshwara (2009) observed that nearly half of the farmers possessed medium level of farming experience (40.83%) followed by high (32.50%) and low (26.67%) farming experience. Mohanand and Rameshkumar (2012) reported that majority of the total farmers (33.89%) and farmers of Vizainagaram (30.00%) and Warangal (40.00%) districts were having 20 years and above farming experience followed by 11-15 years of experience. But, in case of Chittoor district majority (35.00%) of the farmers having 16-20 years experience followed by 11-15years of farming experience. Periyar (2012) stated that nearly half of the tank farmers (45.50%) had medium level of farming experience followed by 40.00 per cent of the farmers with high level of farming experience. The remaining 14.50 per cent of the tank farmers had low level of farming experience.

Annual family income: Annual income of the family refers to the income earned by all the members of the family of the respondents from different sources per year. Jayashree (2004) revealed that majority of the respondents (46.67%) had low level of income, followed by medium (28.33%) and high (25.00%) levels of annual income through paddy cultivation. Amarnath and Karthik Raja (2006) analysed tank rehabilitation in Madurai district of Tamil Nadu. The results indicated that the total annual income has been found higher in the rehabilitated tanks than the non-rehabilitated tanks. The study has suggested that rehabilitation work should be undertaken in all the non-rehabilitated tanks also. Umamaheshwara (2009) reported that, 40.83 per cent of the respondents belonged to high income category (>Rs. 51,000) followed by 29.17 per cent of them belonged to medium income category (Rs. 34,0001 – Rs. 50,000) and 24.17 per cent of them belonged to semi- medium category (Rs. 17,001 – Rs. 34,000), whereas 5.83 per cent of respondents belonged to low annual income category (<Rs. 17,000), respectively. Sasikala (2011) observed that in case of below normal rainfall blocks, 69 per cent of farmers had an annual income below Rs.50, 000 followed by 18 per cent with Rs.50,000-1 lakh and 13 per cent with above 1 lakh as annual income. In above normal rainfall block, 64 per cent of the farmers had an annual income up to Rs.50,000 while 16 per cent had an annual income between Rs.50,000 and 1lakh and 20 per cent had an annual income of above 1 lakh.

Mass media exposure: It refers to the degree to which the respondent was exposed to various mass media channels. Jayasree (2004) stated that nearly half of the respondents (49.17%) had a medium level of exposure to mass media sources followed by nearly one-third (32.50%) of the respondents with low level of mass media exposure and just above one-sixth (18.33%) of the respondents with high level of mass media exposure. Balasubramaniam (2005) reported that more than one-third of the respondents had high and medium levels of mass media exposure followed by low level 27.00 per cent. With regard to the mass media exposure Umamaheshwara (2009) observed in his study that, 80.71 per cent and 47.86 per cent of the respondents possessed television and radio, respectively and among the total respondents, 34.17per cent of respondents were regular readers of newspapers. The agricultural information was read regularly by only 10.00 per cent of the respondents. Mohan and Rameshkumar (2012) stated that mass media exposure of majority of total farmers (66.67%) and farmers of Chittoor (70.00%),Vizainagaram (85.00%) and Warangal (45.00%) districts was medium level followed by high level.

Organizational participation: Organizational participation is the degree of involvement of the farmer in the meetings of local formal organizations like gram panchayat, co-operatives, youth clubs and other unregistered organizations. Senthilvadivoo (2003) found that majority of the respondents (68.33 per cent) had medium to high levels of social participation. Jayasree (2004) revealed that majority of the respondents (62.50 per cent) had medium level of social participation followed by low and high levels of social participation with 30.00 per cent and 7.50 per cent respectively. Umamaheshwara (2009) reported that 7.50 per cent of respondents were members and 10.00 per cent were office bearers in gram panchayat and cent per cent of the respondents were members of tank user group. Further he observed that 66.84 per cent of the respondents had regular participation in tank user meeting while 21.66 and 11.50 per cent of respondents had occasional and no participation respectively.

***Extension agency contact*:** It refers to the frequency of contact by a respondent with various extension functionaries for obtaining information on tank irrigation management activities. Suresh (2011) found that 50.00 per cent of the paddy farmers had medium level of contact with extension agency while 45.00 per cent of the respondents had low level followed by high level (5.00%) of contact with extension agencies. With regard to extension participation Mohan and Rameshkumar (2012) reported that majority of the total farmers (62.22%) and farmers of Chittoor (66.675), Vizainagaram (46.67%) and Warangal (73.33%) districts had low extension participation, followed by medium level of extension participation.

***Economic motivation*:** Economic motivation refers to the profit maximization and relative value placed by a individual on economic ends.

Balasubramaniam (2005) stated that 44.00 per cent of the total respondents had high level of economic motivation followed by low and medium levels. Umamaheshwara (2009) reported that, 40.00 per cent of the respondents had medium level of economic motivation whereas 34.58 per cent and 25.75 per cent of them had high and low level of economic motivation respectively. It was reported by Mohan and Rameshkumar (2012) majority of total farmers (65.00%) and farmers of Chittoor (71.66%), Vizainagaram (75.00%) and Warangal (48.34%) had medium level economic orientation followed by high economic orientation.

Risk orientation: Risk orientation refers to the degree to which an individual were oriented towards risk and uncertainty with courage to face the problems in existence. Lawrance (2000) reported that equal percentage of paddy growers of tank fed area had low and high levels of risk orientation. Floralavanya (2007) revealed that 41.70 per cent of adopters and 42.70 per cent of non adopters possessed medium level of risk orientation. Low level of risk orientation was observed among 31.70 per cent of adopters and 26.70 per cent of non adopters followed by 26.60 per cent of adopters and 30.60 per cent of non adopters with high risk orientation nature. Dev (2009) noted that crop insurance is not the long term solution for yield variability. Risk prevention or de-risking of agriculture is important. In order to de-risk agriculture, we have to focus more on management of land and water, including irrigation development, soil conservation, watershed development, water conservation and improvement in public delivery systems. Rakesh (2010) reported that 45.30 per cent of the respondents had high level of economic motivation followed by medium level (32.00 per cent) and little more than twenty per cent of the respondents come under low level of economic motivation. With respect to risk orientation Mohan and Rameshkumar (2012) revealed in his study on profile characteristics of tank farmers that majority of total farmers (58.89%) and farmers of Chittoor (61.67%), Vizainagaram (46.67%) and Warangal (68.33%) of the respondent farmers has medium risk orientation.

Innovativeness: was operationalised as the degree to which a farmer is relatively earlier in adopting new ideas. Balasubramaniam (2005) reported that medium level of innovativeness was observed among the total respondents. The head and mid reach farmers were having more of medium level innovativeness (78.00%) followed by low and high levels. More than half of the respondents (52.50%) belonged to medium innovativeness category whereas 26.67 per cent and 20.83 per cent of them belonged to high and low level of innovativeness categories respectively (Umamaheshwara, 2009). Mohan and Rameshkumar (2012) stated that majority of total farmers (67.78%), farmers of Chittoor (75.00%), Vizainagaram (61.67%) and Warangal (66.67%) districts had medium innovativeness followed by low level of innovativeness.

Dependency of tank: It refers to the extent to which a tank user farmer depends on the tank for the irrigation purpose. Balasubramanian and Selvaraj (2003) opined that tanks are especially important to marginal and small-scale farmers who largely depend on it.

Equitability of water distribution: This is referred to the perception of the respondents as whether the quantum of water from the tank was equally distributed at all reaches or not. Arumgam *et al.* (1997) stated in his study on sustainable management of tank irrigation system, the practice of field to field irrigation leads to inequity in distribution of water and heavy losses in supply and also there was large disparity in distribution of water in head, middle and tail reaches of the command. Arumugam (2001) reported in his study on water user's association in Tankfed Irrigation System, majority (40.00%) of the paddy farmers had the equitability of water distribution in head, middle and tail reaches. This was followed by head, mid (36.00%) and tail reaches (24.00%) of equitability distribution. Krishnaraj (2004) found that majority (44.00%) of the paddy farmers had the equitability of water distribution in head reach. This was followed by head, middle and tail reaches (38.00%) and head and middle reaches (18.00%) with equitability of water distribution. Balasubramaniam (2005) stated that 60.00 per cent of the respondents reported that equitability of water distribution only at two reaches (head and mid) followed by 31.00 per cent in all reaches and meagre per cent (9.00%) reported that equitability of water distribution at head reach only.

Supplemental irrigation source: This was operationalised as the irrigation source utilized by the farm family other than the tank irrigation sources. Karpagam (2004) inferred that a majority of the encroachers (58.30%) relied upon tank water for irrigating their encroached land followed by 27.10 per cent of the encroachers who used the well water, which is located at their patta land. About 10 per cent of encroachers used both tank and well water. Four per cent of the encroachers had not used any irrigation source. Balasubramaniam and Govindasamy (1991) reported that well in the tank command area supplement the tank irrigation by 16-22 per cent. Balasubramaniam (2005) more than fifty per cent of the total respondents were having bore wells as supplemental irrigation sources followed by 45.00 per cent of respondents possessed wells as supplemental irrigation sources. Shankara (2010) observed that nearly 46.99 per cent of respondents belong to medium level of irrigation potential fallowed by low (32.53 %) and high (20.48 %) level of irrigation potential.

Period of availability of water: This referred to the availability of water in the tank during different seasons. Arumugam (2001) reported in his study on water user's association in Tankfed Irrigation System, majority (36.00%) of the paddy farmers had had water availability was for only one season followed by two seasons (33.00%) and all seasons (31.00%) period of water availability. Krishnaraj (2004) found that majority (53.00%) of the paddy farmers had irrigation water availability in all seasons followed by two seasons (32.00%), one seasons (7.00%) and not available (8.00%). Balasubramaniam (2005) reported that more than 60.00 per cent of the total respondents expressed that the availability of water for two seasons alone followed by one third (33.33%) expressed the availability for one season and 3.33 per cent reported for all seasons.

Timely availability of water: It is referred to the availability of water at all the critical stages of the crop. Balasubramaniam (2005) found that more than sixty per cent of the total respondents expressed that water was not available at critical stages, while 32.00 per cent reported that availability of water in critical stages.

CONSTRAINTS EXPERIENCED BY FARMERS IN TANK IRRIGATION MANAGEMENT

Accordingly, Umashankari (1991) assessed tank irrigation in Chittor district of Andhra Pradesh. The inadequacy in supply of water by feeder chemicals because of non-participation in cleaning, encroachment of tank bed for cultivation and inadequate repairs, weed infestation and siltation are responsible for disintegration of the traditional system. Arumugam and Mohan (1997) examined some major considerations related to tank irrigation systems in south India. The major deficiencies that influence the sustainability are given as inadequate maintenance, reduction in storage capacity, heavy seepage losses in the delivery system, and poor water management techniques. A pressing need is identified to evolve and implement appropriate strategies that are sound on technical, social, institutional and economical dimensions for sustainable development and management of tank systems. Palanisami (2006) reported that encroachment, privatization and government appropriation of the tanks have been the main outcomes of the failure of local authority systems to enforce the institutional arrangements under the common property resources management regime. About 2 per cent of the tanks in the tank less intensive region and 67% of the tanks in the intensive region have become defunct. Wells that are supposed to be security against late season tank water scarcity have of late become a major threat to the very survival of the tanks. Taxes from multiple uses of the tanks, if collected by a single agency are sufficient to meet the operation and maintenance expenditures of the tanks both in the short run and in the long run. Navaneeth *et al.* (2007) conducted a study in the Krishna Basin of Karnataka to document the potential created, utilization and to identify the constraints in the development of minor irrigation. Minor irrigation components considered for the study included tanks, barrages, pick-ups and lift irrigation schemes (LIS). The study was reported that Encroachment and siltation of tank bed, poor maintenance, inadequate power, lack of institutional support were identified as the major constraints in the development of minor irrigation in the basin. From the above reviews, it was concluded that encroachment of tank bed, poor water management techniques and siltation were the important constraints experienced by farmers in irrigation tank management. Singh *et al.* (2008) reported that the major constraints and problems identified specific to land and water management were viz.,scattered and fragmented land holdings, field to field Irrigation, over dependency on unreliable canal water, Reluctance in use of groundwater, Seasonal waterlogging/water congestion near canal and drain, unproportionate outlet sizes, unauthorized cuts in distributaries/sub distributary, ungated outlets, obstruction in canal flow to raise the water level, conflicts amongst water users over water distribution, no representation and lack of coordination among canal managers and water users, low water productivity, lack of awareness about recent water management technologies. The major constraints experienced by farmers were lack of knowledge about tank management practices (79.25%) followed by, lack of required irrigation water (65.17%), lack of free time to participate in tank user group meetings (63.18%), accumulation of silt in command area (61.58%) and low productivity (53.24%) Umamaheshwara (2009).

Implications for Strengthening Community based Tank Irrigation Systems

1. Since the majority of the farmers were middle and old age category they might have got good experience in tank irrigation system. Therefore it is important to utilize their knowledge about tank irrigation system and it should be imparted to young generation. This is the right time for the change agents and policy makers to take necessary action to encourage young generation in participatory tank irrigation management and imparting the knowledge and importance about community based tank irrigation management system.
2. Farming and wage earning was the major source of livelihood in tank command area. However due to inadequate water availability in tanks and lack of rainfall resulted with crop failure and low yield. Due to this condition they ought to seek for alternative livelihood option. In order to improve their livelihood status and mitigate the uncertainty, it is suggested that extension agency should play a crucial role in finding suitable copping pattern, production technology and train the farmers to go for crop diversity.
3. Medium and low level of innovativeness may hinder the early adoption of innovative agricultural practices therefore it is suggested that there is a need to improve their level of organizational participation and extension agency contact to give good exposure about outside

environment and knowledge about innovative agricultural practices which in turn help the farmers to have high level of innovativeness.

4. Mass media participation, extension agency contact, economic motivation, innovativeness and risk orientation were found to have moderate level. It is suggested that extension personnel from the public and private sector should make a good rapport to the farmers and provide advice on new profit oriented technologies and its suitability in a particular ecosystem which in turn influence the farmers to have high level of economic motivation, innovativeness and risk taking ability.
5. Community participation in tank irrigation management should be encouraged for the effective management water resources. There should be a governmental interventions and assistance in formation of water users association, water management committee and farmers associations for the involving community participation in water resource management.
6. Tank user farmers were found to possess moderately favourable attitude towards community based tank irrigation management. This is a critical observation which needs to be addressed through intensification of efforts to change the mindset of tank user farmers towards community managed tank irrigation system.
7. The contribution of tanks plays significant role in improving livelihood of rural people. It is suggested that special attention should be given for renovation of tanks and improve its physical structures which in turn increases the water holding level and ultimately lead to improvement in agricultural productivity
8. Conflict management patterns in terms of sources, nature, pattern and resolution strategies have to be considered. Since community based tank irrigation management involves different status of people, special attention should be given to amicably solve the conflict issues such as inter village conflict, conflict among farmers and conflict among multiple tank users for the smooth functioning of community approach in tank irrigation management system.
9. The major constraints were non-availability of required irrigation water, poor maintenance of tank structures, poor distribution of water and accumulation of silt. It is suggested that proper scheduling of irrigation should be followed and necessary action should be taken to reduce the conveyance loss of water.

The Mahatma Gandhi National Rural Employment Guarantee Programme should be strictly implemented in a community managed tanks which helps to renovate physical structure of tanks and improve its water holding capacity.

10. Levying maintenance charge according to acreage and collection of some amount for irrigating lands according to the acreage should be followed for the effective maintenance of tanks. Besides, government should also allocate necessary budget for maintenance of tanks.
11. It was reported in the study that majority of the tank user farmers depend on supplemental irrigation sources viz., dug well, bore well and tube wells. It shows that less reliability over tank irrigation source therefore tank maintenance should be given more important.
12. Necessary action should be taken for proper channelizing and allocation of water from head end to tail end.
13. Effort should be taken for capacity building of farmers through training and exposure visits in order to involve the farmers in community managed tank irrigation system. It will give good exposure to the farmers about the irrigation management practices followed in other places and will lead them to involve themselves in collective tank irrigation management activities.
14. Importance should be given for the community managed tanks on par with PWD managed tanks, such that, tanks structure can be maintained and it can serve its purpose.
15. Proper training should be given to farmers in selection of crops and varieties, adopting water management practices and improved production technology like System of Rice Intensification (SRI) and Sustainable Sugarcane Initiative techniques (SSI).

CONCLUSION

As a result, a large majority of the tanks in the southern and eastern parts of India suffer from inadequate management and maintenance, some have become dysfunctional while others are even obliterated. At the all India level, the area under tank irrigation declined from 4.6 mn ha to 3.3 mn ha (Narayanamoorthi, 2002 and Janakarajan 1996). In Tamil Nadu the contribution of tank irrigation declined from 40 per cent in 1955 to less than 25 per cent in 2000 (Balasubramanian,and Selvaraj, 2004). In this context, it is perceived that there is urgent need to establish community organization and formulate policy programmes for both participatory and collaborative mode of water resource management. The community approach in tank irrigation management ensures sustainable management of irrigation system and mutual understanding among people in water sharing and developing good personal relationship. It is also reported that community management of water resources had proven over time to be very successful and sustainable. This approach ensures its optimum utilization, conservation, and maximizes the benefits. Large numbers of such example are scattered throughout India (Bhavsar and Bhagale 2007). Scaling-up of ground water level has to be the thrust area for development of farming sectors.

REFERENCES

Amarnath and Karthikraja, K. (2006): An Economic Analysis of Tank Rehabilitation in Madurai District of Tamil Nadu, *Agricultural Economics Research Review*, 19: 187-194.

Anandan, C. (2007): Participatory Approach only Tool for Success Model – TRPP Scheme, Paper Presented at Twelfth National Water Convention, Ministry of Water Resources, Government of India, 384-388.

Anitha, S. (1998): Analysis of Pesticides and Plant Protection Equipment Use Behaviour of Rice Farmers, Unpub. M.Sc. (Ag.) AC & RI, TNAU, Coimbatore.

Ann-Marie, N and J. Strazzabosco. (2009): Group Dynamics and Team Building, Pub. Hemophilia organization development, No 4. pp.1-2.

Arumugam and Mohan. (1997): Tank Irrigation in India: Problems and Prospects, *Water Resource Management*, 6 (3): 211.

Arumugam, N., S. Mohan and R. Ramprasad. (1997): Sustainable Development and Management of Tank Irrigation System in South India, *Water International*, Vol. 22: 2. pp. 90-97.

Arumugam, S. (2001): Water user's Association in Tankfed Irrigation System- An Impact Analysis. Unpub. M.Sc. (Ag.) Thesis, TNAU, Coimbatore.

Arumugam. (2001): Water user's Association in Tank-fed Irrigation System- An Impact Analysis. Unpub. M.Sc. (Ag) Thesis, AC&RI, TNAU, Coimbatore.

Arun, K.P. (2013): The Influence of Organizational Climate for Organizational Success in SCCL, *South Asian Journal of Marketing & Management Research* (SAJMMR), Vol. 3, (7) pp. 45-47.

Asian Development Bank. (2006): Rehabilitation and Management of Tanks: A Study of Selected State, *Asian Development Bank*, Philippines, Publication No. 122605.

Asokhan, M. (2006): Empowerment of Rural Women through Self-Help Groups – An Empirical Analysis, Unpub. Ph.D. Thesis, TNAU, Coimbatore.

Austin, D.L. (1976): Conflict: A more Professional Approach. *Personal Administration*, Vol. 21(2), 16-19.

Balasubramaniam, P. (2005): Developing a Transfer of Technology Strategy for Water Management Technologies in Canal Command Areas. Ph.D. Thesis, TNAU, Coimbatore.

Balasubramaniam, R and Govindasamy. (1991): Ranking Irrigation Tanks for Modernization. Agricultural Water Management, Vol. 20 (2), pp: 155-162.

Balasubramanian, K. and Selvaraj. (2004): Tank Degradation and Poverty Reduction,

The Importance of Common Property Resources in Sustaining the Rural Poor, SANDEE, *Policy Brief*, No. 2.4.

Balasubramanian, R and K.N. Selvaraj. (2003): Poverty, Private Property and Common Pool Resource Management: The Case of Irrigation Tanks in South India, *Working Paper*, No. 2-03. SANDEE.

Balasubramanian, R. and G. Ramu, (1991): Ranking Irrigation Tanks for Modernization, Agricultural Water Management, Vol. 20, pp: 155-162.

Bauman, Z. (1989): Modernity and the Holocaust, *Cornell University Press*, pp: 163.

Bhavsar, C. and P. Bhalge. (2007): Fruits of Participatory Irrigation Management, the 4th Asian Regional Conference and 10th International Seminar on Participatory Irrigation Management, Tehran-Iran may 2-5, 2007.

Blake, R.R. and J.S. Mouton. (1985): The Managerial Grid III (3rd Ed.), *Houston Press*, pp: 172.

Brewer, J.D. and R. Sakthivadivel. (1999): Maintenance Management Process: A Key Factor in Maintenance Improvement under Resource Constraints, Irrigation and Drainage Systems,Vol. 13: pp. 207-227.

Carron, A.V. (1980): Social Psychology of Sport, Ithaca, NY: Movement., 16p.

Cartwright, D. (1968): The Nature of Group Cohesiveness. In D. Cartwright, & A. Zander (Eds.), Group Dynamics: Research and Theory, 3rd.ed, New York: *Harper & Row*, pp: 18.

Chandran, M.K., K.M. Varadan, and T. Valsan. (2001): Evaluation of Farmer's Participation under Command Area Development Programme in Kerala, *J.tropical. agric.* Vol. 39: pp. 38-41.

Chung. K.H. and L.C. Meggison. (1981): Organisational Behaviour, *Harper and Row*, New York.

Coser, L. (1967): Continuities in the Study of Social Conflict, *Free Press*, New York.

Dahama, O.P. and Bhatnagar. (1985): Education and Communication for Development, *Oxford and IBH Publishing Co.*, New Delhi, pp. 232.

Darling, J.R. and W.E Walker. (2001): Effective Conflict Management: Use of the Behavioural Style Model, *Leadership and Organization Development Journal*, Vol. 22 (5): pp. 230-242.

Deetz, S.A. and S.L. Stevenson. (1986): Managing Interpersonal Communication, *Harper and Row*, New York.

Deutsch, M. (1973): Conflicts: Productive and Destructive, In Conflict Resolution through Communication, *Harper and Row*, New York.

Dev, S.M. (2009): Challenges for Revival of Indian Agriculture, *Agricultural Economics Research Review*, Vol. 22: pp. 21-45.

Dubin, R.(1974): Theory Building, *Free press*, New York.

Edwards, A.L. (1969): Techniques of Attitude Scale Construction, *Vakils Feffer and Simmons Private Limited*, Bombay.

Faria, R.G. (1982): An Investigative Analysis of Conflict Management Theory and Practice as Examined from the Operative Position of the Secondary School Assistant Principalship, *Boston College School of Education*, Boston.

Festinger, L. (1954): A Theory of Social Comparison Processes, *Human Relations*, pp: 16.

Floralavanya, V. (2007): Sustainable Water Management through Drip Irrigation in Madurai District – An Explorative Study, Unpub. M.Sc. (Ag.) Thesis, AC&RI, TNAU, Madurai.

Gandhi Vasant. P and N.V. Namboodiri. (2002): Investments and Institutions for Water Management in India's Agriculture: Policies and Behaviour, in Donna Brennan (ed.) Water Policy Reform: A Lesson from Asia and Australia, Australian Centre for International Agricultural Research, Canberra, Austalia.

Garrett, H.E. (1979): Statistics in Psychology and Education. *Vakils, Feffer and Simons Ltd*, Mumbai.

Gibb, C.A. (1947): The Principles and Traits of Leadership. *Journal of Abnormal and Social Psychology*, pp. 268.

Goswami,S. (2011): Tanks in Rural West Bengal: Performance and Institutions for Sustainable Use. Sixth Biennial Conference on "Nature, Economy and Society: Understanding the Linkages". *Centre for Economic and Social Studies* (CESS), Hyderabad.

Goudappa, S.B., S. R. Surekha and A.M. Benki. (2012): Extent of Participation of Farmers in Planning and Implementation of Community Based Tank Management Project in Raichur District, *Indian Research Journal of Extension Education*, Special Issue Vol. 1, pp. 273-274.

Hall, J. (1969): Conflict Management Survey, *Telemetric,* Inc., Austin, Texas.

Harris, P.R. and K.G. Harris. (1996): Managing Effectively through Teams, Team Performance, pp: 16.

Hema, D. (2003): Functioning on Women SHGs in Pondicherry Union Territory-A Critical Analysis, Unpub. M.Sc. (Ag.) Thesis, AC&RI, TNAU, Coimbatore.

Hocker, J.L. and W.W. Wilmot. (1985): Interpersonal Conflict Dubuque, *Brown Publishers,* Iowa.

Hudson and Seekler. (1974): Organisation and Management on An Introduction to Sociology, *Vidya Bhushan, Kitab Mahal,* Allahabad, pp. 312.

James A.F. Stoner, R. Edward Freeman and R. Gilbert. (2006): Management, *Prentice Hall of India Pvt. Ltd,* New Delhi.

Janakarajan, S (1996): Note on Irrigation Experience of Tamil Nadu, Proceedings of the Seminar on Conservation and Development of Tank Irrigation for Livelihood Promotion, July 12, Madurai, Conservation and Development Forum Gainesville, USA.

Janakaran.S. (1993): In Search of Tanks, Some Hidden facts, *Economic and Political Weekly,* Jan. 26, pp. 453-460.

Jayashree, B.S. (2004): A Study on Integrated Water Management Technologies Demonstrated under AICRP on Water Management, Unpub. M.Sc. (Ag.) Thesis, AC&RI, TNAU, Madurai.

Jebamary, K. (2012): Impact of Dynamics of Self-help Group on Rural Women Empowerment-A Critical Analysis: A Case Study, Unpub. Ph.D Thesis, TNAU, Coimbatore.

Jennifer, M. and G.B. Keremane. (2006): Farmers' Perception on Self-created Water Management Rules in a Pioneer Scheme: The Mulla Irrigation Scheme, India, *Irrigation and Drainage Systems,* 20: 205-223. pp. 1-19.

Jodha, N.S. (1986): Rural Common Property Resources and Rural Poor in Dry Regions of India, *Economic and Political Weekly,* Vol. 21 No. 27, p. 1169-1181.

Karpagam, D. (2004): Case Study on Encroachment in Tank Irrigation System and its Consequences on Agriculture, Unpub. M.Sc. (Ag.) Thesis, AC&RI, TNAU, Coimbatore.

Karthikeyan, C. (2000): A Study on the Effectiveness of Tank Irrigation Institutions in Tamil Nadu, Ford Foundation Funded Research Project Report Submitted to TNAU, Coimbatore.

Karthikeyan. C. (2010): Competition and Conflicts among Multiple users, Fourteenth International Water Technology Conference, IWTC 14 2010, Cairo, Egypt, pp. 845-847.

Kavitha, S. (2001): Integrated Water Management-An ex-post facto Study on Differential Knowledge and Adoption Behaviour of Rice Growers, Unpub. M.Sc. (Ag.) Thesis, AC & RI, TNAU, Coimbatore.

Kei Kajisa., Palanisami., K and Takeshi Sakurai. (2006): Effect on Poverty and Equity of the Decline in Collective Tank Irrigation Management in Tamil Nadu, *India Agricultural Economics,* Vol. 36, 347-362.

Kerlinger, F.M. (2002): Foundation of Behavioural Research, *Rinehart and Winston*. Inc. New York.

Kerlinger, F.M. (2007): Foundation of Behavioural Research, Rinehart and Winston, Inc. New York.

Kolavalli, S. (1995): Assessing the Water User association, Paper Presented in IIMIIMI Workshop on Irrigation Management, Transfer in India, Indian Institute of Management, Ahmedabad, pp: 191.

Kolavalli, S. and J.D. Brewer, (1999): Facilitating user Participation in Irrigation Management, *Irrigation and Drainage Systems*, 13: 249-273.

Kondalkar, V.G. 2007. Organizational Behaviour, New *Age International Publishers*, New Delhi.

Koontz, H., H. Weihrich, and A.R. Aryasri. (2008): Principles of Management, *Tata McGraw-Hill Publishing Company Limited*, New Delhi.

Kressel, N. (1996): Mass Hate: The Global Rise of Genocide and Terror, *Plenum Press*, pp: 139.

Krishnaprasad, T. (2005): A Study on Rural Poverty and Sustainable Livelihood in Agrarian Sector of Andhra Pradesh, Ph.D (Agri.) Thesis, Acharya N.G. Ranga Agric. Univ. Hyderabad.

Krishnaraj, A. (2004): Awareness, Knowledge, Extent of Adoption and Consequential Effects of Water Management/Conservation Practices, Unpub. M.Sc. (Ag.) Thesis, TNAU, Coimbatore.

Kurt, L. (1951): Field Theory in Social Science, *Harper and Row*, New York.

Lam, W.F. (1996): Improving the Performance of Small-scale Irrigation Systems: The Effects of Technological Investments and Governance Structure on Irrigation Performance in Nepal, *World Development*, 24(8): 1301-1315.

Lauren. P., R.D. Meinzen, and D. Stephen. (2008): Gender and Collective Action: Motivations, Effectiveness and Impact, *Journal of International Development*, Vol. 20, pp. 1-11.

Lawrance, M. (2000): Integrated Pest Management in Tankfed Rice Cultivation- A Critical Analysis, Unpub. M.Sc (Ag.) Thesis, AC & RI, TNAU, Coimbatore.

Mahendrarajah, S., J. Jakemarie and P.C. Young. (1999): Water Supply in Monsoonal Asia: Modelling and Predicting Small Tank Storage, *Agricultural Economics*, Vol. 84. pp. 127-137.

Matriu, V. (2000): Conflict and Natural Resource Management, *FAO Publication*, pp: 182.

Mayya, S.G. (1987): System Study on Tank irrigation, Ph.D. Thesis, Indian Institute of Science, Bangalore.

McCauley, C. (1989): The Nature of Social Influence on Groupthink: Compliance and Internalization, JPSP, 57, 250-260.

McFarland, L.J., S. Senen and J.R. Childress. (1993): Twenty-first-century Leadership, *Leadership Press*, New York.

Meenu Singh. (2000): An Analysis of Common-Pool –Resources in Institutional Economic Framework: Evidence from Tank Irrigation and Group- Owned-Wells in South India, M.Sc. Degree paper, Michigan State University, pp. 15-5.

Mohan, K and P.R. Rameshkumar. (2012): Profile Characteristics of Farmers under Tank Irrigation Commands, *Karnataka J. Agric. Sci.*, Vol. 25 (3) pp. 359-362.

Mosse. (1999): Colonial and Contemporary Ideologies of 'Community Management':

The Case of Tank Irrigation Development in South India, *Modern Asian Studies*, Vol. 33 (2): 82.

Myers, M.T., and G.E. Myers. (1982): Managing by Communication – An Organizational Approach, *McGraw-Hill Book Company,* New York.

Nagabhushanam., K. (1997): Sustainability of Agriculture in Watershed Environment – An Analysis, Unpub. Ph.D. Thesis, AC&RI, TNAU, Coimbatore.

Naimark, N. (2001): Fires of Hatred: Ethnic Cleansing in Twentieth-century Europe, *Harvard University Press,* Harvard.

Nanthakumaran. A and K. Palanisami. (2010): Farmer Participation on Water Management in the Tank Irrigated Systems in Tamil NADU, International Conference on Sustainable Built Environments (ICSBE-2010), Kandy, 13-14: pp. 1-8.

Narayanamoorthi, A. (2002): Indian Irrigation: Five Decades of Development', *Water Resources Journal,* ESCAP, No. 212.

Narayanamoorthy, A. (2004): Tank Irrigation in the 21st Century: What Next? *Indian Journal of Agricultural Economics,* pp. 183.

Navaneeth, B.S., R.S. Poddar, L.B. Kunnal Hugar, and D.P. Biradar. (2007): Performance of Minor Irrigation in Krishna Basin of Karnataka - An Economic Analysis, *Karnataka J. Agric. Sci.,* Vol. 21: pp. 532-534.

Ostrom, E. (2000): Reformulating the Commons, *Swiss Political Science Review,* Vol. 6(1): pp. 29-52.

Palanisami, K. and K.W. Ester, (2009): Tank Irrigation in the 21st Century: What Next? *Discovery Publishing House Pvt. Ltd.,* New Delhi.

Palanisami, K., (2006): Sustainable Management of Tank Irrigation Systems in India, Water Technology Centre, Tamil Nadu Agric. Univ, Coimbatore.

Palanisami, K., Senthilvel, S., Ranganathan, C. R and T. Ramesh. (2006): Water Productivity at Different Scales under Canal, Tank and Well Irrigation Systems, Centre for Agricultural and Rural Development Studies (CARDS), Tamil Nadu Agricultural University, Coimbatore.

Palaniswamy, K., and K.W. Easter.(1986):The Tanks of South India: A Potential Future Expansion in Irrigation: Economic Report ER 83-1, Department of Agri and Applied Economics, University of Minnesota, U.S.A.

Parker, C., B. Baltes, S.Young, J. Huff, R. Altman, H. Lacost and J. Roberts. (2003): Relationships between Psychological Climate Perceptions and Work Outcomes: A Meta Analytic Review, *Journal of Organizational Behaviour,* Vol. 24 (4), pp. 389-416.

Periyar, R. (2012): Study on the Influence of Climate Change and Socio-economic Factors on the Livelihood of Farmers in Tank Command Area, Ph.D. Thesis, TNAU, Coimbatore.

Prasidha, P.R. (2006): Agricultural Labour in Rice based Farming System: A Gender based Multidimensional Analysis, M.Sc (Ag) Thesis, Kerala Agricultural University, Thrissur, pp. 130.

Rafiepour, F. (1993): Rural Tendency Evaluation to Jahad e-Sazandagi, Tehran, Arganoon Edition, 50-58.

Rakesh, K. (2010): Precision Farming in Sugarcane – A Diagnostic Study, Unpub. M.Sc. (Ag.) Thesis, AC & RI, TNAU, Madurai.

Rao, N.M. (1987): A Study to Identify the Technological Gaps and Constraints in Adoption of Improved Practices in Groundnut Cultivation in Guntur District of Andhra Pradesh, Unpub. M.Sc. (Ag.) Thesis, APAU, Hyderabad.

Reddy, D.N., B.C. Beahrah, and T., Sudhakar. (1993): Decline of Traditional Water Harvesting System: Tanks in the Drought Prone Areas of Andhra Pradesh, *Ind. J. Agric Econ.,* Vol. 48(1): pp. 76-78.

Reddy, R. (2002): Water Institutions: Is Formalisation the Answer?, *Indian Journal of Agricultural Economics*, Vol. 57 (3): 893.

Reddy, V.R. and B. Bhagirath. (2009): Economic and Ecological Impacts of Tank Restoration in South India, *European Journal of Development Research*, Vol. 21, pp. 112-136.

Robbins, S.P. (1974): Managing Organizational Conflict, Englewood Cliffs, N. J.Prentice-Hall, Inc. India.

Robbins, S.P. (2009): Essentials of Organizational Behaviour, Prentice Hall, India.

Rogers, E.M. and R.A. Rogers. (1976): Communication in Organizations, *Free Press*, New York.

Sakthivadivel, R and P. Gomathinayagam, (2006): Rehabilitation and Management of Tanks in India, India Resident Mission and Asian Development Bank, pp. 51-53.

Sakthivadivel, R., P. Gomathinayagam and Tushaar Shah. (2004): Rejuvenating Irrigation Tanks though Local Institutions, *Economic and Political Weekly*, Vol. 39(31): pp. 3521-3526.

Sakthivadivel, R., S. Savadamuthu, C.R, Shanmugam, Balakrishnani and C.Arputharaj. (1982): A Pilot Project Study of Modernization of Tank Irrigation in Tamil Nadu, Workshop on Modernization of Tank Irrigation: Problems and Issues, Centre for Water Resources, Anna University, Madras, India.

Samuel C.C. and S.C.Trevis. (2008): Modern Management, *PHI Learning Private Limited*, New Delhi, San Francisco, CA.

Sangeetha, S. (2009): Study on Factors Influencing the Adoption of Precision Farming Technologies in Tomato Cultivation, Unpub. M.Sc. (Ag.) Thesis, AC&RI, TNAU, Coimbatore.

Saravanakumar. (1996): A Study of the Management of Mango Gardens by Farmers in Krishnagiri Taluk of Dharmapuri District, Tamil Nadu, M.Sc. (Agri.) Thesis, Univ. Agric. Sci., Dharwad.

Sasikala, C. (2011): Vulnerability and Adaptation to Rainfall Variability in Rainfed Tank Irrigated Agriculture in Pudukkottai District of Tamil Nadu, Unpub. M.Sc. (Ag.) Thesis, TNAU, Coimbatore.

Schermerhorn, G. (2009): Organisational Behaviour, Wiley Student Edition, New Delhi.Sci., Dharwad.

Scott, W.E. (1975): The Effects of Extrinsic Rewards on Intrinsic Motivation, Organizational Behaviour and Human Performance, pp: 182.

Sekar, I. (2008): Economic Performance and Promotion of Tank Modernisation Programme for Sustaining Rainfed Agriculture, *Indian Journal of Agricultural Economics*, Vol.63 (3): Pp.533

Sekaran, U. (2010): Organizational Behaviour - Text and Cases, *Tata McGraw Hills Publishing Company Limited*, New Delhi.

Senthilvadivoo, K. (2003): Integrated Wasteland Development Programme-A critical analysis, Unpub. M.Sc. (Ag.) Thesis, AC & RI, TNAU, Madurai.

Shankara. M.H. (2010): Farmers' Perception of Climate Change and their Adaptations, Unpub. M.sc. (Ag.) Thesis, University of Agricultural Sciences, Bengaluru.

Sharma, A. (2001): Greening of Desert, *Deccan Herald*, 15th July, 20. Agri. Sci., Dharwad.

Sharma, M.L., Khan, M.A. (1999): Constraints in Irrigation as Perceived by the Farmers of Raipur District, J. Ravishankar Univ. B. Sci., 11/12: 1-5.

Shashidhara, K.K. (2003): A Study on Socio-economic Profile of Drip Irrigation Farmers in Shimoga and Davangere District of Karnataka, M.Sc. (Agri.) Thesis, Univ. Agri. Sci., Dharward.

Sing, A.K., A.K. Sikka, A. Upadhyaya, P.R. Bhatnagar, S. Dhanphle, M.K Singh, and A.R Singh. (2008): Scientific Perceptions and Community Responses in a Participatory Water Management Endeavour, *Water Resource Management*, Vol. 22. pp. 1173-1159.

Singh, A.K. (2008): Test, Measurements and Research Methods in Behavioural Sciences, *Bharati Bhawan Publishers & Distributors*, New Delhi.

Singh, J.P. (1977): Productivity of Crops in Indian Agriculture, *Productivity*, Vol. 18(2): pp. 169-186.

Singh, K. (1977): A Study on New Marginal Farmers Situations and Socio-economic Impact of New Agricultural Technology, Unpub. M.Sc. (Ag) Thesis, AC&RI, TNAU, Coimbatore.

Smith, B.R. (1856): Irrigation in Southern India, London, U.K: Elder and Co.

Sophia, R. (1991): A Diagnostic Study on the Impact of Factors Associated with Shift from Paddy to Tapioca, unpub. M.Sc.(Ag.) Thesis, Agrl. College and Res. Instt. T.N.A.U., Madurai.

Stoel, L. (2002): Retail Cooperatives: Group Size, Group Identification, Communication Frequency and Relationship Effectiveness, *International Journal of Retail & Distribution Management*, Vol. 30 (1), pp. 51-60.

Stoner, J.A.F., R.D. Freeman and D.R. Gilbert. (1996): Management Eastern Economy Edition, *Prentice Hall of India Private Limited*, New Delhi.

Supe, S.V. (1969): Dynamics of Rational Behaviour, *New Heights Publishers*, New Delhi.

Suresh, R. (2001): Farmers Adoption of Agricultural Technologies in Tank Fed Area of Gundar River Basin of Ramanathapuram District in Tamil Nadu, Unpub. M.Sc. (Ag.) Thesis, AC&RI, TNAU, Madurai.

Suresh, T.V. and B. Ramesh. (2008): Extent of Participation of Farmers in Sujala Kalinganahalli Halla Watershed Project, *Andhra Agric. Journal.*, 55(3): pp. 405-407.

Suresh, S. (2011): Studying Climate Change Pattern through Farmers Participatory Approach, Unpub. M.Sc. (Ag.) Thesis, TNAU, Coimbatore.

Tang, S.Y. (1992): Institutions and Collective Action: Self-governance in Irrigation, *ICS Press*, New York.

Tekynel, O. and M.L. Aksu. (1997): Turkish Experiences in Participatory Irrigation Management, *Med. Sem. Mediterranean*,Vol. 8(2): 23-30.

Thinagaran, M. (1997): Tanks and Social Forestry, The Role of Forest Department, National Seminar on Participation in Tank Rehabilitation and Management Training Institute, Trichy, Tamil Nadu. pp. 24-25.

Thiruchelvam, S. (2004): Economic Effects of Irrigation Management Transfer in Mahaweli System H. Paper Presented at the Water Professionals' Day Symposium, University of Peradeniya, Sri Lanka.

Thirumoorthy,S. (2009): An Economic Study on Effects of Tank Modernisation on Farming in Puducherry Region, Unpub. M.Sc. (Ag.) Thesis, Pandit Jawaharlal Nehru College of Agriculture and Research Institute, Tamil Nadu Agricultural University, Karaikal.

Thomas, K. (1976): Conflict and Conflict Management. Handbook of Industrial and Organizational Psychology, *Rand McNally Press*, Chicago.

Thurstone, L.L. and E.J. Chave. 1929. The Measurement of Attitude, Chicago University, *Chicago Press*, pp: 186.

Trivedi, G. (1963): Measurement and Analysis of Socio-economic Status of Rural Families in Kanjhawala Block, Ph.D., Thesis, Indian Agricultural Research Institute, New Delhi. pp. 67.

Ul-haq, A. and B.A. Shahid. (1997): Public, Private or Participatory: Reforming Irrigation Management in Pakistan, *Int. Comm. Irr. Drain. J.*, 46(1): 37-48.

Umamaheshwara, M.S. (2009): Study on Community Participation in Irrigation Tank Management in Haveri District, M.sc (Ag.) Thesis, College of Agriculture, Dharwad, University of Agricultural Sciences, pp. 63-64.

Umashankari. (1991): Tanks: Major Problems in Miner Irrigation, *Econ and Pol. Weekly.*, A115-A125.

Vasimalai, M.P., C.R. Shanmugam and R. Seenivasan. (1996): Steering the Process of Turnover: A Perspective', in Proceedings of the Workshop on Turnover of Tank Irrigation Systems to Farmers, Water Technology Centre, Tamil Nadu Agricultural University, Coimbatore.

Viswanathan, K.U. and A. Khandge. (2006): Economics of Tank Modernisation Projects under RIDF in Karnataka, *Indian Journal of Agricultural Economics*, Vol. 61 (3): pp. 515-516.

Yasin, M. and S. Ahmad. (1997): Modernization of Irrigation Schemes in Pakistan, *Water Rep.*, 12: pp. 205-219.

Zander, A. (1979) The Psychology of Group Processes, *Annual Review of Psychology*, Vol. 30: 417- 451.

Pages: 52-59

Water and Waste Water: ***Issues and Management***
Edited by: **Dr. Pawan Kumar 'Bharti'**
ISBN: 978-93-88854-15-3
Edition: **2019**
Published by: **Discovery Publishing House Pvt. Ltd., New Delhi (India)**

4

Wastewater Quality Characteristics at Shella (East Khasi Hills), Meghalaya, India

Vijender Singh[1,2]
Pawan Kumar 'Bharti'[2]

ABSTRACT

Umaim river is a major river of East Khasi Hills district in Meghalaya along with many small tributaries near Bangladesh Border. It has a great importance as a natural habitat among the various ecosystems of the region, whereas there is a large scale limestone mining area and no more industrial and agricultural pollution. Anthropogenic factors mainly activities of local people and catchments runoff may influence the index of nutrients in river water and may alter the physico-chemical characteristics and also the whole water quality and the structure of biotic community. Wastewater discharge from the villages of the vicinity may play an important role into the balance of aquatic ecosystem of local rivers, ponds, if discharged directly. Pollution load and nutrients concentration of the wastewater were studied with special reference to physico-chemical parameters and heavy metals in the wastewater generated nearby. The present study deals with the preliminary physico-chemical characteristics of wastewater and exhibits the nature of wastewater due to workshop activities, which contribute in pollution load of an ecosystem.

Keywords: Wastewater quality, Pollution status, microbial contamination, physico-chemical characteristics.

[1] **Green Consultancy and Research Pvt. Ltd., 3263, Urban Estate, Jind (Haryana) (India)**
[2] **Shriram Institute for Industrial Research, 19, University Road, Delhi- 110007 (India)**

INTRODUCTION

Wastewater is the water which is disposed from homes, offices and industry. It comes from toilets, sinks, showers, washing machines and industrial processes and was historically called sewage.

Wastewater (or waste water) is any water that has been affected by human use. Wastewater is used water from any combination of domestic, industrial, commercial or agricultural activities, surface runoff or stormwater, and any sewer inflow or sewer infiltration. Therefore, wastewater is a byproduct of domestic, industrial, commercial or agricultural activities. The characteristics of wastewater vary depending on the source. Types of wastewater include: domestic wastewater from households, municipal wastewater from communities (also called sewage) or industrial wastewater from industrial activities. Wastewater can contain physical, chemical and biological pollutants.

Households may produce wastewater from flush toilets, sinks, dishwashers, washing machines, bath tubs, and showers. Households that use dry toilets produce less wastewater than those that use flush toilets.

Wastewater may be conveyed in a sanitary sewer which conveys only sewage. Alternatively, it can be transported in a combined sewer which includes stormwater runoff and industrial wastewater. After treatment at a wastewater treatment plant, the treated wastewater (also called effluent) is discharged to a receiving water body. The terms wastewater reuse or water reclamation apply if the treated waste is used for another purpose. Wastewater that is discharged to the environment without suitable treatment causes water pollution.

Sources of wastewater include the following domestic or household activities:

- Human excreta (feces and urine) often mixed with used toilet paper or wipes; this is known as blackwater if it is collected with flush toilets.
- Washing water (personal, clothes, floors, dishes, cars, etc.), also known as greywater or sullage
- Surplus manufactured liquids from domestic sources (drinks, cooking oil, pesticides, lubricating oil, paint, cleaning liquids, etc.)

Since all natural waterways contain bacteria and nutrients, almost any waste compounds introduced into such waterways will initiate biochemical reactions (such as shown above). Those biochemical reactions create what is measured in the laboratory as the biochemical oxygen demand (BOD). Such chemicals are also liable to be broken down using strong oxidizing agents and these chemical reactions create what is measured in the laboratory as the chemical oxygen demand (COD). Both the BOD and COD tests are a measure of the relative oxygen-depletion effect of a waste contaminant. Both have been widely adopted as a measure of pollution effect. The BOD test measures the oxygen demand of biodegradable pollutants whereas the COD test measures the oxygen demand of oxidizable pollutants.

At a global level, around 80% of wastewater produced is discharged into the environment untreated, causing widespread water pollution. There are numerous processes that can be used to clean up wastewaters depending on the type and extent of contamination. Wastewater can be treated in wastewater treatment plants which include physical, chemical and biological treatment processes. Municipal wastewater is treated in sewage treatment plants (which may also be referred to as wastewater treatment plants). Agricultural wastewater may be treated in agricultural wastewater treatment processes, whereas industrial wastewater is treated in industrial wastewater treatment processes.

STUDY AREA

The seven states of North East India are quite famous as Seven Sisters, and Meghalaya is very well known for the record of rainfall, the state consists of the two places namely Cherrepunjee (Sohra) and Mawsinram for maximum rainfall throughout the year. So, the maximum water resources are depending chiefly on total precipitations of the region. The Meghalaya has been surrounded by the natural beauties with lovely trees and cool climate, which is not only a pleasant place to live in but relaxing for holiday also. This is not only a popular state but also valuable or important place for tourism, Shillong is the capital of Meghalaya state. Mowlong Cherra Cement Ltd and Lafarge Umaim Mining Ltd are the major industries of the region.

Umaim river is originating from the hills of Assam-Meghalaya basically and flowing along with many villages of the region. *Geologically,* North-east hills are enriched with various minerals and the hills near Bangladesh are rich in limestone. *Geographically,* the study area is situated in the globe on a Latitude 25° 11′ 40.8″ N & Longitude 91° 38′ 16.4″ E for Upstream site and Latitude 25° 10′ 43.8″ N & Longitude 91° 38′ 19.2″ E for Downstream site. *Meteorologically,* region has a cool & pleasant climate.

MATERIALS AND METHODS

The wastewater samples were collected from workshop pit of mining site near Shella Bazar according to the analytical requirement.

The samples for physico-chemical parameters and Heavy Metals were collected by using rinsed Borosil glassware, and analyzed with the help of the procedure described by APHA (1995) and Trivedi and Goel (1984). Colour, odour, turbidity, velocity, temperature and Dissolved oxygen were analyzed on site. Sample was collected and immediately preserved in ice boxes, and transfer to the lab for further analysis (Bharti, 2004). Wastewater sample was digested and heavy metals were detected using Atomic absorption spectrophotometer (Bharti, 2007a).

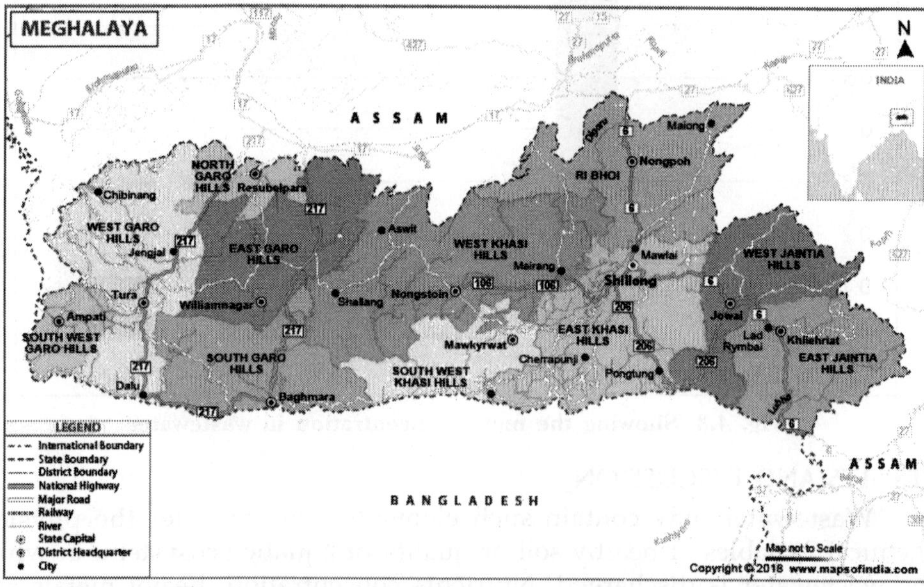

Fig. 4.1: District map of Meghalaya (*Source:* www.mapsonindia.com)

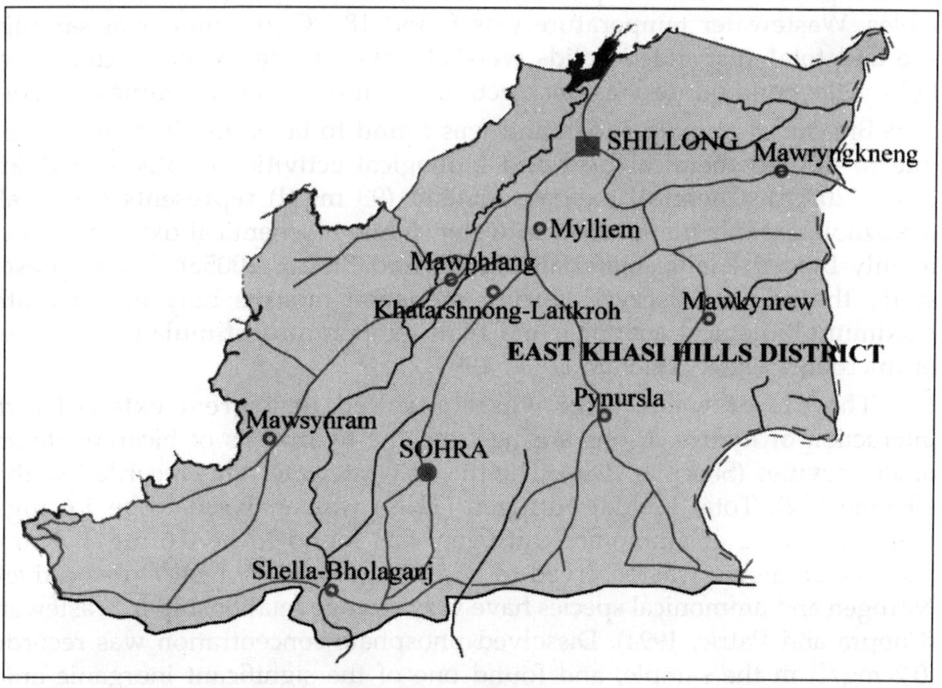

Fig. 4.2: Map of district East Khasi Hills (*Source:* www.meghalaya.gov.in)

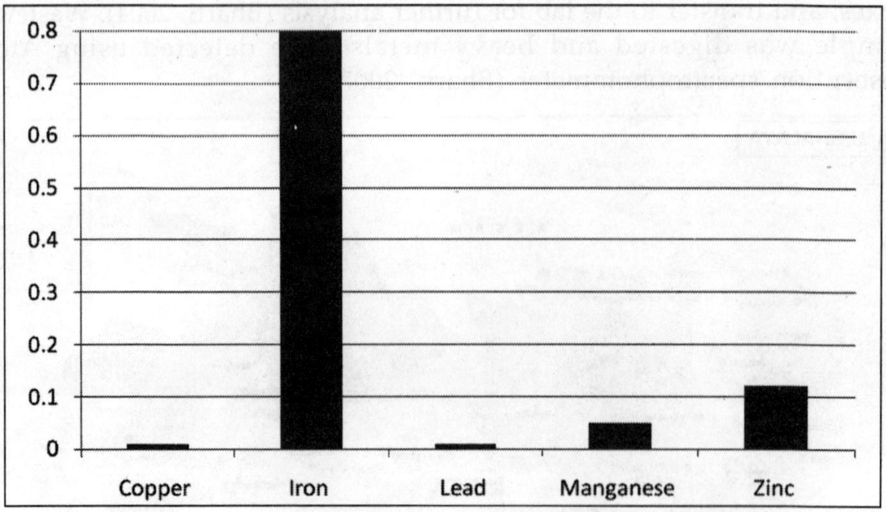

Fig. 4.3: Showing the metal concentration in wastewater

RESULTS AND DISCUSSION

Wastewater may contain such elements that can alter the physico-chemical variables of nearby soil or quality of aquatic ecosystem, in which the wastewater is discharged. Nutrients concentration, heavy metals and related physico-chemical parameters of collected sample are depicted in tables. Wastewater temperature was found 18- °C in summer at sampling site and total suspended solids were observed to be 48 mg/l. colour was light yellow and odour was unobjectionable at the time of sample collection.

Bio-chemical oxygen demand was found to be 30 mg/l in the sample, due to the bio-chemical load and biol;ogical activities (Malik and Bharti, 2005a; 2005b). Chemical oxygen demand (93 mg/l) represents chemically oxidizable organic matter load in water, while biochemical oxygen demand is only biodegradable materials (Malik and Bharti, 2005c). In the present study the values observed during monsoon months may be attributed maximum biological activities and high temperature, stimulate the growth of microorganisms (William *et al.*, 1993).

The pH of wastewater was controlled in a great extent by the interaction of hydroxyl ions arising from the hydrolysis of bicarbonate and other activities (Sharma, 1986). The pH of wastewater was recorded slightly alkaline (7.2). Total Kjeldal Nitrogen (TKN) was analysed to be 1.6 mg/l, while the value of ammonical nitrogen was found to be 0.6 mg/l. Nitrate and free ammonia was observed to be 1.0 mg/l and <0.1 mg/l respectively. Nitrogen and ammonical species have very strange relationship in wastewater (Chopra and Patric, 1994). Dissolved phosphate concentration was recorded (0.2 mg/l) in the sample, and found one of the significant inorganic anion present in natural water (Malik and Bharti, 2009; Bharti, 2004).

Table 4.1: Physical characteristics of waste water

S. N.	Parameters	Unit	Observed Value	Desirable Limit	Analytical Protocol
1.	Temperature	°C	18	40	IS: 3025, Part-9
2.	Colour	–	Light Yellow	–	Visual
3.	Odour	–	Unobjectionable	–	IS: 3025, Part-5
4.	TSS	Mg/l	48	100	IS: 3025, Part-17

Table 4.2: Chemical characteristics of wastewater

S.N.	Parameters	Unit	Observed Value	Desirable Limit	Analytical Protocol
1.	pH	–	7.2	5.5-9.0	IS: 3025, Part-11
2.	Oil and Grease	Mg/l	<1	10	APHA (2005)
3.	Dissolved Phosphate	Mg/l	0.2	–	
4.	Total residual chlorine	Mg/l	<0.1	1.0	IS: 3025, Part-26
5.	Ammonical nitrogen	Mg/l	0.6	50	IS: 3025, Part-34
6.	Total Kjeldal nitrogen	Mg/l	1.6	100	IS: 3025, Part-34
7.	Free ammonia	Mg/l	<0.1	–	IS: 2488, Part-4
8.	Nitrate	Mg/l	1.0		IS: 3025, Part-34
9.	Phoenolic compounds	Mg/l	<0.001	1.0	APHA (2005)
10.	Cyanide	Mg/l	<0.01	0.2	APHA (2005)
11.	Sulphide	Mg/l	<0.1	2.8	APHA (2005)
12.	Fluoride	Mg/l	0.1	2.0	APHA (2005)
	Arsenic	Mg/l	<0.005	0.2	APHA (2005)
13.	Biochemical Oxygen Demand	Mg/l	30	30	IS: 3025, Part-44
14.	Chemical Oxygen Demand	Mg/l	93	250	APHA (2005)

Table 4.3: Heavy Metals in wastewater

S.N.	Parameters	Unit	Observed Value	Desirable Limit	Analytical Protocol
1.	Cadmium	Mg/l	<0.01	1.0	APHA (2005)
2.	Copper	Mg/l	0.01	3.0	APHA (2005)
3.	Chromium	Mg/l	<0.01	2.0	APHA (2005)
4.	Iron	Mg/l	0.8		APHA (2005)
5.	Lead	Mg/l	0.01	0.1	APHA (2005)
6.	Manganese	Mg/l	0.05		APHA (2005)
7.	Mercury	Mg/l	<0.001	0.01	APHA (2005)
8.	Selenium	Mg/l	<0.005	0.05	APHA (2005)
9.	Nickel	Mg/l	<0.01	3.0	APHA (2005)
10.	Vanadium	Mg/l	<0.1		APHA (2005)
11.	Zinc	Mg/l	0.12	5.0	APHA (2005)

Table 4.4: Other important characteristics of wastewater

S.N.	Parameters	Unit	Observed value	Analytical protocol
1.	Bio-assay (survival of fish in 100% sample after 96 hours)	%	100	IS: 6582 & MoEF guideline
2.	Particle size of suspended solids		Passed through 850 micron IS sieve	IS: 2488, Part-1

Heavy metals like, copper, iron, manganese, lead and zinc were not found in high concentration in the sample. Cadmium was absolutely absent, while copper, lead and manganese concentrations were also found to be 0.01 mg/l, 0.01 mg/l and 0.05 mg/l respectively. Mercury, Selenium, Chromium, Nickel and Vanadium were observed below detection limit in sample. The concentration of iron was maximum observed 0.8 mg/l due to vehicular handling at workshop. Zinc concentration was found to be 0.12 mg/l in collected wastewater sample. Malik *et al.*, (2009) described the role of heavy metals in the surface water of north India. The results of Bharti *et al.*, (2010) were also indicated the relation of heavy metals and living organisms in a north Indian water body. Bioassay study was also conducted for fish survival rate, where 100% survival of fish was observed. Sample was passed through 850 micron sieve size during particle size analysis.

The present results conclude that significant concentrations of elements and other physico-chemical variables are having potential to pollute a natural water body, if the wastewater is discharged directly into water body (Odum, 1971). Absence or low concentration of heavy metals shows that the wastewater has no big industrial pollution. However, the Indian standards are not so strict (Bharti, 2007b), but heavy metals never cross the limits in the sample during the study period. On the basis of nutrients and heavy metals, the wastewater may be considered for discharging into lotic aquatic ecosystem, as it has self-purification power over the significant spatial variations.

REFERENCES

APHA (1995): Standard methods for Examination of Water and Waste Water. *American Public Health Association, 19th Edition. Inc, New York.* pp: 1970.

Bharti, P.K. (2004): Limnobiological Study of Sahastradhara Hill-stream at Dehradun, *M.Sc. Dissertation*, Submitted to Gurukula Kangri University, Hardwar, pp: 102.

Bharti, P.K. (2007a): Effect of Textile Industrial Effluents on Ground Water and Soil Quality in Panipat Region (Haryana), *Ph.D. Thesis*, Submitted to Gurukula Kangri University, Hardwar, pp: 191.

Bharti, P.K. (2007b): Why Indian Standards are not so Strict?, *Current Science*, 93(9): 1202.

Bharti, P.K., Malik, D.S. and Rashmi Yadav (2010): Influence of Heavy Metals on Abundance of Cyanophyceae Members in Three Spring-fed Lake in Kempty, Dehradun, In: 'Advances in Aquatic Ecology, Vol-III' ed. by V.B. Sakhare, *Daya Publishing House, New Delhi*, pp: 107-111.

Chopra, A.K. and Patrick, N.J. (1994): Effect of Domestic Sewage on Self-purification of Ganga Water at Rishikesh. *A. Bio. Science.* 13(11): 75-82.

Malik, D.S. and Bharti, Pawan K. (2005a): Nutrient Dynamics in Rhithron Zone of Shivalik Himalayan Stream Sahastradhara, Dehradun (Uttaranchal), *Env. Cons. J.* 6 (2): 63-68.

Malik, D.S. and Bharti, P.K. (2005b): Fluctuation in Planktonic Population of Sahastradhara Hill-stream at Dehradun (Uttaranchal), *Aquacult.* 6 (2): 191-198.

Malik, D.S. and Bharti, P.K. (2005c): Primary Production Efficiency of Sahstradhara Hill-stream, Dehradun, *Env. Cons. J.* 6 (3): 117-121.

Malik, D.S. and Bharti, P.K. (2009): Ecology of Sahastradhara Hill-stream at Dehradun (Uttaranchal), In: 'Advances in Aquatic Ecology, Vol. I' ed. by V.B. Sakhare, *Daya Publishing House, New Delhi,* pp: 1-11.

Malik, D.S. and Bharti, P.K., Negi, K.S. and Rashmi Yadav (2009): Distribution of Metals in Water of an Artificial Lake at Mussoorie, Uttarakhand, In: 'Aquatic Biology and Aquaculture' edited by V.B. Sakhare, Ambajoagi, MS, *Manglam Publication, New Delhi,* pp: 77-95.

Odum, E.P. (1971): Fundamentals of Ecology. New York. W.B. *Saunders and Co.* pp: 1-344.

Trivedi, R.K. and Goel, P.K. (1984): Chemical and Biological methods for Water Pollution Studies. Karad. Environmental Publication. pp: 1-25.

William, M.W., Brown, A. & Melack, J.M. (1993). Geochemical and Hydrologic Controls on the Composition of Surface Water in the High Elevation Basin, *Sierra Navada. Limnol. Oceanogr,* 38: 775-797.

Pages: 60-73

Water and Waste Water: ***Issues and Management***
Edited by: **Dr. Pawan Kumar 'Bharti'**
ISBN: 978-93-88854-15-3
Edition: **2019**
Published by: **Discovery Publishing House Pvt. Ltd., New Delhi (India)**

5

Bioremediation
Green Technology for Wastewater Treatment

Shivani Garg[*1]
Sikander[2]

ABSTRACT

Increased discharges of ineffectively treated wastewater are contributing to the further degradation of water quality in surface and groundwater. As water pollution critically affects water availability, it needs to be properly managed in order to mitigate the impacts of increasing water scarcity. According to an estimate of Central Pollution Control Board, 38354 million litres per day, produced in sewage but the available sewage treatment capacity is only of 11786 million litres per day (~30%), similarly, only 60% of industrial wastewater, mostly from large scale industries, is generated in major cities of India. So it is necessary to treat/recycle wastewater before discharge. Biological method is a natural way to treat wastewater. Bioremediation means elimination of pollutants from soil, groundwater, wastewater, air using microorganisms. Bioremediation requires fewer resources and less energy than conventional technology, and doesn't accumulate hazardous by-products as waste. The objective of the biological treatment or bioremediation of wastewater is to remove organic matter from the wastewater which is present in the soluble and colloidal form or to remove nutrients such as nitrogen and phosphorous from the wastewater. In the biological treatment methods, pollutants in wastewater can be resolved, detoxified, and separated by using mainly microorganisms. Biological processes like nitrification, denitrification, anaerobic biological treatment, activated sludge (aerobic treatment) are some

[*1] **Institute of Environmental Studies, Kurukshetra University, Kurukshetra, Haryana, Pin - 136 119 (India)**
[2] **Department of Geology, Kurukshetra University, Kurukshetra, Haryana, Pin - 136 119 (India)**

processes being used to treat wastewater during bioremediation of wastewater. The study includes all the aspects of treatment of wastewater biologically with the help of microorganisms and natural processes.

Keywords: Bioremediation, biological treatment, nitrification, denitrification, anaerobic biological treatment.

INTRODUCTION

The rapid expansion and increasing sophistication of the chemical industries in the last century has meant that there has been increasing levels of complex toxic effluents being released into the environment (Vidali 2001). The waste generated and discharged into natural water bodies has recently indicated the need for different strategies to solve water quality challenges in the regions (Olguin, 2003). Agricultural runoff is a major sources of pesticide accumulation in the aquatic environments, effluents from agrochemical (pesticide/fertilizers/herbicides) industry cause a high risk for water bodies (Rajeswari and Kanmani, 2009). Bioremediation can be defined as the action of microbes or other biological systems to degrade environmental pollutants. Bioremediation uses biological agents, mainly microorganisms i.e. yeast, fungi or bacteria to clean up contaminated soil and water (Strong and Burgess, 2008). Microorganism has the capability of degrading all naturally occurring compounds; this is known as the principle of microbial infallibility proposed by Alexander in 1965. Today, biotechnology is being considered as emerging science for environmental protection. Biotechnological techniques for treatment of hazardous waste under controlled environmental conditions have been found to reduce the pollution potential of wastewater, leading to enhanced public awareness and compliance with environmental legislation (Fulekar, 2010). The main aim of bioremediation of wastewater is to reduce the organic content (i.e. reduction of biological oxygen demand (BOD) and chemical oxygen demand (COD)), reduction of trace organic compounds that are recalcitrant to biodegradation and may be toxic or carcinogenic and inactivation of pathogenic microorganisms and parasites. In order to treat the wastewater having pollutants (organic and inorganic compounds) with the help of microorganism by bioremediation the favourable conditions such as temperature, nutrients and amount of oxygen are desired (Abdel-Raouf *et al.*, 2012). Microbes consume the organic contaminants and bind the less soluble fractions, which can then be sieved off. The process can either be performed in-situ or ex-situ. Living microorganisms are directly added to contaminated sites during in-situ remediation processes, and contaminated sites are treated elsewhere during ex-situ remediation. The fundamental objective of this chapter is to discuss various kinds of bioremediation processes which may prove to be efficacious in coping with problem of industrial wastewater that cannot be treated with the natural processes and causes a long term environmental destruction.

BIOREMEDIATION

Bioremediation is the treatment of wastewater with the help of biological processes and microorganisms to conserve the water resources. It is a biological process occurs by natural phenomenon. The main objective of the biological processes in wastewater treatment is to remove organic matter which is present in the soluble and colloidal form or to remove nutrients such as nitrogen and phosphorous from the wastewater. The microorganisms (principally bacteria) are used to convert the colloidal and dissolved carbonaceous organic matter into simpler form so that they release into the environment without any harm. Toxicity studies of the biologically treated wastewaters also suggested that the process is efficient enough to reduce the toxicity of the spent wash by around 80 % (Kaushik, 2015). The Energy and Resources Institute (TERI) in India has treated 48,914 tons of waste oily sludge in batches at various oil refineries using bioremediation technology (Mandal *et al.*, 2012). The principal applications of the biological processes are biochemical oxygen demand (BOD) removal, nitrification, denitrification, stabilization, and phosphorous removal (Pokhrel and Viraraghavan, 2004). The classification of biological processes broadly is aerobic or anaerobic (anoxic and anaerobic). Both the processes are very common and used in all the effluent treatment plants but there are some differences between both the processes briefly explained in table 5.1.

Table 5.1: General comparison between aerobic and anaerobic biological processes and their quality parameters

Parameters	Aerobic Processes	Anaerobic Processes
Organic removal efficiency	High	High
Energy requirement	High	Low to moderate
Sludge production	High	Low
Odour	Less odours	Potential odour
Temperature sensitivity	Low	High
Effluent Quality	Excellent	Moderate to poor

Factors Affecting Bioremediation Process

Some of the conditions needed for optimal efficiency of the microorganisms and their proliferation in the processing system are enlisted below:

- A constant temperature
- Dissolved oxygen content
- pH
- Nutrient levels

Bioremediation Process used to Treat the Wastewater

The biodegradation/bioremediation of industrial wastes is challenging task because there is no authentic technology till date which is efficient enough to completely remove the pollutants from these industrial wastes. Eventually, a diverse group of microorganism present in the nature may provide solution for this problem (Garg, 2017). Biological treatment can be divided into aerobic and anaerobic depending on the availability of oxygen. Among both these treatments processes one thing is common, use of microbes (Pokhrel and Viraraghavan 2004). Bioremediation of wastewater to remove pesticides can be enhanced by using lignolytic enzymes such as Laccases. Removal of phenolic or xenobiotic pollutants from wastewater using Laccase can be eventuated in several ways *viz.* (1) using purified immobilised enzyme; (2) using purified free enzyme; (3) using enzyme obtained directly from culture broths; and (4) bioremediation in reactors with immobilized or free cells (Majeau, Satinder and Tyagi, 2010). A number of fungi, bacteria, yeast, and algae have been reported to have effluent-treatment capabilities. Few processes those include use of microorganisms in bioremediation of wastewater are explained below:

1. **Decolourization of Effluents:**
   (a) Decolourization of effluents with Bacteria
   (b) Decolourization of effluents with Fungi
   (c) Decolourization of effluents with Algae
2. **Anaerobic Process:**
   (a) Upflow sludge blanket (UASB)
   (b) Fluidized bed,
   (c) Anaerobic lagoon, and
   (d) Anaerobic contact reactors
3. **Aerobic Process:**
   (i) **Suspended Growth System**
      (a) Activated sludge
      (b) Oxidation ditches
      (c) Oxidation pond
   (ii) **Attached growth system**
      (a) Trickling filters
      (b) Rotating biological contactor

A. DECOLOURIZATION OF EFFLUENTS

The public demand for treated colourless waste discharge to receiving waters and colour standards given by international organizations have made decolourization of a variety of industrial wastes a top priority. Colour-causing compounds present in waste are complex so; the decolourization of these wastes is a difficult and challenging task. Colour is contributed by phenolic compounds such as tannins, lignins (2-3%) and organic colorants (3-4%) and with a maximum contribution from dye and dye intermediates. Due to their complex structure, synthetic origin and recalcitrant nature, dyes are difficult to be decolourized. These dyes include several structures such as acidic, reactive, basic, disperse, azo, diazo, anthraquinone based and metal-complex dyes. The ability of biological treatment process for decolourization of industrial effluents is ambiguous, different and divergent. Most recently used laboratory technique for biodegradation involve aerobic microorganisms, which utilize molecular oxygen as reducing equivalent acceptor during the respiration process. In these anoxic and hypoxic environments, microorganisms survive by using sulphates, nitrates and carbon dioxide etc. as electron acceptors.

(a) Decolourization of effluents with Bacteria

Dyes are the most commonly used in printing, colour, textile, rubber product, paper and pharmaceutical industries (Holey, 2015). In addition to the genotoxic. carcinogenic and mutagenic properties of the dyes, their presence with intense coloration in aqueous ecosystems blocks sunlight penetration into deep layers which affects photosynthetic activity, deteriorates water quality and also lowers the gas solubility, harmful for the growth of aquatic animals (Zahrim and Hilal, 2013). Bacteria can degrade and even completely convert whole dyes into minerals under certain conditions and the products of intermediate metabolism during the decolourization process, such as aromatic amines, can be degraded by the enzymes produced by bacteria (Asad, 2007). The study showed that the removal, degradation and decolourization of 98.62% and 96.31% of Congo Red dye with concentration of 100 mg/L and 200 mg/L respectively after 48 h. was done by the bacteria *Acinetobacterbaumannii* YNWH 226 (Li *et al.*, 2015). Different studies and researches have revealed isolation of various bacterial strains acclimatized on higher concentrations of distillery mill effluent. Some examples of such bacterial strains are *Lactobacillus hilgardii* (Ohmomo *et al.* 1988), *Bacillus sp.* (Kambe *et al.* 1999; Kaushik and Thakur 2009), *Pseudomonas putida* (Ghosh *et al.* 2002), *Bacillus thuringiensis*(Kumar and Chandra 2006), and *Pseudomonas aeruginosa* (Mohana *et al.* 2007).

(b) Decolourization of effluents with Fungi

Filamentous fungi have lower sensitivity to variations in temperature, pH, nutrients, and aeration, and have lower nucleic acid content in the biomass (Knapp *et al.* 2001). Azo dyes can be degraded by lignin degrading fungi, white rot fungi, capable of producing reduced flavins and hydroquinones. Fungal degradation of azo dyes mainly occurs from the lignin peroxidase activity under aerobic conditions (Chen, 2006). The Different studies showed that the fungi strains *Aspergillusfumigatus*G-2-6

(Ohmomo *et al.* 1987), *Aspergillusniger* (Patil *et al.* 2003), *Flavodonflavus* (Raghukumar *et al.*, 2004), and *Phanerochaetechrysosporium* (Thakkar *et al.*, 2006) are used to treat and decolorized the distilleries wastewater.

(c) Decolourization of effluents with Algae

Cyanobacteria are considered the best technique for treatment of distillery effluent as they apart from degrading the polymers also oxygenate water bodies, thus reduce the BOD and COD levels. The cyanobacteria *Anabaena flosaquae* UTCC64, *Phormidiumautumnale* UTEX1580 and *Synechococcus sp.* PCC7942 was estimated for degradation of three textile dyes (Indigo, RBBR and Sulphur Black), and the dye-containing liquid effluent and solid waste from the Municipal Treatment Station, Americana, São Paulo, Brazil (Dellamatrice, 2017). A marine filamentous, non heterocystous form *Oscillatoriaboryana*BDU 92181 used the recalcitrant biopolymer melanoidin as nitrogen and carbon source leading to decolourization. The species of *Chlorella, Anabaena inaequalis, Westiellopsisprolifica, Stigeocloniumtenue, Synechococcus sp.* tolerate heavy metals. However, several species of *Chlorella, Anabaena and* marine algae have been used for the removal of heavy metals (Garg, 2017).

B. ANAEROBIC PROCESSES

Anaerobic degradation occurs in the absence of oxygen. The anaerobic treatments are used to treat wastewaters rich in biodegradable organic matter and for further treatment of sludge. Agricultural and food processing industries discharge wastewaters containing higher amounts of biodegradable material and solid organic matter. Although the anaerobic treatment is time-consuming, it has a multitude of advantages in treating strong organic wastewaters. The following methods are biological treatment methods works in anaerobic condition to treat such type of wastewater:

(a) Up flow sludge blanket (UASB)

The UASB reactor is a methanogens (methane-producing) digester that evolved from the clarifier. UASB uses an anaerobic process whilst forming a blanket of granular sludge which suspends in the tank (Figure 5.2). Wastewater flows upwards through the blanket and is degraded by microorganisms. The upward flow combined with the settling action of gravity suspends the blanket with the aid of flocculants. The blanket starts to reach its maturity at around 3 months. The flow conditions create a selective environment in which only those microorganisms, capable of attaching to each other, survive and proliferate. Biogas produced from this technique can be used for domestic or commercial purposes in household industries (Figure 5.1).

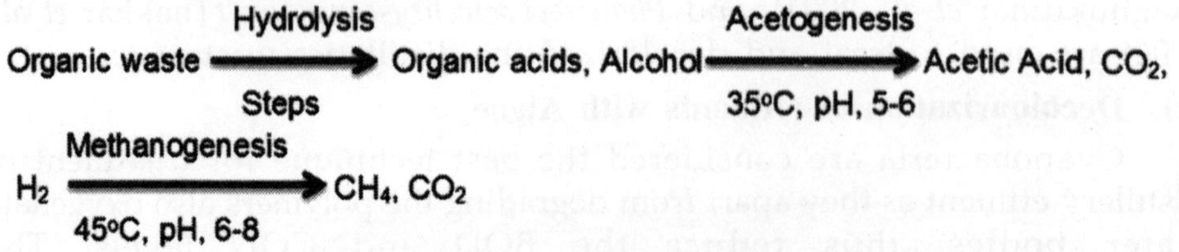

Fig. 5.1: General steps involved in the process of anaerobic digestion (Garg, 2017)

The aggregates formed into dense compact biofilms referred to as "granules". The government of India has made a major commitment to anaerobic treatment technology in its National River Basin Improvement Program.

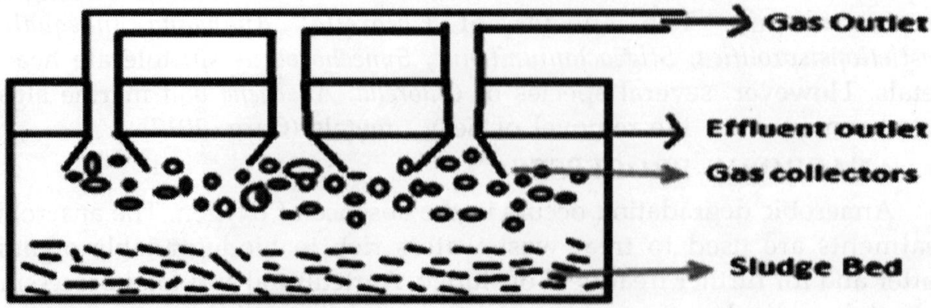

Fig. 5.2: General model of up flow anaerobic sludge bioreactor for treatment of wastewater (Garg, 2017)

(b) Fluidized bed reactor

A reactor in which the filled packing material expands and gets fluidized when the wastewater to be treated moves upward in the reactor is called a fluidized bed reactor (FBR). Carrier particles develop a biofilm composed of bacteria and other microbes in this process. The excellent mixing and mass transfer characteristics inherent to fluidization make this process very effective at treating both municipal and industrial wastewater (Nelson, 2017). The use of fluidized bed reactor particularly Advanced Oxidation Processes and biological treatment, represents a cost-effective treatment of wastewater containing recalcitrant pollutants. Although the application of fluidized bed reactor in biological wastewater treatment is well established with many large-scale plants in existence, but it is used mostly at laboratory-scale (Bello *et al.*, 2017).

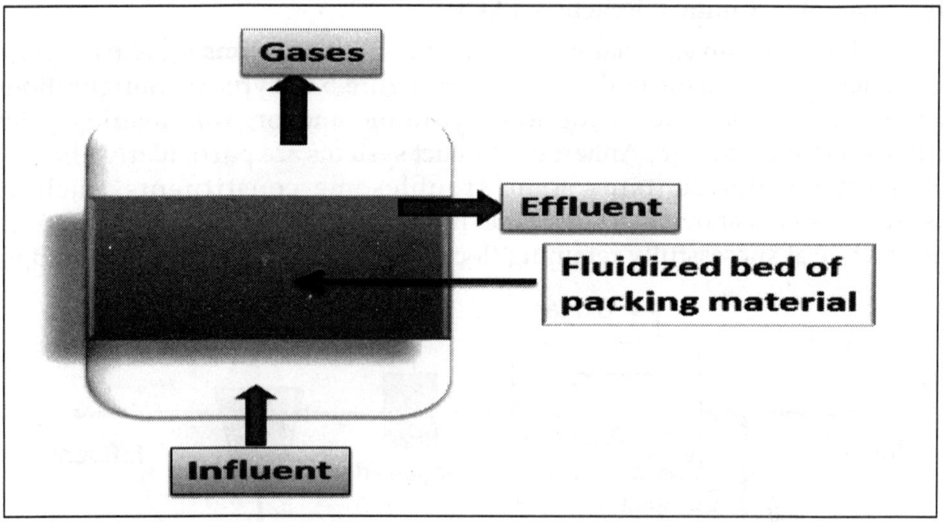

Fig. 5.3: General schematic model of Fluidized bed reactor (Garg, 2017)

(c) Anaerobic lagoon

These lagoons are typically 6 to 30 feet deep. They have no aerobic zones, which may cause the production of odours. The detention time can vary from 20-50 days. These systems have typically been used to treat high strength wastewater. The low-rate anaerobic process stabilizes organic matter, converting it to carbon dioxide and methane. If sulphur is present, hydrogen sulphide, an odorous compound, may be produced. Particulate matter that does not get degraded will settle to the bottom with time. An anaerobic lagoon is a deep lagoon, fundamentally without dissolved oxygen, that enforces anaerobic conditions. The depth of an anaerobic lagoon should be deeper than 2.5 m, as deeper lagoons are more efficient. Such depths reduce oxygen mixing from the surface, allowing anaerobic condition.

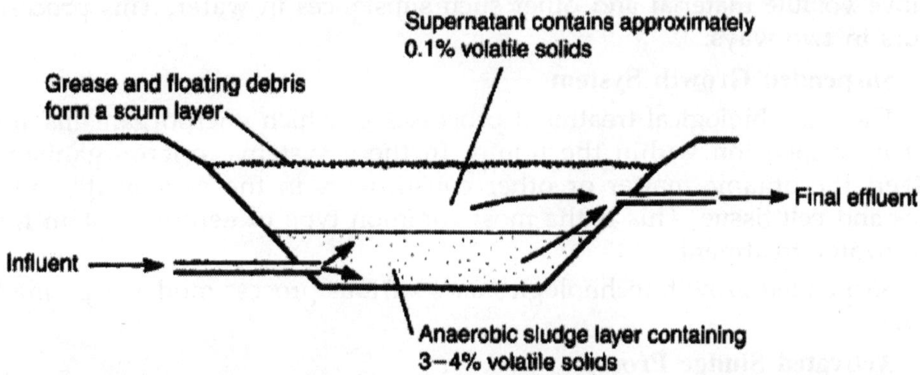

Fig. 5.4: Anaerobic lagoon for strong wastewater treatment, such as meat processing wastewater (Samer, 2015)

(d) Anaerobic Contact Reactors (ACR)

ACR employ an external vessel to settle solids and consequently recycle them back to the reactor tank as shown in figure 5.5. Typical configurations include large tanks due to the low hydraulic and organic loading rates employed in their design. Anaerobic contact systems are particularly efficient when wastewater contains some troublesome constituents, such as suspended solids above their desirable limits. Anaerobic contact alternatives are effective at successfully retaining flocculent, such as non-granular sludge.

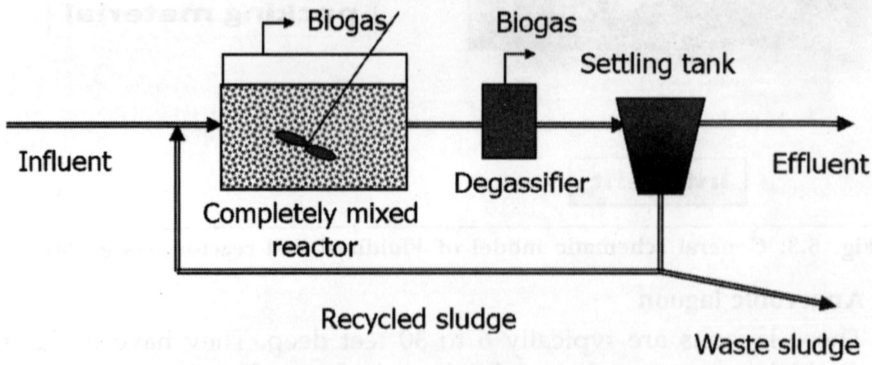

Fig. 5.5: Schematic diagram of Anaerobic contact reactors

C. AEROBIC PROCESSES

Unlike Anaerobic process, aerobic process used oxygen in its process. Aeration has been used to remove trace organic volatile compounds (VOCs) in water. It has also been employed to transfer a substance, such as oxygen, from air or a gas phase into water in a process called "gas adsorption" or "oxidation", i.e., to oxidize iron and/or manganese. Aeration also provides the evaporation of dissolved gases, such as CO_2 and H_2S. Air stripping has also been used effectively to remove ammonia from wastewater and to remove volatile material and other such substances in water. This process occurs in two ways:

1. Suspended Growth System

These are biological treatment processes in which microorganisms are kept in suspension within the liquid. In these systems, microorganisms convert the organic matter or other constituents in the wastewater into gases and cell tissue. This is the most common type of aerobic system for wastewater treatment.

Suspended growth technologies uses various process modes explained below:

(a) Activated Sludge Process

Activated sludge is probably the most adaptable process of the biological wastewater treatment processes capable of producing an effluent with desired BOD. The process has wide application among domestic wastewater and industrial wastewater treatment like the trickling filter, activated sludge in which a number of microorganisms such as bacteria, fungi, protozoa and small organisms such as rotifers and nematode worms are commonly found. The bacteria are the most important and common group of microorganisms which are responsible for the structural and functional activity of the activated sludge floc. All types of bacteria make up activated sludge. When present, most common type of the fungi found to be the filamentous forms which prevent good floc formation and therefore reduces the efficiency of the plant. A high concentration of carbohydrate, unusual organic compounds, low pH and dissolved oxygen concentrations, and nutrient deficiencies stimulate fungi growths. The other forms of microorganisms present in activated sludge play a fewroles in stabilization of the organic compounds in wastewater.

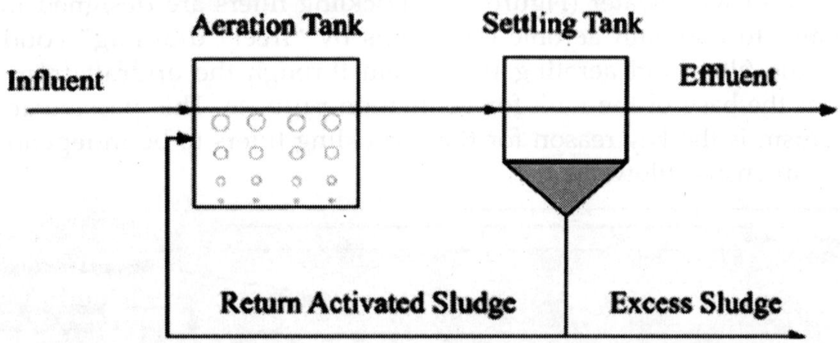

Fig. 5.6: Schematic diagram of Activated sludge process in wastewater treatment plants (Samer, 2015)

(b) Oxidation ditches (OD)

The oxidation ditches are a sort of equipments consisting of a long channel of elliptical or circular shape having aeration equipment called rotor for generating a water flow and stirring water in the channel to supply oxygen. Though, it requires a relatively large area, it has a very simple structure and can be easily operated as well as being able to remove nitrogen easily. Thus, it has recently been widely used in relatively small wastewater treatment plants.

(c) Oxidation Ponds

Oxidation ponds are aerobic systems where the oxygen required by the heterotrophic bacteria is provided not only by injecting from the atmosphere but also by photosynthetic algae. The algae are restricted to the euphotic zone (sunlight zone), which is often only a few centimetres deep. Ponds are constructed to a depth of between 1.2 and 1.8 m to ensure maximum penetration of sunlight, and appear dark green in colour due to dense algal bloom.

2. Attached Growth System

Attached growth systems are a wastewater treatment process in which the microorganisms and bacteria are attached to waste substrates in the reactor for treatment of wastes. The wastes being treated flow over the media. Trickling filters and rotating biological contactors are attached growth reactors. These reactors can be used for BOD removal, nitrification, and denitrification.

(a) Trickling filters

Trickling filters operated by continuously pouring wastewater uniformly over substrate made up of plastic or traditional stone/rock that is generally 2-6m in thickness. Microorganisms and slime molds are grow on the media and uses contaminants present in the wastewater as food when wastewater percolates through the assembly, thereby providing treatment of wastewater (Figure 5.7). Trickling filters are designed in such a manner to maintain aerobic conditions by "freely draining" conditions within the filter, and aerating the system through the updraft from holes made at the base of the tank for ventilation purpose. This passive aeration mechanism is the key reason for these trickling filters to be independent of energy intensive blowers.

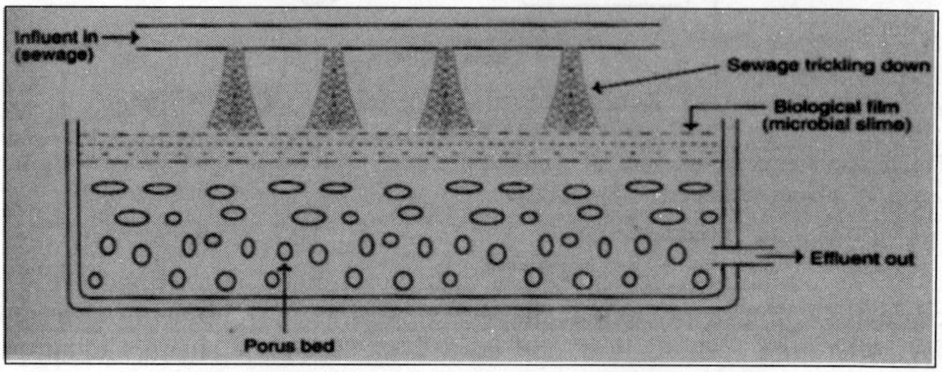

Fig. 5.7: Outline Diagram of process of Trickling Filters

(b) The rotating biological contactors (RBC) system

In this process, a fixed-biofilm of either aerobic or anaerobic biological treatment system is used for removal of nitrogenous and carbonaceous compounds from wastewater. The RBC system can be implemented to modify and then improve the available treatment processes such as the secondary or tertiary treatment processes. The three steps of the biological treatment involved in this process are BOD removal, nitrification, and denitrification. All three steps of the biological treatment *i.e.* BOD removal, nitrification, and denitrification can be successfully done with the help of RBC system.

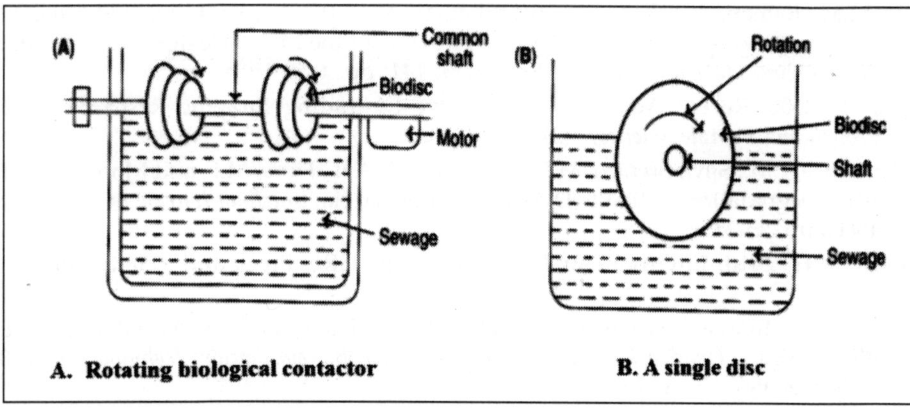

Fig. 5.8: General diagram of the rotating biological contactors (RBC) system

PHYTOREMEDIATION

Phytoremediation is a treatment process that solves environmental problems by using plants that solve the problems of environmental pollution without disposing pollutants elsewhere. Phytoremediation is the abatement of pollutant concentrations in contaminated soils or water using plants that are able to accumulate, degrade, or eliminate heavy metals, pesticides, solvents, explosives, crude oils and its derivatives, and a multitude of other contaminants and pollutants from water and soils. Now a days, this process is used everywhere to restore the contaminated sites. But this is a very time consuming process as plants take a very long time to grow. For the removal of toxic hexavalent chromium from mines wastewater, Sukinda mines, Orissa, *Eichhorniacrassipes*used(Saha *et al.*, 2017).

CONCLUSION

Bioremediation is a biological process and used widely to treat wastewater, reuse it for different purposes. The implementation of bioremediation, phytoremediation, and mycoremediation is to reduce the use of chemicals, which leads to the "Green Development Technology". Microbial fuel cells, phytoremediation, and mycoremediation are the focus of the future development in this field. Phytoremediation is ecologically a better and promising choice with bright future. Efforts should be focused on exploring and utilizing this technology to get treated water meeting the standards and thus conserve the environment aiming at sustainable development and reduce stress on natural resources.

REFERENCES

Abdel-Raouf, N., Al-Homaidan, A.A. and Ibraheem, I.B.M., 2012.Microalgae and Wastewater Treatment. *Saudi journal of Biological Sciences*, *19*(3), pp. 257-275.

Asad, S., Amoozegar, M.A., Pourbabaee, A., Sarbolouki, M.N. and Dastgheib, S.M.M., 2007. Decolorization of Textile azo dyes by Newly Isolated Halophilic and Halotolerant Bacteria. *Bioresource Technology*, 98(11), pp. 2082-2088.

Bello, M.M., Raman, A.A.A. and Purushothaman, M., 2017. Applications of Fluidized Bed Reactors in Wastewater Treatment – A Review of the Major Design and Operational Parameters. *Journal of Cleaner Production, 141*, pp. 1492-1514.

Chen, H., 2006. Recent Advances in azo Dye Degrading Enzyme Research. *Current Protein and Peptide Science, 7*(2), pp. 101-111.

Dellamatrice, P.M., Silva-Stenico, M.E., de Moraes, L.A.B., Fiore, M.F. and Monteiro, R.T.R., 2017. Degradation of Textile Dyes by Cyanobacteria. *Brazilian Journal of Microbiology*, 48(1), pp. 25-31.

Fulekar M.H. 2010. Environmental Biotechnology. CRC Press and Science Publisher, USA.

Garg, S. 2017. Bioremediation of Agricultural, Municipal, and Industrial Wastes. In J. Bhakta (Ed.), *Handbook of Research on Inventive Bioremediation Techniques* (pp. 341-363). Hershey, PA: IGI Global.

Ghosh, M., Ganguli, A. and Tripathi, A.K., 2002. Treatment of Anaerobically Digested Distillery Spentwash in a Two-stage Bioreactor using *Pseudomonas putida and Aeromonas sp. Process Biochemistry, 37*(8), pp. 857-862.

Holey, B.A., 2015. Decolourization of Congo Red dye by Bacteria and Consortium Isolated from Dye Contaminated Soil. Int. Res. J. Sci. Eng., 3, 107-112.

Kaushik, G. and Thakur, I.S., 2009. Isolation and Characterization of Distillery Spent Wash Color Reducing Bacteria and Process Optimization by Taguchi Approach. *International Biodeterioration & Biodegradation*, 63(4), pp. 420-426.

Kaushik, G., 2015. Bioremediation of Industrial Effluents: Distillery Effluent. In *Applied Environmental Biotechnology: Present Scenario and Future Trends* (pp. 19-32). Springer, New Delhi.

KNAPP, J.S., 2001. Use of Wood-rotting Fungi for the Decolorization of Dyes and Industrial. *Fungi in Bioremediation*, (23), p. 242.

Kumar, P. and Chandra, R., 2004. Detoxification of Distillery Effluent through Bacillus thuringiensis (MTCC 4714) enhanced Phytoremediation Potential of Spirodelapolyrrhiza (L.) Schliden. *Bulletin of Environmental Contamination and Toxicology*, 73(5), pp. 903-910.

Li, R., Ning, X.A., Sun, J., Wang, Y., Liang, J., Lin, M. and Zhang, Y., 2015. Decolorization and Biodegradation of the Congo red by *Acinetobacterbaumannii* YNWH 226 and its Polymer Production's Flocculation and Dewatering Potential. *Bioresource Technology*, 194, pp. 233-239.

Mandal, A.K., Sarma, P.M., Jeyaseelan, C.P., Channashettar, V.A., Singh, B., Lal, B. and Datta, J., 2012. Large Scale Bioremediation of Petroleum Hydrocarbon Contaminated Waste at Indian Oil Refineries: Case Studies. *Int. J. Life Sci. Pharm. Res*, 2(4), pp. L114-L128.

Mohana, S., Desai, C. and Madamwar, D., 2007. Biodegradation and Decolourization of Anaerobically Treated Distillery Spent Wash by a Novel Bacterial Consortium. *Bioresource Technology, 98*(2), pp. 333-339.

Nakajima-Kambe, T., Shimomura, M., Nomura, N., Chanpornpong, T. and Nakahara, T., 1999. Decolorization of Molasses Wastewater by Bacillus sp. under Thermophilic and Anaerobic Conditions. *Journal of Bioscience and Bioengineering, 87*(1), pp. 119-121.

Nelson, M.J., Nakhla, G. and Zhu, J., 2017. Fluidized-Bed Bioreactor Applications for Biological Wastewater Treatment: A Review of Research and Developments. *Engineering*, 3(3), pp. 330-342.

Ohmomo, S., Daengsubha, W., Yoshikawa, H., Yui, M., Nozaki, K., Nakajima, T. and Nakamura, I., 1988.Screening of Anaerobic Bacteria with the Ability to Decolorize Molasses Melanoidin. *Agricultural and Biological Chemistry*, 52(10), pp. 2429-2435.

Olguìn, E.J., 2003. Phycoremediation: Key Issues for Cost-effective Nutrient Removal Processes. *Biotechnology Advances*, 22 (1-2), pp. 81-91.

Patil, P.U., Kapadnis, B.P. and Dhamankar, V.S., 2003. Decolorisation of Synthetic Melanoidin and Biogas Effluent by Immobilised Fungal Isolate of Aspergillusniger UM2. *International Sugar Journal*, 105(1249), pp. 8-13.

Pokhrel D. and Viraraghavan T., 2004. Treatment of Pulp and Paper Mill Wastewater: A Review. *Sci Total Environ* 333: 37-58.

Raghukumar, C., Mohandass, C., Kamat, S. and Shailaja, M.S., 2004. Simultaneous Detoxification and Decolorization of Molasses Spent Wash by the Immobilized White-rot Fungus Flavodonflavus Isolated from a Marine Habitat. *Enzyme and Microbial Technology*, *35*(2-3), pp. 197-202.

Rajeswari, R. and Kanmani, S., 2009. A Study on Degradation of Pesticide Wastewater by TiO_2photocatalysis.

Saha, P., Shinde, O. and Sarkar, S., 2017. Phytoremediation of Industrial Mines Wastewater using Water Hyacinth. *International Journal of Phytoremediation*, 19(1), pp. 87-96.

Samer, M., 2015. Biological and Chemical Wastewater Treatment Processes. In *Wastewater Treatment Engineering*. InTech.

Strong, P.J. and Burgess, J.E., 2008. Treatment methods for Wine-related and Distillery Wastewaters: A Review. *Bioremediation Journal*, 12(2), pp. 70-87.

Thakkar, A.P., Dhamankar, V.S. and Kapadnis, B.P., 2006. Biocatalytic Decolourisation of Molasses by Phanerochaetechrysosporium. *Bioresource Technology*, 97(12), pp. 1377-1381.

Zahrim, A.Y. and Hilal, N., 2013. Treatment of Highly Concentrated Dye Solution by Coagulation/Flocculation-sand Filtration and Nanofiltration. Water Resour. Ind., 3, 23-34.

Pages: 74-132

Water and Waste Water: *Issues and Management*
Edited by: **Dr. Pawan Kumar 'Bharti'**
ISBN: 978-93-88854-15-3
Edition: **2019**
Published by: **Discovery Publishing House Pvt. Ltd., New Delhi (India)**

6

Water and Wastewater Management
A Case Study of Delhi

M.S. Rawat[1]
P.K. 'Bharti'[2]

ABSTRACT

Water is a prime requirement for all living organisms and for any residential establishment, colony or city. Delhi is also a super residential area with very high population density. Management and utilization of water and wastewater is a prime issue in Delhi.

This article highlighted the current status of water supply, water uses, treatment, management and water loss in metro city Delhi, India. All the water sources have been described in the article. Similarly, wastewater is also the second face of water management; hence the present condition of wastewater generation, treatment and reuse of total wastewater of city is being described in the present article. All the CETP/STP of city are being explained with their respective capacity and other relevant information.

INTRODUCTION

Water

Water is crucial for all aspects of life, an earth around 97.5% of all water is found in the oceans, the remaining freshwater only 1% is accessible for extraction and use. During the last few decades the world is facing a water crisis, due to continuous population growth, industrialization, food production, increased living standards and poor water use strategies. Lack of wastewater management has a direct impact on the aquatic ecosystems, disrupting the biological system of our life support systems. A wide range of activities such as urban development, food production and industrial

[1] Delhi Pollution control committee, 5th floor, ISBT building, Kashmiri Gate, Delhi – 110006, India
[2] R&D Division, Shriram Institute for Industrial Research, Delhi – 110007, India

development depend on it. It is essential that wastewater management is considered as part of integrated, ecosystem-based management.

Domestic water supplies are one of the fundamental requirements for human life. Without domestic water, human life cannot be sustained and the lack of access to adequate water supplies leads to disease hunger, death etc. In its "Guidelines for Drinking-Water Quality", WHO defines domestic water as being 'water used for all usual domestic purposes including consumption, bathing and food preparation' (WHO, 1993; 2002).

Globally, 10% water is being used for domestic purpose, 20% utilize for industrial purpose and major part of about 70% in agriculture practices. In developed countries, 13% water is being used for domestic purpose, 42% utilize for industrial purpose and major part of about 46% in agriculture practices. In developing countries, 8% water is being used for domestic purpose, 11% utilize for industrial purpose and major part of about 81% in agriculture practices as per UNWD.

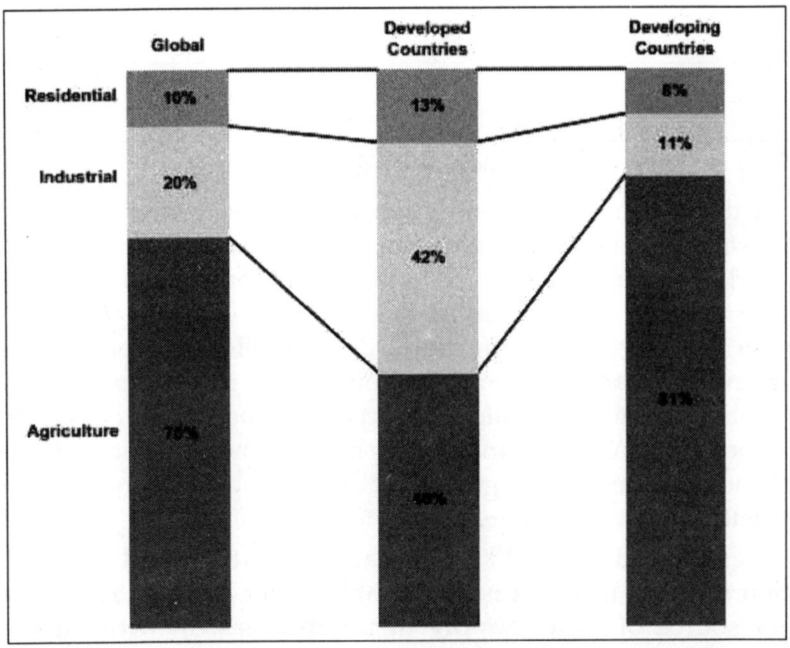

Source: UN Water Development

Fig. 6.1: Water requirement for various sectors in the world

In India, around 38% population live in urban area and is increasing in every year with rapid rate. Water supply and sanitation are basic needs for the quality of life and enhancement of productive efficiency of the urban people. In urban areas, water is used from rivers, streams, wells and lakes for domestic and industrial purpose. Almost 80% of the water supplied for domestic use comes out as waste water. In many times wastewater is let out untreated and it either sinks into the ground as a potential pollutes of ground water or is discharged into the natural drainage system causing pollution in downstream areas.

Water requirement for various sector such as irrigation, domestic water, industry, energy and other sector are mentioned in table 6.1. Domestic water demand will be almost doubled by 2050 as predicted by MOWR and NCIWRD.

Table 6.1: Water requirements for various sectors in India

Sector	Water demand in km³ (or BCM)					
	Standing Sub-Committee of MoWR			NCIWRD		
Year	2010	2025	2050	2010	2025	2050
Irrigation	688	910	1072	557	611	807
Domestic Water	56	73	102	43	62	111
Industry	12	23	63	37	67	81
Energy	5	15	130	19	33	70
Others	52	72	80	54	70	111
Total	813	1093	1447	710	843	1180

Source: Website of MOWR, Govt. of India, NCIWRD)

With the increase in consumption of drinking water in urban areas, the wastewater generation is increasing. If such wastewater is not collected, treated and disposed properly, it will contaminate the locally available freshwater source. Additionally, the cumulative impact of untreated wastewater can have large effects on both public health and ecosystem. Management of urban environment is one of the most important issues in today's world. The major challenges faced by urban planners are the need to ensure ongoing basic human services such as the provision of safe water and sanitation. The miss-management of domestic wastewater in many areas may present a major challenge.

It is estimated that 31% of rural population and 77% of urban population in India have access to potable water supply. Surface water is the major source of water supply in urban areas. In rural area ground water is the basic source. Municipalities and State Water Supply and sewerage boards own and operate the urban water supply schemes, however in rural areas there is no such organized water supply.

Wastewater

Waste water generated from industrial, commercial, municipal sewage systems and agricultural establishment release a variety of inorganic, organic and biological contaminants. Sewage is generally a mixture of domestic waste water of cities. Its main sources are from baths, sinks, washing and toilets, industry and rainwater run-off from roads and other areas. They require physical, chemical and biological treatment depending on the nature of pollutants before discharge to river and lakes.

Quantitative assessment of wastewater is necessary to understand quality of wastewater with respect to physical, chemical and biological parameters. This helps in deciding treatment strategies for wastewater. Hence, wastewater characteristics can be envisaged after studying process details and raw material requirement during the process.

Water supply and sanitation are important basic needs for the improvement of the quality of life in city. In urban areas, water is tapped for domestic uses from rivers, streams, wells, groundwater, lakes etc. Almost 80% of the water supplied for domestic use, comes out as wastewater. In most of the cases wastewater is also let out untreated and it either sinks into the ground as a potential pollutant of ground water or is discharged into the natural drainage system causing pollution in downstream areas.

It is major source of water pollution in India, particularly in urban areas. In India about 78% of the urban population has access to safe drinking water and about 38% of the urban population has no access to basic sanitation services. The water requirement for various sectors is given in table 6.1. This indicates that demand for drinking water is increasing, since the population in urban areas is increasing.

Domestic Wastewater

In India, domestic sewage and sludge is the main source of water pollution, especially in urban cities. Water supply has been significantly increased during the last few decades. This has resulted in generation of huge amount of wastewater without adequate arrangements for collection, treatment and disposal. Assessment of total sewage generation, its collection, treatment and disposal is essential for rational planning of a comprehensive strategy to cope up with this problem. In the present article, an attempt has also been made to identify the gap between wastewater generation and existing treatment in Delhi.

Urban centers are discharging wastewater in the water bodies and also in the agriculture fields. In the early stages of human history, wastewater discharges did not pose problem to water bodies as the nature had the capacity and the system to degrade wastes and restore normal condition. Nature still does, but with the advent of urbanization, industrialization and resultant concentrated massive wastewater discharges, the aquatic systems are overloaded. The major source of organic pollution in fresh water bodies is sewage. In India, most of the cities and towns did not have sewage treatment facilities. Untreated human waste is being disposed into aquatic resources from where the city's water requirements are drawn. This constitutes a big public health hazard in terms of their potential for spreading water borne diseases.

Sewerage system in Delhi

Delhi being the capital of India and a state itself is very important Metropolitan City. The city is located at 28°22′48″ N latitude and 77°7′12″ E longitude and occupies an area of about 1483 km^2. It is the third largest town in India (population wise). The population of Delhi is rapidly growing. As per the 2011 census, the population of the metropolitan city of Delhi is 16.7 million. It increases up to 500% from 1961-2011 and it will be expected to reach about 19.1 million in 2021.

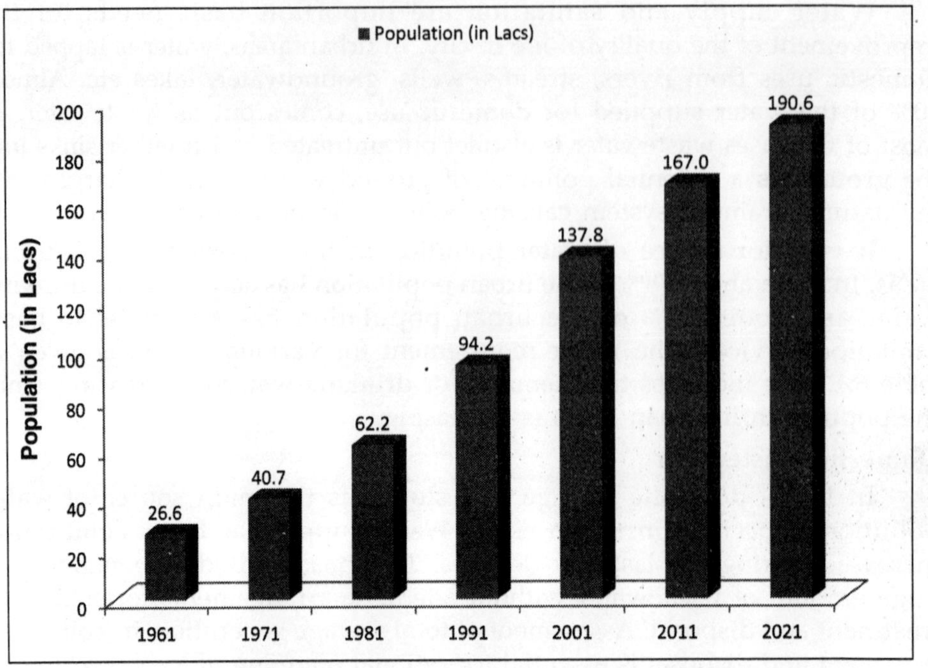

Fig. 6.2: Trends in population growth of Delhi (Source: CPCB, 2004)

The development of sewerage system in Delhi was started soon after New Delhi was Built in 1938. A sewage treatment plant of 18 MGD Capacity was constructed at Okhla. By 1956, the capacity of this plant was augmented to 30 MGD. Additional STPs were later constructed at Coronation Pillar (10 MGD) and at Keshopur (12 MGD) in 1957 and 1958 respectively. The treatment capacity increased from 52 MGD in 1961 to 283 MGD in 1993. The present sewage treatment capacity in Delhi stands at around 594.72 MGD. Presently the urban area of Delhi is served by a gravity collection sewerage system involving a large network of branch sewers, intercepting sewers, peripheral and trunk sewers of about 6000 km length. For the purposes of sewerage and drainage, Delhi can be divided into six zones: (1) Rithala, (2) Coronation Pillar (3) Keshopur; (4) Okhla; (5) Trans Yamuna; and (6) Outer Delhi. Besides this, there are newly developed areas or urban extensions mostly continuous with urban limits such as Narela, Pappan Kalan, Nazafgarh, Ghitroni, Vasant Kunj, Mehrauli & Sarita Vihar.

At present STPs are located at 23 different places in Delhi with a cumulative treatment capacity of around 5594.72 MGD. Water requirement will be increased from 2001-2021 about 60% and sewage generation will also increased upto 85%. Wastewater from their respective catchment areas finds its way into the river through storm water drains. As per figure 6.3, Domestic water requirement in Delhi is rising with the rate of 30-40% per decade. Waste water generation is increasing with the rate of 25-35% per decade in Delhi.

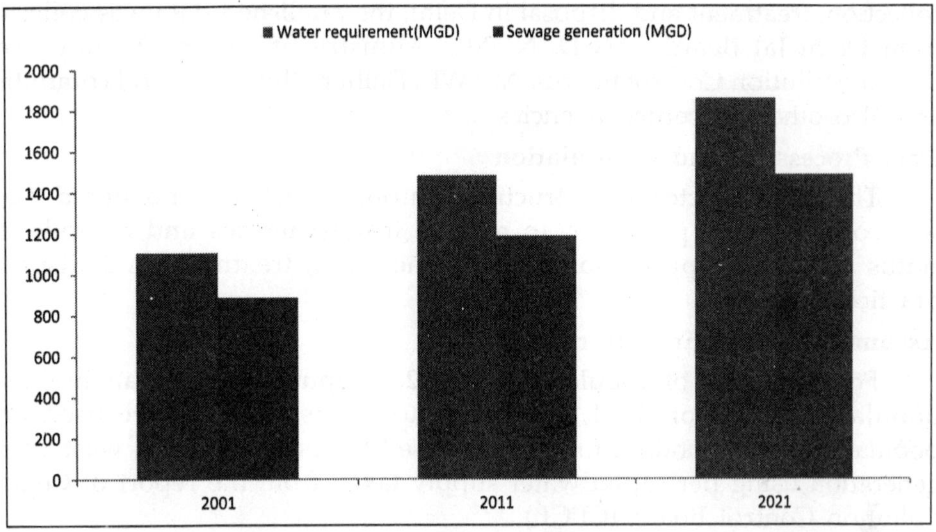

Fig. 6.3: Water requirement and domestic waste water generation in Delhi (Source: Delhi Jal Board)

Disposal of Treated Waste Water

Delhi being highly urbanized city, a huge amount of waste water is generated by domestic human activities. This domestic waste water goes to sewage treatment plant for treatment and discharge through various drains and nallahs and finally gets discharge into the Yamuna River. Some important drains are eastern and western Yamuna canals and Agra canal, Bawana, Rajpur and Lampur distributaries. Auchandi, Budhanpur, Sultanpur Mundka, Mongolpur, Nahari, Dhansa and Surkhpur are some of important minor's drains.

Objectives

The study was carried out keeping following objectives:

- To collect the data on status of water supply and domestic waste water generation in Delhi;

- To assess the existing domestic wastewater treatment capacity (plant-wise) in Delhi;
- To collect the data on disposal of domestic wastewater water, treatment, recycling and its utilization.

METHODOLOGY

The methodology adopted for collection of information and preparation of this work is as follows:

Source of Information and Data Collection

To collect information/data on water supply, wastewater generation, collection, treatment and disposal in Delhi, the published data was collected from Delhi Jal Boards, MCD, NDMC, Ministry of Urban Development, Central Pollution Control Boards, MOWR, Delhi pollution control committee and also other concerned agencies.

Data Processing and Compilation

The data collected was structured through MS-Excel and stored. Data was compiled and processed to remove inconsistencies and compile the status of water supply, wastewater generation, treatment and disposal practices.

Assumption and Limitations

For estimation of population for 2012, computed growth rate in Urban population based on 1991, 2001 and 2011 census data were used and population corresponding to 2012 was used for estimation viz. wastewater generation using per capita water supply taken from the report of Central Pollution Control Board (CPCB).

WATER: SUPPLY AND WASTE GENERATION

Water Supply Source

Water requirement for drinking purpose in Delhi is mainly met from river source. As per the information available from Delhi Jal Board, the availability of water from surface water sources viz. Yamuna, western Yamuna Canal, Ganga canal and Bhakra- Sutluj system is 745 MGD. Surface water contributes to over 86% of Delhi's Total water supply. Delhi's share of Yamuna river total water is 4.6%. Other sources include subsurface sources like Renny wells and tube well. The Ground water available in the Delhi is 100 MGD. However; groundwater is also used for drinking purpose in few areas. The main use of groundwater is in agriculture, horticulture and industries. The gross per capita availability of filtered water is about 200 LPCD.

Table 6.2: Water Resources in Delhi (Source: Delhi Jal Board)

S. No.	Source	Quantity (MGD)
1.	Yamuna	235
2.	Upper Ganga canal	245
3.	Bhakhara Storage	265
4.	Renny Wells/Tube well (Ground water)	100
	Total	**845**

Water requirement and availability of water is given in table 6.3. As the population of Delhi is increasing, water requirement will be increased from 211 MGD (Year 1961) to 1840 MGD (Year 2021). Availability of water has also been reached from 77 MGD (Year 1961) to 845 MGD (Year 2012).

Table 6.3: Water supply status in Delhi

Year	Population (in lacs)	Water requirement (MGD)	Availability of water (MGD)
1961	26.59	211	77
1971	40.66	324	173
1981	62.20	495	252
1991	93.70	749	469
2001	137.80	986	650
2011	167.00	1020	845
2021	191.00	1840	—

Source: DDA Delhi Master Plan

Table 6.4: Drinking water treatment plant capacity in Delhi

S. No.	Location of water treatment plant	Installed capacity as on June, 2012, (MGD)	Source of water
1.	Chandrawal I & II	103	River Yamuna
2.	Wazirabad I, II, III	132	River Yamuna
3.	Hyderpur/Dwarka	225	Bhakra Storage (WYC)
4.	Nangloi/Bawana	40	Bhakra Storage (WYC)
5.	Bhagirathi	105	Upper Ganga Canal
6.	Sonia Vihar	140	Upper Ganga Canal
7.	Renny well/Tubewells	100	Groundwater
Total Available		**845**	
Total Demand		**1020**	
Short fall		**175**	

Source: Delhi Jal Baord, June 2012

There are six water treatment plants in Delhi. Installed capacity of Hyderpur/Dwarka water treatment is 225 MGD. This is biggest water treatment plant. Installed capacity of smallest water treatment at Nangloi/Bawana is 40 MGD. Locations of water treatment plants are given in figure 6.4.

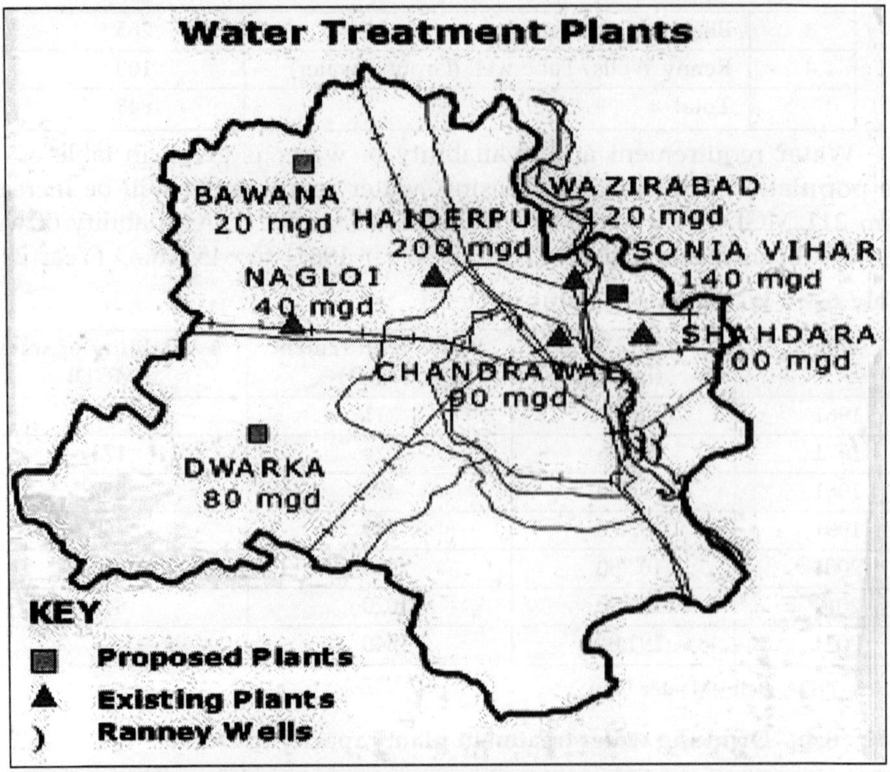

Fig. 6.4: Location of Water Treatment Plant in Delhi

Classification of Water (Based on Quality Standards)

Water can be categorized in several classes on the basis of water quality and utilization of water. The classes are:

- Class A: Drinking water Source without Conventional treatment
- Class B: Outdoor bathing
- Class C: Drinking water source with conventional treatment
- Class D: Wildlife, Fisheries
- Class E: Recreation and Aesthetic, Irrigation, Industrial cooling

Table 6.5: Specified Limits for various parameters of Quality for Different Classes of Water

S.N.	Water Quality Parameter	Characteristic of Water Body				
		A	B	C	D	E
1.	Dissolved Oxygen (DO) mg/l (min)	6	5	4	4	3
2.	BOD, mg/l (max)	2	3	3	-	-
3.	Total Coliform organisms * MPN/100ml (max)	50 *	500	500	-	-
4.	TDS mg/l (max)	500	-	1500	-	2100
5.	Chlorides (as Cl^-) mg/l (max)	250	-	600	-	600
6.	Colour, Hazen units (max)	-	10	300	300	-
7.	Sodium Absorption Ratio (max)	-	-	-	-	20
8.	Boron (as B), mg/l (max)	-	-	-	-	-
9.	Sulphates (as SO_4^{-2}), mg/l (max)	400	-	400	-	1000
10.	Nitrates (as NO_3^-) mg/l (max)	20	-	50	-	-
11.	Free Ammonia (as NH_3) mg/l (max)	-	-	-	1.2	-
12.	Conductivity at 25°C μmhos/cm (max)	-	-	-	1000	2500
13.	pH value	6.5-8.5	6.5-8.5	6.5-8.5	6.5-8.5	6.0-8.5
14.	Arsenic (as As), mg/l (max)	0.05	0.2	0.2	-	-
15.	Iron (as Fe), mg/l (max)	0.3	-	-	0.5	-
16.	Fluoride (as F), mg/l (max)	1.5	1.5	1.5	-	-
17.	Lead (as Pb), mg/l (max)	0.1	-	0.1	-	-

(Water quality criteria for different uses specified by CPCB, 1979 and the Bureau of Indian Standards, 1982)

* If the coliform is found to be more than the prescribed tolerance limits, the criteria for coliforms shall be satisfied if not more than 20 percent of samples show more than the tolerance limits specified and not more than 5 percent of samples show values more than 4 times the tolerance limits. There should be no visible discharge of domestic and industrial waste into class "A" waters. In case of classes "B" and "C" the discharge shall be so regulated/treated as to ensure maintenance of the stream standards.

Waste Water Generation

The wastewater is the major cause of water pollution in Delhi. About 1.99 and 0.32 MCM/day of wastewater is generated from municipal and industrial sectors respectively. Delhi Jal Board is responsible for treatment and disposal of wastewater through an efficient network of about 5600 km of internal, peripheral and trunk sewers. The capacity of Sewage Treatment Plants has been raised from 458 MGD to 518 MGD during the year 2005-2011. Presently about 21 Sewage Treatment Plants are working in the city.

The capacity of the present wastewater treatment plants in Delhi is about 595 MGD. Moreover, only primary wastewater treatment is carried out in these wastewater treatment plants; with exception in few where secondary treatment facility exists. No treatment plant is equipped with tertiary water treatment facility. In this way, the untreated or partially treated wastewater is discharged in to the Yamuna River.

Table 6.6: Trend and prediction of Waste Water Generation (Source: DJB, 2012)

Source of Waste Water	Volume, MGD				
	2004	2005	2006	2012	2021
Total water Demand	597	836	909	1020	1394
Total net water supply	503	525	547	854	1169
Waste water generation	403	669	727	680	1115
Outside sewer area	56	67	67	65	47
Net generated wastewater	302	383	400	403	720
Infiltration	115	115	115	115	115
Gross waste water to treatment	417	498	515	518	836

DOMESTIC WASTEWATER TREATMENT

Waste Water Treatment

With the enhancement of drinking water supply to the urban areas, the waste water generation is also increasing. Therefore, with increasing waste water generation, the collection and appropriate treatment of waste water has become pertinent to reduce the degeneration impact on both public and eco-system at large.

Treatment is the process of removing contaminants from wastewater and household sewage, both runoff (effluents) and domestic. It includes physical, chemical, and biological processes to remove physical, chemical and biological contaminants. Its objective is to produce an environmentally-safe fluid waste stream (or treated effluent) and a solid waste (or treated sludge) suitable for disposal or reuse (usually as farm fertilizer). Using advanced technology it is now possible to re-use sewage effluent for drinking water. For the most economic disposal of wastewater from various sources, recycling, reuse, renovation and regeneration must be practiced with utmost keenness. Recycling refers to repeating the same use; reuse is done by using waste water for other purpose; renovation refers to treatment to the (tertiary) level so that it is fit for use like fresh water, and regeneration refers of a water source in a natural manner. Recycling and reuse is a process, which reduce the burden of water supply. The existing treatment capacity and the additional capacity requirement of India are depicted in figure 6.5.

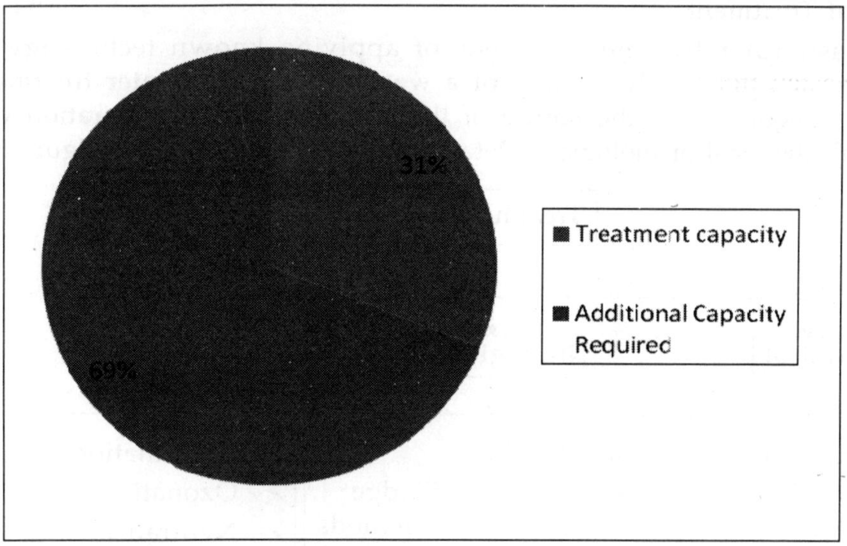

Fig. 6.5: Status of wastewater treatment plant in India

Delhi being fast growing city is facing severe problem of untreated sewage. Since the untreated sewage is discharged into the Yamuna river, the river is severely polluted. Delhi has the maximum constructed treatment capacity of 518 MGD, Followed by Mumbai at 473 MGD.

Table 6.7: Status of Sewage treatment capacity of metropolitan cities (CPCB, 2009)

S.No.	Name of City	Sewage Generation (MLD)	Sewage Treatment (MLD)	Percent Treatment Capacity (%)
1.	Hyderabad	95	132	100
2.	Vadodara	40	46	100
3.	Ahemadabad	105	108	100
4.	Ludhiana	52	69	100
5.	Chennai	57	59	100
6.	Mumbai	594	473	80
7.	Delhi	845	518	61
8.	Kolkata	157	38	24

Certain cities like Hyderabad, Vadodara, Chennai, Ludhiana and Ahemadabad has the treatment capacity, which meets the volume of generation. However, the total treatment capacity in the metropolitan cities is only half of the sewage generation. On account of absence of treatment capacity the sewage is discharged without treatment. Even the facilities constructed to treat wastewater do not operate at their optimum capacity due to improper maintenance, together with no-technical and unskilled approach.

Types of Treatment

Wastewater treatment consists of applying known technology to improve or upgrade the quality of a wastewater. Wastewater treatment can be categorized by the nature of the treatment process operation viz. physical, chemical or biological. Detail methods are described in figure 6.6.

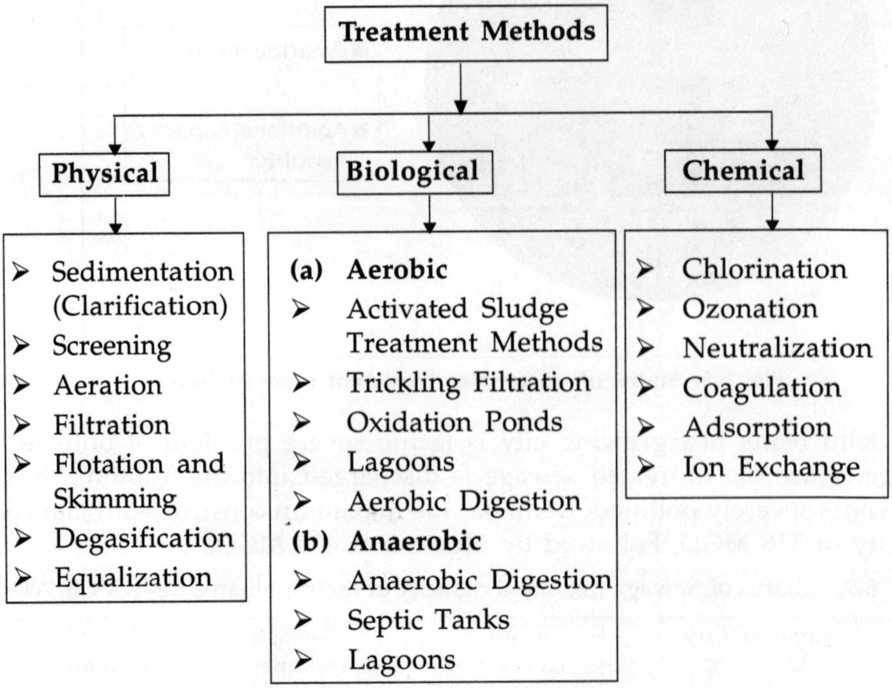

Fig 6.6: Methods of wastewater treatment

Following treatment technologies are generally used in Delhi for waste water treatment:

A. Preliminary Treatment

At most plants preliminary treatment is used to protect pumping equipment and facilitate subsequent treatment processes. Preliminary devices are designed to remove or cut up the larger suspended and floating solids, to remove the heavy inorganic solids, and to remove excessive amounts of oils or greases.

In preliminary treatment, the following devices are commonly used:

1. Screens - rack, bar or fine
2. Comminuting devices - grinders, cutters, shredders
3. Grit chambers
4. Pre-aeration tanks

In addition to the above, chlorination may be used in preliminary treatment. Since chlorination may be used at all stages in treatment, it is considered to be a method by itself. Preliminary treatment devices require careful design and operation.

B. Primary Treatment

In this treatment, most of the settleable solids are separated or removed from the wastewater by the physical process of sedimentation. When certain chemicals are used with primary sedimentation tanks, some of the colloidal solids are also removed. Biological activity of the wastewater in primary treatment is of negligible importance.

The purpose of primary treatment is to reduce the velocity of the wastewater sufficiently to permit solids to settle and floatable material to surface. Therefore, primary devices may consist of settling tanks, clarifiers or sedimentation tanks. Because of variations in design, operation, and application, settling tanks can be divided into four general groups:

1. Septic tanks
2. Two story tanks — Imhoff and several proprietary or patented units
3. Plain sedimentation tank with mechanical sludge removal
4. Upward flow clarifiers with mechanical sludge removal

When chemicals are used, other auxiliary units are employed. These are:

1. Chemical feed units
2. Mixing devices
3. Flocculators

The results obtained by primary treatment, together with anaerobic sludge digestion as described later, are such that they can be compared with the zone of degradation in stream self-purification. The use of chlorine with primary treatment is discussed under the section on Preliminary Treatment.

C. Secondary Treatment

(i) Activated sludge process

The Activated Sludge Process is the one of the main process in waste water treatment. Activated sludge process was developed in England in 1914 and was so named because it involved the production of an activated mass of microorganisms capable of aerobically stabilizing the organic content of waste water. Activated Sludge Process in waste water treatment is the most versatile of the biological water treatment processes capable of producing an effluent with any desired BOD (Biological Oxidation Demand).

The Activated Sludge Process is an aerobic biological waste water treatment process that uses microorganisms, including bacteria, fungi, and protozoa, to speed up decomposition of organic matter requiring oxygen for treatment. In this activated sludge process, microorganisms are thoroughly mixed with organics under conditions that stimulate their growth and waste materials are removed. As the microorganisms grow and are mixed by the agitation of the air, the individual microorganisms clump (or flocculate) together to form a mass of microbes called activated sludge.

(ii) Activated Sludge-Extended Aeration

The Extended Aeration is the most common variation of the Activated Sludge Process. It is a biological treatment process, which is able to produce high quality effluent for a reasonable operating and maintenance costs. In the process, large quantities of air are bubbled through wastewaters that contain dissolved organic substances in open aeration tanks.

Oxygen is required by bacteria and other types of microorganisms present in the system to live, grow, and multiply in order to consume the dissolved organic "food", or pollutants in the waste. After several hours in a large holding tank, the water is separated from the sludge of bacteria and discharged from the system. Extended Aeration process are its stability, the ease of installation and operation of systems, the low construction operating and maintenance costs, the low sludge yield and the odorless operation.

(iii) High Rate Bio-Filter

The High Rate Bio-Filter (HRBF) technology has been designed for the efficient reduction of BOD, nitrification of ammonia and denitrification systems.

(iv) Oxidation Pond

Oxidation Ponds (or Stabilization Ponds) are a popular sewage treatment method for small communities because of their low construction and operating costs. New oxidation ponds can treat sewage but require maintenance and periodic de-sludging. Oxidation ponds, also called lagoons or stabilization ponds, are large, shallow ponds designed to treat wastewater through the interaction of sunlight, bacteria, and algae. Algae grow using energy from the sun and carbon dioxide and inorganic compounds released by bacteria in water. During the process of photosynthesis, the algae release oxygen needed by aerobic bacteria. Mechanical aerators are sometimes installed to supply yet more oxygen, thereby reducing the required size of the pond. Sludge deposits in the pond must eventually be removed by dredging. Algae remaining in the pond effluent can be removed by filtration or by a combination of chemical treatment and settling.

(v) Trickling Filter

The terms trickle filter, trickling biofilter, biofilter, biological filter and biological trickling filter are often used to refer to a trickling filter.

These systems have also been described as roughing filters, intermittent filters, packed media bed filters, alternative septic systems, percolating filters, attached growth processes, and fixed film processes

A trickling filter consists of a fixed bed of rocks, lava, coke, gravel, slag, polyurethane foam, sphagnum peat moss, ceramic, or plastic media over which sewage or other wastewater flows downward and causes a layer of microbial slime (biofilm) to grow, covering the bed of media. Aerobic conditions are maintained by splashing, diffusion, and either by forced air flowing through the bed or natural convection of air if the filter medium is porous.

The removal of pollutants from the wastewater stream involves both absorption and adsorption of organic compounds by the layer of microbial biofilm. The filter media is typically chosen to provide a very high surface area to volume. Typical materials are often porous and have considerable internal surface area in addition to the external surface of the medium. Passage of the wastewater over the media furnishes dissolved air, the oxygen which the slime layer requires for the biochemical oxidation of the organic compounds and releases carbon dioxide gas, water and other oxidized end products. As the biofilm layer thickens, it eventually sloughs off into the treated effluent and subsequently forms part of the secondary sludge. Typically, a trickling filter is followed by a clarifier or sedimentation tank for the separation and removal of the sloughing. Other filters utilizing higher-density media such as sand, foam and peat moss do not produce a sludge that must be removed, but require forced air blowers and backwashing or an enclosed anaerobic environment. The treatment of sewage or other wastewater with trickling filters is among the oldest and most well characterized treatment technologies.

Table 6.8: Expected Efficiencies of Various Treatment Units

S.No.	Process	% Reduction		
		TSS	BOD	Total coliform
1.	Primary Treatment (Sedimentation)	45-60	30-45	40-60
2.	Chemical Treatment	60-80	45-65	60-90
3.	Secondary Treatment			
	(i) Slandered Trickling Filter	75-85	70-90	80-90
	(ii) High rate trickling filter			
	(a) Single stage	75-85	75-80	80-90
	(b) Two Stage	90-95	90-95	90-96
	(iii) Activated Sludge process	85-90	85-90	90-95
	(iv) Stabilization pond (Single cell)	80-90	90-95	90-95
	(v) Stabilization pond (Two cell)	90-95	95-97	95-98

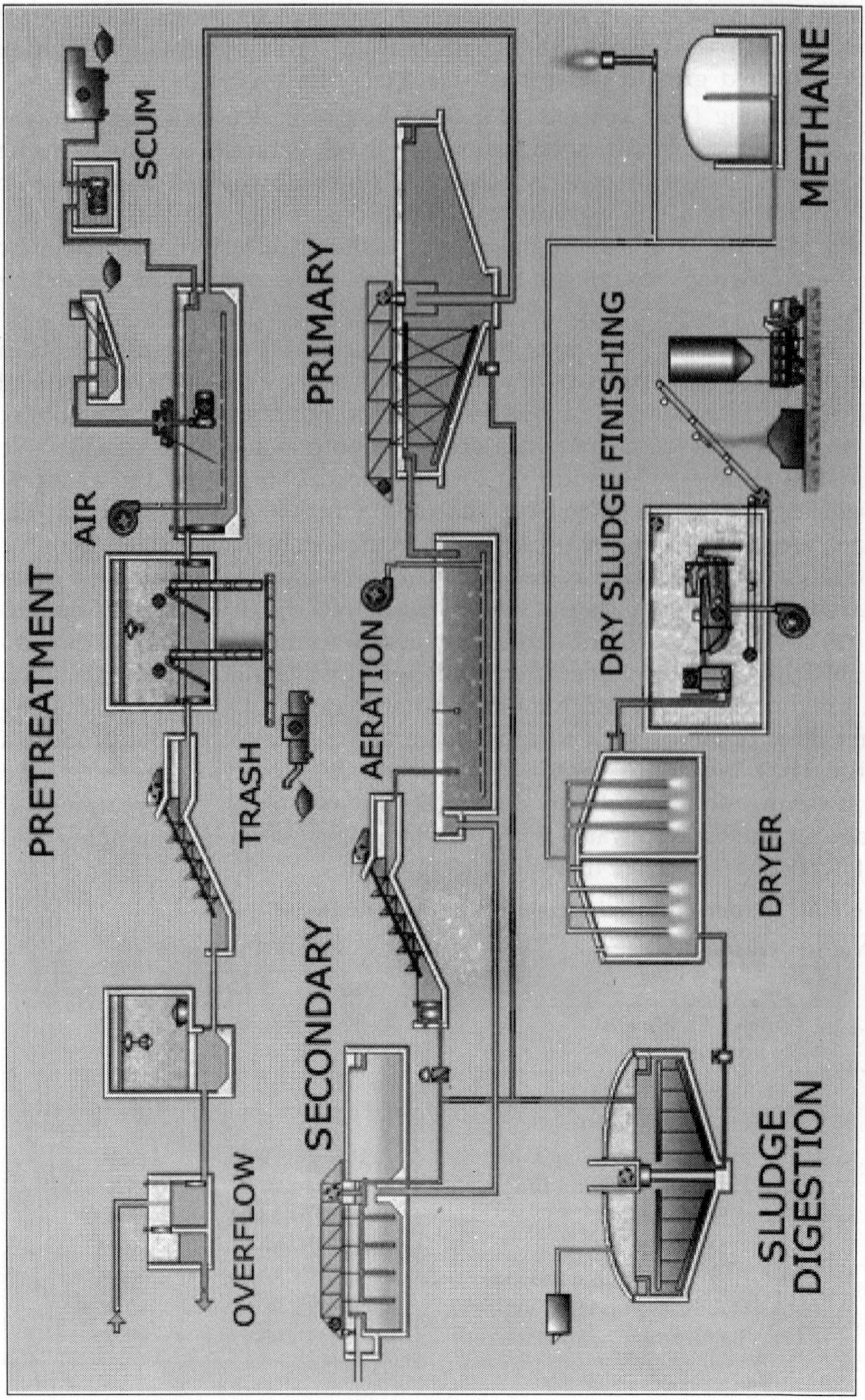

6.7: Flow diagram of a sewage treatment plant

Table 6.9: Unit operation/process, their function and devices used for Domestic Wastewater Treatment

S.No.	Unit operation and process	Functions	Treatment Device
1.	Screening	Removal of large floating, suspended and settleable solids	Bar racks and screens of various description
2.	Grit Removal	Removal of inorganic suspended solids	Grit chamber
3.	Primary Sedimentation	Removal of organic and inorganic settlement solids	Primary Sedimentation Tank
4.	Aerobic biological suspended growth process	Conversation of colloidal, dissolved and residual suspended organic matter into settleable biofloc and stable inorganic	Activated sludge process units and its modifications, Waste stabilization ponds, Aerated Lagoons
	Aerobic biological growth process	Conversation of colloidal, dissolved and residual suspended organic matter into settleable biofloc and stable inorganic	Trickling filter, Rotating Biological Contactor
5.	Anaerobic biological growth process	Conversion of organic matter in to CH_4 & CO_2 and organic relatively stable organic residue	Anaerobic filter, Fluid bed submerged media, Anaerobic Reactor, Upflow Anaerobic Sludge, Blanket Reactor, Anaerobic Rotating Biological Contractor
6.	Anaerobic stabilization of organic sludge	Conversion of organic matter in to CH4 & CO_2 and organic relatively stable organic residue	Anaerobic digester

Table 6.10: Installed capacity of the Sewage Treatment Plants (DJB, 2012)

Name of the plant	No. of Plant (Year of establishment)	Capacity (MGD)	Type of STP
Sen Nursing Home	One (1998)	2.2	Densadag Technology
Delhi Gate STP	One (1998)	2.2	Densadag Technology
Kondli STP	Four (10+25+10+45) (1987,1989, 2001, 2013)	90	Activated Sludge Process
Coronation Pillar STP	Three (10+20+10) (1957, 1999, 2000)	40	Activated Sludge Process, (ASP), Trickling filter
Oxidation pond, STP	One (T.O. from MCD)	6	Oxidation Pond
Narela, STP	One (2001)	10	Activated Sludge Process
Okhla STP	Six(30+12+37+45+16+30) (1937, 82, 93, 1993, 2001, 2012)	170	Activated Sludge Process
Vasant Kunj STP	Two (2.2+3.0) (1982, 2001)	5.2	Activated Sludge Process & Extended Aeration
Mehrauli STP	One (2003)	5.0	Extended Aeration
Yamuna Vihar STP	Two (10+10) (1999, 2001)	20	Activated Sludge Process
Rithala STP	Two (40+40) (1989, 2002)	80	ASP & High rate aerobic ASP & Biofilter
Keshopur STP	Three (12+20+40) (1958, 1975, 1990)	72	Activated Sludge Process
Ghitorni	One (1997)	5	Extended Aeration
Nilothi STP	One (2002)	40	Activated Sludge Process
Pappan kalan STP	One (2000)	20	Activated Sludge Process
Najafgarh STP	One (2002)	5	Extended Aeration
Rohini STP	One (2002)	15	Activated Sludge Process
Akshardham (CWG)	One (2010)	1.0	MBR (Membrane Bioreactor)
Kapashera	One (2013)	5.0	Activated Sludge Process
Molarband	One (T.O. from MCD)	0.66	FAB (fluidize Aeration Bed)
Bakkerwala	One (T.O. from MCD)	0.66	FAB (fluidize Aeration Bed)
Total 21		**594.72**	

Sewage Treatment Plants (STPs)

About 21 Sewage Treatment Plants are working in the Delhi and details are given below:

(i) Okhla STP (170 MGD)

This is the largest STP of Delhi having ring road catchment area contribute pollution through 12 open sewer drains. Although a number of sewage pumping stations exist in its command area, three most important sewage pumping stations pumping sewage to Okhla STP are at ring road,

Kilokri and Andrewganj. The design treatment capacity of Okhla STP is 140 MGD. 30 MGD is recently increased into this capacity and now it has been reached 170 MGD. Besides, East Kailash and Okhla Industrial estate pumping stations, the catchment area includes Qudsia drain, Civil mill drain, Delhi gate nall, Sen nursing home, Drain no. 14 and Barapulla drain.. The treatment process is conventional aeration. The raw sewage inlet is common for all the units from where the sewage is distributed after screening. Treatment system comprises of bar screens followed by grit chambers and primary settling tanks (PSTs).

(ii) Keshopur STP (72 MGD)

This STP is located to the west of outer ring road and to the south and east of Najafgarh drain. The existing capacity is 72 MGD and was built up in three stages of 12 MGD, 20 MGD and 40 MGD each. All the three sewage treatment plants are based on conventional activated sludge process systems. The treatment system comprises of inlet chamber, bar screen followed by grit chambers and the primary settling tanks. The wastewater of primary settling tank is then taken to conventional type surface aerators (aeration tank) and finally to final settling tanks. The plant also has digesters for digestion of the sludge from primary settling tanks and gasholders. The gas generated from the digesters is hold in these tanks and is disposed off by burning. The wastewater from the plant is finally discharged into Najafgarh drain. As indicated above, Keshopur STP receives sewage from:

(i) Najafgarh road trunk sewer

(ii) Relieving trunk sewer

(iii) Punjabi Bagh sewer

The average in-flow of sewage ate the STP is about 45 MGD against the capacity of 72 MGD.

(iii) Coronation pillar STP (40 MGD)

The catchment area of this plant includes Jahangirpuri, Adarsh Nagar, Nehru Vihar, Rajsthan Udyog Nagar, Sanjay Gandhi Transport Nagar and Old Model Town. The drainage zone of Coronation sewage treatment plant comprises of Sanjay Gandhi Transport Nagar in north-west, Delhi-Ambal railway line on the western side, old Subzi Mandi in south and Timarpur in north-east. The drainage zone is predominantly residential and has educational institutions such as Delhi University, St. Stephen College, Shriram college of Commerce, Delhi School of Economics, Hindu College and several other Colleges, Institute of Nuclear Medicine besides industrial area along GT Karnal road and GT road. The treatment capacity of Coronation pillar is 40 MGD. This sewage treatment plant receives sewage through main trunk sewers namely University sewer and north Delhi trunk sewer besides sewage from Adarsh Nagar and Model Town sewage pumping station. Sewage from 12 tributary drains in civil lines zones of

MCD is outfalling into Najafgarh drain. All the tributary drains from Timarpur drain to Shaktinagar drain no. 1 are connected to Najafgarh drain on its right bank, while Poor House drain to Rana Pratap Bagh drain are connected on the left bank of Najafgarh drain. The wastewater from Wazirpur drain is being taken to Wazirpur CETP for treatment. Sewage from the sewage pumping station located in Rana Pratap Bagh is also being pumped into Najafgarh drain, while sewage pumping station in Timarpur, Mukharjee Nagar and Tagore Garden are pumping into trunk sewers. Trapping arrangements of the drains connected on the right bank of Najafgarh drain are made with the University trunk sewer and those on the left bank with the north Delhi trunk sewer. Both trunk sewers convey the sewage to the University sewage pumping station and the sewage further pumped to the Coronation pillar sewage treatment plant. The sewage from the local sewage pumping stations located in Model town, Azadpur, Kewal Park, Adarsh nagar is pumped directly to the sewage treatment plant. The drains which are trapped to convey sewage to Coronation pillar sewage treatment plant are given in the table below:

Table 6.11: Trapping of drains into sewers in Coronation Pillar catchments

S.N.	Name of Drain	Trapping existed into
1.	Gurmandi drain	North Delhi trunk sewer
2.	Vijay Nagar drain	North Delhi trunk sewer
3.	Mall road drain No. I	North Delhi trunk sewer
4.	Poor House drain	North Delhi trunk sewer
5.	Kamala Nagar drain	University trunk sewer
6.	Hansraj drain	University trunk sewer
7.	Patel Chest drain	University trunk sewer
8.	G.T. Road drain	North Delhi trunk sewer
9.	Shastri Nagar drain No. I	North Delhi trunk sewer
10.	Shastri Nagar drain No. II	University trunk sewer
11.	Mall road drain No. II	University trunk sewer
12.	Roop Nagar drain	Not trapped
13.	Rana Pratap Bagh drain	Not trapped
14.	Wazirpur drain	Wazirpur CETP drainage zone

The two units having 40 MGD capacity is with activated sludge process, while 6 MGD is based on trickling filter technology treatment system comprises of inlet chamber, grit chamber then followed by primary settling tank. The wastewater of the primary settling tank is then taken at aeration tank and finally to final settling tanks. The excess sludge is dried in sludge drying beds. This sewage treatment plant receives sewage from University trunk sewer and north Delhi trunk sewer besides direct pumping from sewage pumping stations at Model Town, Adarsh Nagar, etc. there are thirteen drains with an average of 95 MLD (21 MGD) approximately of sewage flow reaches the sewage treatment plant as against existing capacity of 46 MGD of secondary treatment.

(iv) Oxidation pond STP (6 MGD)

The Timarpur oxidation is located in north Delhi near Nehru Vihar. The catchment area of this sewage treatment plant is same as Coronation Pillar sewage treatment plant. Approximately 6 MGD sewage is diverted to this sewage treatment plant (Oxydation Pond) from the sewage pumping station and rest goes to Coronation Pillar sewage treatment plant. There are total 18 oxidation ponds in series.

(v) Rithala- STP (80 MGD)

The catchment area of this plant includes the area of seven sewage pumping stations i.e. Rithala, Haiderpuri, Bharat Nagar, Shalimar Bagh, Rohini sector-17 and Pitampura. Rithala drainage zone lies between Coronation Pillar zone and keshopur drainage zones. This zone lies in the north-west of Delhi and is bounded between the two northern railway lines going towards Ambala and Rohtak respectively. Rithala sewage treatment plant is situated in the north-west of Delhi in Rohini area of design capacity of 80 MGD. Rithala drainage zone mainly covers Rajendranagar, Karol Bagh, Sarai Rohilla, Pratap nagar, Vardhman Nagar, Shastri Nagar, Trinagar, Bharat Nagar, Wazirpur, Ashok Vihar, Lawrence road, Raja Park, Rani Bagh, Raj nagar, Shalimar Bagh, Pitampura, Saraswati Vihar, Prashant Vihar, Mangolpuri, Sultanpuri, Haiderpuri, Rithala and Rohini sector 16, 17 & 19 areas. The wastewater from these are as finally goes to the Rithala wastewater treatment plant through 12 major sewage pumping stations located at various places in the zone. Rithala-Rohini drainage zone is mainly a residential area with small pockets of three industrial areas i.e. Wazirpur industrial estate, Lawrence road industrial estate and Mangolpuri industrial area. The major sewage pumping station to Rithala treatment plant is Bharat nagar, Trinagar, Lawrence road, Rampura, Shalimar Bagh, Pitampura, Rithala, Haiderpuri, Avantika, Nangloi, Rohini sector 17 & 19. The existing capacities of the five terminal sewage pumping station are Rithala sewage pumping station of 481 MLD, Haiderpur sewage pumping station of 245 MLD, Avantika sewage pumping station of 200 MLD, Rohini sector 17 sewage pumping station of 123 MLD and Rohini sector 19 sewage pumping station of 54 MLD. The combined average and peak capacities of these sewage pumping stations are 554 MLD and 1103 MLD respectively. The existing capacities of the two terminal sewage pumping stations i.e. Rohini sector 23 & 25 are 68 MLD respectively. Rithala sewage treatment plant is hardly getting an average of 182 MLD (40 MGD) of sewage as against total existing capacity of 364 MLD (80 MGD).

(vi) Rohini STP (15 MGD)

The existing capacity of the Rohini sewage treatment plant is 15 MGD. The three industrial pockets in this drainage zone are Wazirpur industrial estate, Lawrence road industrial estate and Mangolpuri industrial estate. The Wazirpur industrial estate (24 MLD), and Mangolpuri industrial estate (2.4 MLD) has already been commissioned. The untreated effluent of this industrial area is discharging to the sewer finally finds its way into the open drain. The sewage treatment technology includes old and new with activated sludge process (ASP) and high load ASP & biofilter respectively. This comprises of bar screen, grit chamber, primary settling tank followed by aeration, clari-flocculation and secondary settling (activated sludge process). The high load ASP system comprises of 3 bar screens followed by four aeration tanks. The wastewater of aeration tank is then distributed in sedimentation tank consisting of 8 nos. of partitions and having 24 surface aerators. The wastewater from the sedimentation tank is then taken to 4 floatation thickeners (FTs). The sewage treatment plant has 24 sludge drying beds. The sludge produced is thickened and then digested in the digesters (9 Nos.). The digested sludge is stored and de-watered. Electricity is to be generated by the production of bio-gas in the digesters. The secondary treatment is given by bio-filtration. From the areas of Pitampura, Rohini, Ashok Vihar, Lawrence road, Shalimar Bagh, Trinagar group of colonies, Sarai Rohilla, Shastri Nagar, Shakurbasti group of colonies, J.J. resettlement colonies of Nangloi, Sultanpuri, Mangolpuri, etc., sewage generated is to be conveyed for treatment at Rithala sewage treatment plant.

(vii) Vasant Kunj STP (5.2 MGD)

The catchment area of this sewage treatment plant is mainly from Kishangarh village and surroundings and wastewater is being pumped from sewage pumping stations of B1 & B2, B3 & B4, B5 & B6 and C-9 blocks of Vasant Vihar. The design capacity of sewage treatment plants is 5 MGD. Treatment is through extended aeration, activated sludge process comprises of bar screen and grit chambers and aeration tank followed by secondary settling tanks. The wastewater from the grit chambers is then taken to final settling tanks. The sludge is dried in sludge drying beds. As there is no primary settling tank, digesters, gasholders are not installed in this plant.

(viii) Narela STP (10 MGD)

The catchment area comprises whole Narela drainage zone and the treatment system comprises of 2 bar screens followed by two grit chambers and two primary settling tanks. Wastewater from primary settling tank is taken to aeration tank consisting of 2 compartments and having 20 numbers of surface aerators (10 nos. each). The wastewater from the aeration tank is then taken to final settling tanks (2 Nos.). The designed treatment capacity is 10 MGD. The excess sludge is dried in sludge drying beds (20 Nos.) Dried sludge is being sold as manure. There are two sludge digesters and 2 gasholders for holding the gas from digesters.

(ix) Nilothi STP (40 MGD)

A sewage treatment plant of 40 MGD capacity receiving wastewater from sewage pumping station of at Sayed Nangloi. The flow from the entire area north of Najafgarh drain will be diverted from the existing Keshopur pumping station and sewage treatment plant. The sewage treatment plant comprises of bar screen, grit chambers, primary settling tank followed by aeration tank. Sewage from aeration tank is then taken to secondary settling tank (SST). The raw sludge collected from primary settling tank and excess sludge from SST is then taken to the sludge drying beds. Bio-gas collected in gasholder is finally flared off into the atmosphere.

(x) Pappankalan STP (20 MGD)

Papankala zone lies in the southwest side of Delhi. DDA has developed the Dwarka township covering a total area of 5600 hectare. The area is bounded on the north by Najafgarh road and Pankha road on the east by Rewari railway line running in a south north-easterly direction and on the west by the Najafgarh drain. The design capacity of Papankala sewage treatment plant is 20 MGD. The catchment area includes Palam drain, Madhu Vihar, Dabri Mod, sector 13, 14, 3 and 4 of Papankalan. There are four sewage pumping stations to cater this entire area of Dwarka township covering census towns of Palam, Bindapur, Nasirpur and adjacent villages such as Dabri, Sagarpur, Matiyala, Amber hai, Pochanpur, Dhul Siras, Bamnoli and Bharthal. The treatment system comprises of bar screens followed by grit chamber and 2 nos. of primary settling tanks. Sewage from primary settling tank is then taken to aeration tank consisting of 2 compartments and 24 surface aerators (12 Nos. each). The wastewater from aeration tank is then taken to Final settling tanks (2 Nos.). The sludge generated in the process is dried in sludge drying beds. The plant has 8 nos. of digesters for digestion of sludge from primary settling tank and gasholder. The gas generated in the digesters is collected in the gasholder and is recycled to digesters for mixing the digester contents with the help of compressors. The excess quantity of gas is being burnt in gas burners.

(xi) Najafgarh STP (5 MGD)

Najafgarh zone lies in the western part of NCT of Delhi. There is only one sewage pumping station catering to the entire Najafgarh sub-city. This sewage pumping station covers the town of Roshanpur Ali (Dech Khurd) and village Khera, Paprawat etc. There is one sewage treatment plant of 5 MGD capacity located in Najafgarh zone. The average flow generated in these areas is less than 23 MLD. The treatment system comprises of bar screens followed by grit chamber, primary settling tank and aeration tank consisting of 2 compartments and having 16 surface aerators (8 Nos. each). The wastewater from aeration tank is then taken to 2 Nos. of Final settling tanks. The sludge generated in the process is dried in sludge drying beds.

(xii) Yamuna Vihar STP (20 MGD)

The catchment area covers Kaboolnagar, Naveen Shahdra, Rohtash Nagar, Gorakhpark, Babarpur, Balbirnagar, Panchsheel Park, Shivaji Park, Panchsheel Garden, Mohan Park, Dwarkapuri and Seelampur resettlement colonies Ph.-III and IV. The treatment is activated sludge process for two sewage treatment plants. The design capacity of each sewage treatment plant is 20 MGD. The treatment system comprises of grit chamber followed by primary settling tanks and then aeration tank consisting of 4 compartments. The wastewater from aeration tank is then taken to 2 Nos. of secondary settling tanks.

(xiii) Kondli STP (90 MGD)

The 10 MGD Kondli sewage treatment plant unit receives sewage from Preet Vihar sewage pumping station having catchment areas spread over Geeta Colony, Laxmi Nagar, Shakarpur, Preet Vihar, Krishna Nagar and Bihari Colony. The other two 113 MLD and 45 MLD units recieves sewage through sewage pumping station of Jagrati enclave, Kalyanpuri, Dallupura, Mansarovar, Ram Nagar and Kondli sewage pumping station having catchment area of Kailash Nagar, east End enclave, Jagrati enclave, Anand Vihar, Mayur Vihar I & II and all colonies of south of GT road. The sewage treatment plant is a conventional activated sludge includes bar screens, grit chambers, primary settling tanks, aeration tanks and secondary settling tanks. After primary treatment, the combined flow is sent to the aeration tank and the wastewater of the outlet of aeration tank is again equally distributed to the two secondary settling tanks. The design treatment capacity is 45 MGD. The sludge generated is being sent to digesters and digested sludge is then sent to sludge drying beds. There are 3 numbers of gasholders and gas is being flaring off into the atmosphere.

(xiv) Mehrauli STP (5 MGD)

The catchment area of these sewage treatment plants covers partly outer Delhi drainage zone. However, these sewage treatment plants falls under the catchment of Okhla sewage treatment plant and all along the ring road trunk sewer starting from Timarpur to Okhla catchment. The command areas of this sewage treatment plant area Mehrauli and adjacent urban centers. The system of this sewage treatment plants are extended aeration and ASP respectively. Mehrauli sewage treatment plant is extended aeration comprising of screen bars, grit chambers, and aeration tanks. Wastewater from aeration tanks is then flows to secondary settling tanks. There is no primary settling tank exists. Installed capacity of this plant is 5 MGD.

(xv) Delhi Gate STP (2.2 MGD)

This sewage treatment plants comprising of inlet course screen, medium screens, fine screens, and grease & grit removal chamber. Wastewater then flow to flash mixer for polyelectrolyte dosing. After chemical dosing the wastewater then flows to Densadeg reactors and classifier and finally bio-filtration stage I and stage II (Biofor). Sludge generated from the Densadeg clarifier goes to sludge pit and then de-watering unit. Finally sludge cake produced and disposed off. This sewage treatment plants are running on their designed capacity.

(xvi) Dr. Sen Nursing home STP (2.2 MGD)

This sewage treatment also works as like Delhi gate mechanism. Its Installed capacity is 2.2 MGD. It is running on their installed capacity.

(xvii) Ghitorni STP (5 MGD)

Ghitorni sewage treatment plant is based on activated sludge type. This sewage treatment plant comprises of screen bars, grit chambers, and aeration tanks. The wastewater then flows to secondary settling tanks. Treatment capacity of this plant of is 5 MGD.

(xviii) Akshardham STP (1 MGD)

This plant is situated at in Akshardham Temple. It is very small treatment plant and capacity of this plant is 1.0 MGD. Activated sludge process is utilized for treatment of sewage.

(xix) Kapashera STP (5 MGD)

The IGI Airport and its neighboring villages have a proper outlet for sewage and storm water, with the DJB having a 5 MGD sewage treatment plant (STP) at Kapashera. Sewage pipelines are currently being laid around six villages around the airport - Mehram Nagar, Mahipalpur, Samal Khan, Shahbad Mohammadpur, Bijwasan and Kapashera- to collect sewage and transport it to the Kapashera STP.

(xx) Molarband STP (0.66 MGD)

Treatment capacity of this sewage plant is 0.66 MGD. Treatment process of this plant is activated sludge process.

(xxi) Bakkerwala STP (0.66 MGD)

Treatment capacity of this sewage plant is 0.66 MGD. Treatment process of this plant is activated sludge process.

Table 6.12: Details of wastewater generation and treatment in Delhi

S.N.	Variable	Value
1.	Water consumption (MGD)	845
2.	Sewage Generation (MGD)	680
3.	Sewage Treatment Capacity (MGD)	594
4.	Treatment Capacity (%)	61
5.	Per Capita Sewage (LPCD)	258.48

Table 6.13: Sewage Treatment Plant Capacity in different regions of Delhi (Source: Delhi Jal Board)

S.N.	Name of STP	Installed Capacity (MGD)	Actual Treatment (MGD)	Remark
1.	Okhla	170	128.57	Under Utilized
2.	Keshopur	72	45.39	Under Utilized
3.	Coronation pillar with	40	11.33	Under Utilized
4.	Oxidation Pond Timarpur	6	1.5	Under Utilized
5.	Rithala	80	46.39	Under Utilized
6.	Kondli I,II, III, IV	90	41.08	Under Utilized
7.	Yamuna Vihar I, II	20	11.63	Under Utilized
8.	Vasant Kunj	5.2	3.99	Under Utilized
9.	Ghitorni	5	–	Not in operation
10.	Pappankalan	20	18.20	Under Utilized
11.	Narela	10	1.08	Under Utilized
12.	Najafgarh	5	0.90	Under Utilized
13.	Delhi gate	2.2	2.38	Over Utilized
14.	Sen Nursing Home	2.2	2.40	Over Utilized
15.	Rohini	15.0	—	Not in operation
16.	Nilothi	40	12.50	Under Utilized
17.	Meharouli	5.0	2.33	Under Utilized
18.	Bakarwala	0.66	0.12	Under Utilized
19.	Molarband	0.66	0.50	Under Utilized
20.	Akshardham	1.0	0.12	Under Utilized
21.	Kapashera	5.0	—	Not in operation
	Total	**594.72**	**328.91**	

Table 6.14: Proposed capacity of under construction Sewage Treatment Plants (Source: DJB, 2012)

S.No.	Name of STP	Proposed capacity of STP (MGD)	Expected date of commissioning
1.	Chilla	9	December 2013
2.	Yamuna Vihar III	25	March 2014
3.	Nilothi Ph. II	20	June 2014
4.	Pappan Kalan Ph. II	20	March 2014
5.	Delhi Gate Ph. II	15	June 2014
6.	*Coronation Pillar	40*	–
7.	*Delhi Cantt.	8*	–
	Total	**89+48***	

*Under proposal

Augmentation of Capacity of STPs:

Sewage treatment plants shall be augmented from 594.72 MGD to 683.72 MGD by June 2014 after commissioning of Sewage treatment plants at Yamuna Vihar (25 MGD), Nilothi (20 MGD), Pappankalan (20 MGD) Delhi Gate (15 MGD) and Chilla (9 MGD). To match the quantity of sewage generated in future, the STPs are under construction and Coronation Pillar (40 MGD) and Delhi Cantt. (8 MGD) have been proposed, which will create the total treatment capacity of 731.72 MGD in addition to CETPs (40 MGD) in industrial areas and few decentralized STPs likely to be proposed in unsewered areas.

Table 6.15: Performance Evaluation of Sewage Treatment Plant in Delhi (Month-April, 2011)

Name of STP		pH	TSS (mg/l)	BOD (mg/l)	COD (mg/l)	Oil and grease (mg/l)	Ammonical Nitrogen (mg/l)	Phosphate (mg/l)
(1)	(2)	(3)	(4)	(5)	(6)	(7)	(8)	(9)
Sen Nursing Home	Inlet	7.6	-	200	472	26.0	8.6	-
	Outlet	8.1	-	21	76	3.6	1.2	-
Delhi Gate STP	Inlet	7.8	-	225	496	23.6	7.6	-
	Outlet	7.3	-	22	152	4.4	1.1	-
Kondli STP (Ph- I (20))	Inlet	7.5	-	160	364	25.2	9.9	-
	Outlet	7.5	-	25	76	3.2	2.7	-
Kondli STP (Ph- II (25))	Inlet	8.0	-	150	344	27.2	9.7	-
	Outlet	8.5	-	28	132	3.2	2.1	-
Kondli STP (Ph- III (20))	Inlet	8.0	-	150	344	27.2	9.7	-
	Outlet	8.3	-	23	116	4.0	2.3	-
Coronation Pillar STP (Phase-I,II(20))	Inlet	7.7	-	60	296	26.8	9.7	-
	Outlet	8.1	-	28	80	3.2	3.4	-
Coronation Pillar STP (Phase-III(10))	Inlet	7.7	-	280	1004	25.2	9.7	-
	Outlet	8.1	-	16	76	4.0	2.1	-
Coronation Pillar STP* (Old Clarifier(10))	Inlet	-	-	-	-	-	-	-
	Outlet	-	-	-	-	-	-	-
Oxidation Pond (Nehru Vihar) STP *	Inlet	-	-	-	-	-	-	-
	Outlet	-	-	-	-	-	-	-
Narela STP(10)	Inlet	7.7	-	50	152	24.4	12.2	-
	Outlet	8.4	-	16	44	3.2	2.0	-
Okhla STP Plant-I(12)	Inlet	7.4	-	210	612	24.4	8.6	-
	Outlet	7.5	-	16	104	4.0	2.3	-
Okhla STP Plant-II(30)	Inlet	7.4	-	210	612	24.4	8.6	-
	Outlet	7.8	-	28	104	3.6	2.4	-
Okhla STP Plant-III(37)	Inlet	7.4	-	210	612	24.4	8.6	-
	Outlet	8.3	-	14	80	3.2	2.6	-

(Table Contd...)

(1)	(2)	(3)	(4)	(5)	(6)	(7)	(8)	(9)
Okhla STP Plant-IV(45)	Inlet	7.4	-	210	612	24.4	8.6	-
	Outlet	7.8	-	29	132	4.0	2.7	-
Okhla STP Plant-V(16)	Inlet	7.4	-	210	612	24.4	8.6	-
	Outlet	7.9	-	16	96	3.2	2.7	-
Vasant Kunj STP) Plant-I(2.2)	Inlet	8.8	-	170	456	24.8	8.1	-
	Outlet	8.8	-	18	56	3.2	3.0	-
Vasant Kunj STP) Plant-II(3.0)	Inlet	7.5	-	270	460	25.6	11.9	-
	Outlet	8.3	-	28	92	3.6	3.0	-
Mehrauli STP	Inlet	7.8	-	225	496	23.6	7.6	-
	Outlet	7.3	-	22	152	4.4	1.1	-
Yamuna Vihar STP Plant-I(10)	Inlet	7.9	-	245	610	23.2	7.6	-
	Outlet	7.5	-	28	116	4.0	2.1	-
Yamuna Vihar STP Plant-II(10)	Inlet	8.0	-	200	492	25.6	10.3	-
	Outlet	7.7	-	20	64	3.2	3.0	-
Rithala STP Plant-I(40)	Inlet	8.4	-	105	324	26.8	8.1	-
	Outlet	7.7	-	18	46	4.0	2.6	-
Rithala STP Plant-II (40)	Inlet	8.4	-	105	324	26.8	8.1	-
	Outlet	7.7	-	27	94	3.6	2.4	-
Keshopur STP* Plant-I(12)	Inlet	-	-	-	-	-	-	-
	Outlet	-	-	-	-	-	-	-
Keshopur STP* Plant-II(40)	Inlet	-	-	-	-	-	-	-
	Outlet	-	-	-	-	-	-	-
Nilothi STP	Inlet	7.8	-	110	820	23.2	10.4	-
	Outlet	8.4	-	16	76	3.6	2.9	-
Pappankala STP	Inlet	8.2	-	145	468	24.8	9.3	-
	Outlet	7.8	-	12	42	3.2	2.4	-
Najafgarh STP	Inlet	8.1	-	115	410	23.6	9.3	-
	Outlet	7.7	-	18	128	3.6	2.0	-
Rohini STP*	Inlet	-	-	-	-	-	-	-
	Outlet	-	-	-	-	-	-	-
STP standard		5.5-9.0	50	30	250	10	50	5

* Plant was not operational

Source: Delhi Pollution Control Committee

Table 6.16: Performance Evaluation of Sewage Treatment Plant in Delhi (Month-May, 2011)

Name of STP		pH	TSS (mg/l)	BOD (mg/l)	COD (mg/l)	Oil and grease (mg/l)	Ammonical Nitrogen (mg/l)	Phosphate (mg/l)
(1)	(2)	(3)	(4)	(5)	(6)	(7)	(8)	(9)
Sen Nursing Home	Inlet	7.9	-	200	444	11.6	7.2	4.4
	Outlet	8.1	-	11	60	2.0	2.1	1.1
Delhi Gate STP	Inlet	7.6	-	170	440	25.6	7.7	4.4
	Outlet	8.4	-	15	64	2.0	2.3	1.1
Kondli STP (Ph- I (20))	Inlet	7.4	-	190	520	23.6	21.4	6.4
	Outlet	7.3	-	20	76	3.2	8.6	1.6
Kondli STP (Ph- II (25))	Inlet	7.3	-	210	476	25.6	28.1	6.5
	Outlet	7.5	-	19	64	4.0	5.4	2.9
Kondli STP (Ph- III (20))	Inlet	7.3	-	210	476	25.6	28.1	6.5
	Outlet	7.3	-	34	132	3.6	2.9	2.0
Coronation Pillar STP (Phase-I,II(20))	Inlet	7.7	-	125	444	26.8	8.1	4.4
	Outlet	8.1	-	20	76	4.4	3.0	1.3
Coronation Pillar STP (Phase-III(10))	Inlet	7.6	-	120	392	24.8	8.0	4.8
	Outlet	8.1	-	22	96	4.0	2.8	1.1
Coronation Pillar STP* (Old Clarifier(10))	Inlet	-	-	-	-	-	-	-
	Outlet	-	-	-	-	-	-	-
Oxidation Pond (Nehru Vihar) STP *	Inlet	-	-	-	-	-	-	-
	Outlet	-	-	-	-	-	-	-
Narela STP(10)	Inlet	7.5	-	90	248	24.4	17.0	2.6
	Outlet	8.8	-	21	72	2.0	5.6	1.5
Okhla STP Plant-I(12)	Inlet	7.1	-	140	560	25.6	7.8	6.5
	Outlet	8.0	-	22	48	3.2	2.3	3.3
Okhla STP Plant-II(30)	Inlet	7.1	-	140	560	25.6	7.8	6.5
	Outlet	7.8	-	28	96	2.4	0.3	2.0
Okhla STP Plant-III(37)	Inlet	7.1	-	140	560	25.6	7.8	6.5
	Outlet	8.0	-	17	84	3.0	0.5	1.5
Okhla STP Plant-IV(45)	Inlet	7.1	-	140	560	25.6	7.8	6.5
	Outlet	7.8	-	26	120	3.6	0.3	2.8
Okhla STP Plant-V(16)	Inlet	7.1	-	140	560	25.6	7.8	6.5
	Outlet	8.0	-	36	120	3.6	0.9	2.5
Vasant Kunj STP) Plant-I(2.2)	Inlet	7.3	-	165	452	25.2	5.5	6.5
	Outlet	8.0	-	24	92	3.2	1.6	2.8
Vasant Kunj STP) Plant-II(3.0)	Inlet	7.1	-	195	372	26.4	4.6	6.4
	Outlet	7.2	-	33	132	4.0	0.4	2.7
Mehrauli STP	Inlet	7.7	-	135	444	23.6	5.3	5.6
	Outlet	6.8	-	24	96	3.6	0.2	4.7

(Table Contd...)

(1)	(2)	(3)	(4)	(5)	(6)	(7)	(8)	(9)
Yamuna Vihar STP Plant-I(10)	Inlet	7.2	-	180	416	24.8	9.5	4.7
	Outlet	7.3	-	25	104	3.6	3.2	1.8
Yamuna Vihar STP* Plant-II(10)	Inlet	-	-	-	-	-	-	-
	Outlet	-	-	-	-	-	-	-
Rithala STP Plant-I(40)	Inlet	8.1	-	170	352	24.8	7.6	6.0
	Outlet	7.7	-	23	72	3.2	2.1	3.3
Rithala STP Plant-II (40)	Inlet	8.1	-	170	352	24.8	7.6	6.0
	Outlet	7.7	-	24	96	4.0	4.8	2.5
Keshopur STP* Plant-I(12)	Inlet	-	-	-	-	-	-	-
	Outlet	-	-	-	-	-	-	-
Keshopur STP* Plant-II(40)	Inlet	-	-	-	-	-	-	-
	Outlet	-	-	-	-	-	-	-
Nilothi STP	Inlet	7.8	-	175	372	24.8	7.5	4.1
	Outlet	8.4	-	25	84	3.2	2.7	1.3
Pappankala STP	Inlet	7.7	-	130	360	25.2	7.3	4.4
	Outlet	7.6	-	25	92	4.0	2.2	1.1
Najafgarh STP	Inlet	8.1	-	95	260	23.2	7.6	4.4
	Outlet	7.7	-	24	76	3.2	2.0	1.0
Rohini STP *	Inlet	-	-	-	-	-	-	4.4
	Outlet	-	-	-	-	-	-	1.0
STP standard		5.5-9.0	50	30	250	10	50	5

* Plant was not operational

Source: Delhi Pollution Control Committee

Table 6.17: Performance Evaluation of Sewage Treatment Plant in Delhi (Month-June, 2011)

Name of STP		pH	TSS (mg/l)	BOD (mg/l)	COD (mg/l)	Oil and grease (mg/l)	Ammonical Nitrogen (mg/l)	Phosphate (mg/l)
(1)	(2)	(3)	(4)	(5)	(6)	(7)	(8)	(9)
Sen Nursing Home	Inlet	7.3	-	140	228	23.6	7.7	9.2
	Outlet	7.6	-	11	24	4.0	2.2	3.8
Delhi Gate STP	Inlet	7.2	-	155	360	25.6	7.7	16.8
	Outlet	7.3	-	28	104	3.6	2.1	4.3
Kondli STP (Ph- I (20))	Inlet	7.4	-	120	284	26.0	8.5	10.6
	Outlet	7.2	-	27	84	3.6	3.7	**6.0**
Kondli STP (Ph- II (25))	Inlet	7.0	-	155	312	27.2	7.4	12.9
	Outlet	7.9	-	29	92	3.6	2.5	**7.0**
Kondli STP (Ph- III (20))	Inlet	7.0	-	155	312	27.2	7.4	12.9
	Outlet	7.5	-	30	104	4.0	3.1	2.0

(Table Contd...)

(1)	(2)	(3)	(4)	(5)	(6)	(7)	(8)	(9)
Coronation Pillar STP* (Phase-I,II(20))	Inlet	-	-	-	-	-	-	-
	Outlet	-	-	-	-	-	-	-
Coronation Pillar STP (Phase-III(10))	Inlet	7.3	-	125	212	23.2	6.0	17.9
	Outlet	8.4	-	28	128	3.2	1.8	**9.0**
Coronation Pillar STP* (Old Clarifier(10))	Inlet	-	-	-	-	-	-	-
	Outlet	-	-	-	-	-	-	-
Oxidation Pond (Nehru Vihar) STP *	Inlet	-	-	-	-	-	-	-
	Outlet	-	-	-	-	-	-	-
Narela STP(10)	Inlet	8.1	-	150	456	25.6	7.7	14.8
	Outlet	8.8	-	18	72	4.0	2.1	**7.7**
Okhla STP Plant-I(12)	Inlet	7.3	-	105	240	23.6	6.1	13.0
	Outlet	7.9	-	11	52	4.0	4.0	2.2
Okhla STP Plant-II(30)	Inlet	7.3	-	105	240	23.6	6.1	13.0
	Outlet	7.8	-	19	80	4.4	3.5	1.3
Okhla STP Plant-III(37)	Inlet	7.3	-	105	240	23.6	6.1	13.0
	Outlet	7.6	-	**42**	164	3.2	3.3	1.5
Okhla STP Plant-IV(45)	Inlet	7.3	-	105	240	23.6	6.1	13.0
	Outlet	7.7	-	17	72	4.0	2.8	2.9
Okhla STP Plant-V(16)	Inlet	7.3	-	105	240	23.6	6.1	13.0
	Outlet	8.1	-	21	112	4.0	3.4	1.9
Vasant Kunj STP) Piant-I(2.2)	Inlet	7.5	-	80	200	26.0	7.3	17.9
	Outlet	8.0	-	16	40	4.0	2.6	4.8
Vasant Kunj STP)Plant-II(3.0)	Inlet	8.0	-	68	148	24.4	7.4	11.2
	Outlet	8.5	-	22	64	3.6	3.3	2.8
Mehrauli STP	Inlet	7.6	-	60	152	24.8	7.0	14.8
	Outlet	8.5	-	20	72	3.6	4.9	2.4
Yamuna Vihar STP Plant-I(10)	Inlet	8.0	-	205	464	24.8	7.7	7.2
	Outlet	7.8	-	29	112	4.0	2.1	2.0
Yamuna Vihar STP Plant-II(10)	Inlet	7.2	-	90	144	23.6	7.1	17.0
	Outlet	7.5	-	11	28	3.6	2.9	**8.4**
Rithala STP Plant-I(40)	Inlet	8.3	-	135	268	25.2	8.0	7.2
	Outlet	7.8	-	30	120	4.0	2.4	3.8
Rithala STP Plant-II (40)	Inlet	8.3	-	135	268	25.2	8.0	7.2
	Outlet	7.5	-	13	52	3.2	2.7	2.0
Keshopur STP* Plant-I(12)	Inlet	-	-	-	-	-	-	-
	Outlet	-	-	-	-	-	-	-
Keshopur STP* Plant-II(40)	Inlet	-	-	-	-	-	-	-
	Outlet	-	-	-	-	-	-	-
Nilothi STP	Inlet	7.1	-	155	324	25.6	8.0	12.6
	Outlet	7.7	-	21	64	4.4	2.1	3.2

(Table Contd...)

(1)	(2)	(3)	(4)	(5)	(6)	(7)	(8)	(9)
Pappankala STP	Inlet	8.2	-	120	312	23.2	7.4	13.0
	Outlet	7.8	-	16	52	4.0	3.0	2.8
Najafgarh STP	Inlet	8.2	-	155	376	25.2	8.7	7.4
	Outlet	7.1	-	29	112	4.0	0.7	2.4
Rohini STP *	Inlet	-	-	-	-	-	-	-
	Outlet	-	-	-	-	-	-	-
STP standard		5.5-9.0	50	30	250	10	50	5

* Plant was not operational

Source: Delhi Pollution Control Committee

Table 6.18: Performance Evaluation of Sewage Treatment Plant in Delhi (Month-July, 2011)

Name of STP		pH	TSS (mg/l)	BOD (mg/l)	COD (mg/l)	Oil and grease (mg/l)	Ammonical Nitrogen (mg/l)	Phosphate (mg/l)
(1)	(2)	(3)	(4)	(5)	(6)	(7)	(8)	(9)
Sen Nursing Home	Inlet	7.2	192	105	280	17.6	7.1	16.5
	Outlet	7.6	24	11	40	2.4	2.5	3.2
Delhi Gate STP	Inlet	7.3	168	165	460	10.8	7.2	17.8
	Outlet	7.4	14	18	72	2.8	3.7	2.6
Kondli STP (Ph- I (20))	Inlet	7.5	1272	180	464	22.8	6.9	11.1
	Outlet	7.4	42	30	156	3.2	1.7	2.4
Kondli STP (Ph- II (25))	Inlet	8.1	344	145	428	25.6	7.2	7.8
	Outlet	8.5	54	24	108	4.0	2.0	2.1
Kondli STP (Ph- III (20))	Inlet	8.1	344	145	428	25.6	7.2	7.8
	Outlet	8.3	44	22	120	3.2	3.1	3.5
Coronation Pillar STP (Phase-I,II(20))	Inlet	7.9	136	105	324	25.2	6.5	8.9
	Outlet	8.4	46	25	104	4.0	2.2	3.5
Coronation Pillar STP (Phase-III(10))	Inlet	7.	108	125	284	23.2	7.1	7.1
	Outlet	38.1	36	17	84	3.2	2.6	2.2
Coronation Pillar STP* (Old Clarifier(10))	Inlet	-	-	-	-	-	-	-
	Outlet	-	-	-	-	-	-	-
Oxidation Pond (Nehru Vihar) STP*	Inlet	-	-	-	-	-	-	-
	Outlet	-	-	-	-	-	-	-
Narela STP(10)	Inlet	8.1	140	72	184	24.4	6.0	8.5
	Outlet	8.9	36	17	68	4.4	2.0	1.3
Okhla STP Plant-I(12)	Inlet	7.4	376	160	576	24.4	7.8	16.7
	Outlet	7.8	32	13	64	2.0	3.1	1.7
Okhla STP Plant-II(30)	Inlet	7.4	376	160	576	24.4	7.8	16.7
	Outlet	8.0	46	28	132	2.8	2.2	4.3

(Table Contd...)

(1)	(2)	(3)	(4)	(5)	(6)	(7)	(8)	(9)
Okhla STP Plant-III(37)	Inlet	7.4	376	160	576	24.4	7.8	16.7
	Outlet	8.0	56	24	112	3.2	2.6	4.1
Okhla STP Plant-IV(45)	Inlet	7.4	376	160	576	24.4	7.8	16.7
	Outlet	7.7	40	16	80	2.4	2.1	3.5
Okhla STP Plant-V(16)	Inlet	7.4	376	160	576	24.4	7.8	16.7
	Outlet	7.8	26	15	100	3.6	2.8	3.9
Vasant Kunj STP) Plant-I(2.2)	Inlet	8.1	172	175	472	24.8	5.2	9.2
	Outlet	7.9	38	30	72	4.4	2.1	3.2
Vasant Kunj STP) Plant-II(3.0)	Inlet	7.3	118	160	376	6.9	8.6	8.6
	Outlet	7.1	42	20	64	3.6	3.0	3.4
Mehrauli STP	Inlet	8.2	116	175	440	25.5	1.5	7.0
	Outlet	7.7	38	25	64	3.2	ND	3.8
Yamuna Vihar STP Plant-I(10)	Inlet	8.4	96	150	324	24.4	1.7	7.4
	Outlet	7.8	16	14	52	4.0	0.6	2.2
Yamuna Vihar STP Plant-II(10)	Inlet	7.5	372	190	464	23.2	2.0	6.2
	Outlet	7.2	50	26	76	3.6	0.7	1.6
Rithala STP Plant-I(40)	Inlet	8.2	144	175	420	26.0	3.0	7.0
	Outlet	7.5	42	30	116	4.4	0.7	2.6
Rithala STP Plant-II (40)	Inlet	8.2	144	175	420	26.0	3.0	7.0
	Outlet	7.2	26	28	80	3.2	ND	4.0
Keshopur STP* Plant-I(12)	Inlet	-	-	-	-	-	-	-
	Outlet	-	-	-	-	-	-	-
Keshopur STP* Plant-II(40)	Inlet	-	-	-	-	-	-	-
	Outlet	-	-	-	-	-	-	-
Nilothi STP	Inlet	7.8	400	110	420	23.6	7.1	9.2
	Outlet	8.4	22	16	76	4.4	2.1	2.1
Pappankala STP	Inlet	7.6	180	150	448	8.8	7.9	10.4
	Outlet	7.1	38	27	116	2.8	2.7	2.7
Najafgarh STP	Inlet	7.8	120	125	464	22.4	7.3	7.2
	Outlet	7.2	30	28	128	4.0	2.3	2.9
Rohini STP*	Inlet	-	-	-	-	-	-	-
	Outlet	-	-	-	-	-	-	-
STP standard		5.5-9.0	50	30	250	10	50	5

* Plant was not operational

Source: Delhi Pollution Control Committee

Table 6.19: Performance Evaluation of Sewage Treatment Plant in Delhi (Month-August, 2011)

Name of STP		pH	TSS (mg/l)	BOD (mg/l)	COD (mg/l)	Oil and grease (mg/l)	Ammonical Nitrogen (mg/l)	Phosphate (mg/l)
(1)	(2)	(3)	(4)	(5)	(6)	(7)	(8)	(9)
Sen Nursing Home	Inlet	7.4	140	165	324	26.8	8.6	24.1
	Outlet	7.6	36	23	72	1.6	3.4	**11.0**
Delhi Gate STP	Inlet	7.3	144	155	364	25.6	7.6	26.8
	Outlet	7.6	24	28	124	3.6	2.1	14.3
Kondli STP (Ph- I (20))	Inlet	7.5	156	220	508	24.0	19.0	10.1
	Outlet	7.4	44	27	92	3.2	13.1	6.4
Kondli STP (Ph- II (25))	Inlet	8.0	268	145	472	25.2	24.9	12.7
	Outlet	8.3	74	20	88	4.0	17.7	7.4
Kondli STP (Ph- III (20))	Inlet	8.0	268	145	472	25.2	24.9	12.7
	Outlet	8.4	50	18	60	1.6	23.1	2.2
Coronation Pillar STP (Phase-I,II(20))	Inlet	7.7	40	280	468	26.8	17.1	42.4
	Outlet	8.1	18	**43**	160	4.0	0.7	**11.3**
Coronation Pillar STP (Phase-III(10))	Inlet	7.7	256	125	304	24.8	17.9	46.5
	Outlet	8.4	30	23	56	4.4	1.4	**11.0**
Coronation Pillar STP* (Old Clarifier(10))	Inlet	-	-	-	-	-	-	-
	Outlet	-	-	-	-	-	-	-
Oxidation Pond (Nehru Vihar) STP *	Inlet	-	-	-	-	-	-	-
	Outlet	-	-	-	-	-	-	-
Narela STP(10)	Inlet	8.1	680	210	612	13.9	15.2	15.2
	Outlet	8.7	164	23	96	5.6	3.5	4.5
Okhla STP Plant-I(12)	Inlet	7.9	228	120	344	24.4	1.1	5.6
	Outlet	8.1	44	23	52	3.2	0.9	4.7
Okhla STP Plant-II(30)	Inlet	7.9	228	120	344	24.4	1.1	5.6
	Outlet	8.4	**66**	23	80	3.2	2.1	4.8
Okhla STP Plant-III(37)	Inlet	7.9	228	120	344	24.4	1.1	5.6
	Outlet	8.3	40	27	92	0.8	2.1	4.8
Okhla STP Plant-IV(45)	Inlet	7.9	228	120	344	24.4	1.1	5.6
	Outlet	8.2	**62**	28	88	3.2	3.3	3.3
Okhla STP Plant-V(16)	Inlet	7.9	228	120	344	24.4	1.1	5.6
	Outlet	8.3	40	11	44	2.4	3.0	3.4
Vasant Kunj STP) Plant-I(2.2)	Inlet	8.1	180	130	316	4.4	15.0	25.6
	Outlet	8.6	32	27	68	2.4	9.1	11.6
Vasant Kunj STP) Plant-II(3.0)	Inlet	8.0	112	100	268	10.0	10.3	15.4
	Outlet	8.0	64	30	88	5.2	7.4	2.7
Mehrauli STP	Inlet	8.2	136	135	248	8.8	10.0	19.2
	Outlet	8.3	38	21	128	5.2	6.3	3.3

(Table Contd...)

(1)	(2)	(3)	(4)	(5)	(6)	(7)	(8)	(9)
Yamuna Vihar STP Plant-I(10)	Inlet	7.7	104	150	340	24.8	31.5	7.4
	Outlet	7.5	36	25	72	4.4	21.7	3.5
Yamuna Vihar STP Plant-II(10)	Inlet	8.0	90	135	372	12.4	38.0	15.2
	Outlet	7.6	44	19	120	4.4	31.2	3.2
Rithala STP Plant-I(40)	Inlet	8.2	464	150	364	10.4	41.6	29.9
	Outlet	7.3	**112**	28	52	1.6	39.3	**12.0**
Rithala STP Plant-II (40)	Inlet	8.2	464	150	364	10.4	41.6	29.9
	Outlet	7.2	18	22	66	4.8	10.3	**13.9**
Keshopur STP* Plant-I(12)	Inlet	-	-	-	-	-	-	-
	Outlet	-	-	-	-	-	-	-
Keshopur STP* Plant-II(40)	Inlet	-	-	-	-	-	-	-
	Outlet	-	-	-	-	-	-	-
Nilothi STP	Inlet	7.1	96	145	364	24.4	7.5	24.2
	Outiet	7.3	14	26	92	3.2	2.7	8.2
Pappankala STP	Inlet	8.2	160	130	364	14.0	76.3	36.7
	Outlet	7.3	54	24	84	6.0	33.8	12.8
Najafgarh STP	Inlet	8.1	168	115	244	10.0	38.2	29.9
	Outlet	7.7	44	13	64	2.8	5.7	4.3
Rohini STP*	Inlet	-	-	-	-	-	-	-
	Outlet	-	-	-	-	-	-	-
STP standard		5.5-9.0	50	30	250	10	50	5

* Plant was not operational

Source: Delhi Pollution Control Committee

Table 6.20: Performance Evaluation of Sewage Treatment Plant in Delhi (Month-September, 2011)

Name of STP		pH	TSS (mg/l)	BOD (mg/l)	COD (mg/l)	Oil and grease (mg/l)	Ammonical Nitrogen (mg/l)	Phosphate (mg/l)
(1)	(2)	(3)	(4)	(5)	(6)	(7)	(8)	(9)
Sen Nursing Home	Inlet	7.5	160	175	448	16.0	3.4	1.6
	Outlet	7.9	20	18	60	2.0	0.3	1.5
Delhi Gate STP	Inlet	7.3	182	170	460	26.8	1.9	4.0
	Outlet	7.1	24	20	72	2.4	0.3	0.7
Kondli STP (Ph- I (20))	Inlet	7.8	288	175	488	25.2	4.8	1.3
	Outlet	7.7	50	23	72	2.4	0.7	1.2
Kondli STP (Ph- II (25))	Inlet	7.8	220	115	248	27.2	3.2	4.5
	Outlet	7.8	**76**	30	100	4.8	0.1	1.7
Kondli STP (Ph- III (20))	Inlet	7.8	220	115	248	27.2	3.2	4.5
	Outlet	7.0	28	26	60	3.2	1.2	1.2

(Table Contd...)

(1)	(2)	(3)	(4)	(5)	(6)	(7)	(8)	(9)
Coronation Pillar STP (Phase-I,II(20))	Inlet	7.6	196	110	336	23.2	1.0	3.3
	Outlet	7.7	44	23	72	3.6	0.05	1.8
Coronation Pillar STP (Phase-III(10))	Inlet	7.5	316	150	480	25.2	2.7	1.5
	Outlet	7.7	28	18	40	4.4	0.2	1.2
Coronation Pillar STP* (Old Clarifier(10))	Inlet	-	-	-	-	-	-	-
	Outlet	-	-	-	-	-	-	-
Oxidation Pond (Nehru Vihar) STP	Inlet	7.7	180	120	316	26.8	0.05	2.5
	Outlet	7.9	14	18	68	3.6	0.03	1.8
Narela STP(10)	Inlet	7.4	176	180	420	24.4	0.04	11.3
	Outlet	7.9	30	26	72	3.2	0.01	1.8
Okhla STP Plant-I(12)	Inlet	7.5	244	125	368	25.6	4.2	11.3
	Outlet	7.6	26	20	72	3.6	2.7	5.0
Okhla STP Plant-II(30)	Inlet	7.5	244	125	368	25.6	4.2	11.3
	Outlet	7.2	48	22	76	3.2	3.8	1.9
Okhla STP Plant-III(37)	Inlet	7.5	244	125	368	25.6	4.2	11.3
	Outlet	7.6	**62**	24	64	4.4	3.3	2.4
Okhla STP Plant-IV(45)	Inlet	7.5	244	125	368	25.6	4.2	11.3
	Outlet	7.4	28	16	44	3.6	3.7	1.0
Okhla STP Plant-V(16)	Inlet	7.5	244	125	368	25.6	4.2	11.3
	Outlet	7.4	44	30	128	2.4	0.07	2.7
Vasant Kunj STP) Plant-I(2.2)	Inlet	7.6	108	140	356	22.0	2.4	11.3
	Outlet	7.9	22	25	84	2.8	0.3	3.0
Vasant Kunj STP) Plant-II(3.0)	Inlet	7.6	108	135	336	24.4	1.0	11.3
	Outlet	7.4	32	26	84	3.2	0.6	1.5
Mehrauli STP	Inlet	7.6	220	90	276	25.6	2.4	11.3
	Outlet	7.4	36	20	112	3.2	0.7	1.4
Yamuna Vihar STP Plant-I(10)	Inlet	7.6	132	140	344	25.2	0.4	11.0
	Outlet	7.8	14	27	80	4.0	0.1	**7.3**
Yamuna Vihar STP Plant-II(10)	Inlet	7.5	300	150	448	15.6	0.9	3.8
	Outlet	7.7	32	21	88	4.4	0.07	0.6
Rithala STP Plant-I(40)	Inlet	7.6	168	130	356	24.8	0.5	11.0
	Outlet	7.7	24	25	96	4.4	0.2	3.2
Rithala STP Plant-II (40)	Inlet	7.6	168	130	356	24.8	0.5	11.0
	Outlet	7.7	28	28	104	4.0	0.03	1.4
Keshopur STP* Plant-I(12)	Inlet	-	-	-	-	-	-	-
	Outlet	-	-	-	-	-	-	-
Keshopur STP* Plant-II(40)	Inlet	-	-	-	-	-	-	-
	Outlet	-	-	-	-	-	-	-
Nilothi STP	Inlet	7.3	112	135	392	23.2	1.5	3.2
	Outlet	7.2	18	24	64	3.6	ND	2.2

(Table Contd...)

(1)	(2)	(3)	(4)	(5)	(6)	(7)	(8)	(9)
Pappankala STP	Inlet	7.4	116	100	264	16.0	2.4	7.9
	Outlet	7.4	28	23	88	2.8	1.3	1.9
Najafgarh STP	Inlet	7.0	182	120	324	18.8	1.8	5.9
	Outlet	7.1	32	18	64	2.8	0.2	3.2
Rohini STP*	Inlet	-	-	-	-	-	-	-
	Outlet	-	-	-	-	-	-	-
STP standard		5.5-9.0	50	30	250	10	50	5

* Plant was not operational

Source: Delhi Pollution Control Committee

Table 6.21: Performance Evaluation of Sewage Treatment Plant in Delhi (Month-October, 2011)

Name of STP		pH	TSS (mg/l)	BOD (mg/l)	COD (mg/l)	Oil and grease (mg/l)	Ammonical Nitrogen (mg/l)	Phosphate (mg/l)
(1)	(2)	(3)	(4)	(5)	(6)	(7)	(8)	(9)
Sen Nursing Home	Inlet	7.7	132	195	-	16.0	3.13	11.34
	Outlet	8.0	12	9	-	1.6	0.02	1.17
Delhi Gate STP	Inlet	7.6	112	220	-	17.2	4.55	11.34
	Outlet	7.7	15	11	-	2.0	0.1	1.28
Kondli STP# (Ph- I (20))	Inlet	-	-	-	-	-	-	-
	Outlet	-	-	-	-	-	-	-
Kondli STP# (Ph- II (25))	Inlet	-	-	-	-	-	-	-
	Outlet	-	-	-	-	-	-	-
Kondli STP# (Ph- III (20))	Inlet	-	-	-	-	-	-	-
	Outlet	-	-	-	-	-	-	-
Coronation Pillar STP (Phase-I,II(20))	Inlet	7.6	128	150	-	4.8	1.5	3.7
	Outlet	7.8	38	27	-	3.6	0.02	1.6
Coronation Pillar STP (Phase-III(10))	Inlet	7.7	124	125	-	4.4	1.1	4.7
	Outlet	7.6	36	28	-	4.0	0.07	0.58
Coronation Pillar STP* (Old Clarifier(10))	Inlet	-	-	-	-	-	-	-
	Outlet	-	-	-	-	-	-	-
Oxidation Pond (Nehru Vihar) STP#	Inlet	-	-	-	-	-	-	-
	Outlet	-	-	-	-	-	-	-
Narela STP# (10)	Inlet	-	-	-	-	-	-	-
	Outlet	-	-	-	-	-	-	-
Okhla STP Plant-I(12)	Inlet	7.5	252	130	-	16.0	11.86	11.34
	Outlet	7.8	52	32	-	3.2	2.86	3.47
Okhla STP Plant-II(30)	Inlet	7.5	252	130	-	16.0	11.86	11.34
	Outlet	7.7	84	26	-	2.8	1.45	1.0

(Table Contd...)

(1)	(2)	(3)	(4)	(5)	(6)	(7)	(8)	(9)
Okhla STP Plant-III(37)	Inlet	7.5	252	130	-	16.0	11.86	11.34
	Outlet	7.8	50	18	-	4.4	1.2	1.34
Okhla STP Plant-IV(45)	Inlet	7.5	252	130	-	16.0	11.86	11.34
	Outlet	7.8	76	20	-	3.6	2.1	0.54
Okhla STP Plant-V(16)	Inlet	7.5	252	130	-	16.0	11.86	11.34
	Outlet	7.8	18	24	-	3.2	3.49	7.39
Vasant Kunj STP# Plant-I(2.2)	Inlet	-	-	-	-	-	-	-
	Outlet	-	-	-	-	-	-	-
Vasant Kunj STP# Plant-II(3.0)	Inlet	-	-	-	-	-	-	-
	Outlet	-	-	-	-	-	-	-
Mehrauli STP#	Inlet	-	-	-	-	-	-	-
	Outlet	-	-	-	-	-	-	-
Yamuna Vihar STP Plant-I(10)	Inlet	6.0	136	185	-	24.4	3.8	6.16
	Outlet	7.2	44	15	-	4.4	0.3	1.9
Yamuna Vihar STP Plant-II(10)	Inlet	7.1	94	135	-	12.4	3.1	4.4
	Outlet	7.6	32	26	-	3.2	0.36	1.0
Rithala STP Plant-I(40)	Inlet	7.3	208	130	-	12.4	2.4	11.34
	Outlet	7.5	32	30	-	5.6	1.2	3.5
Rithala STP Plant-II (40)	Inlet	7.3	208	130	-	12.4	2.4	11.34
	Outlet	7.3	30	28	-	4.4	1.2	4.7
Keshopur STP# Plant-I(12)	Inlet	-	-	-	-	-	-	-
	Outlet	-	-	-	-	-	-	-
Keshopur STP# Plant-II(40)	Inlet	-	-	-	-	-	-	-
	Outlet	-	-	-	-	-	-	-
Keshopur STP# Plant-III(12)	Inlet	-	-	-	-	-	-	-
	Outlet	-	-	-	-	-	-	-
Nilothi STP#	Inlet	-	-	-	-	-	-	-
	Outlet	-	-	-	-	-	-	-
Pappankala STP	Inlet	7.0	344	105	-	25.2	2.1	11.34
	Outlet	7.3	54	26	-	3.2	1.6	4.7
Najafgarh STP	Inlet	7.5	80	110	-	3.6	1.2	11.34
	Outlet	7.4	46	26	-	2.8	0.4	2.5
Rohini STP*	Inlet	-	-	-	-	-	-	-
	Outlet	-	-	-	-	-	-	-
STP standard		5.5-9.0	50	30	250	10	50	5

* Plant was not operational

\# Data not provided

Source: Delhi Pollution Control Committee

Table 6.22: Performance Evaluation of Sewage Treatment Plant in Delhi (Month-November, 2011)

Name of STP		pH	TSS (mg/l)	BOD (mg/l)	COD (mg/l)	Oil and grease (mg/l)	Ammonical Nitrogen (mg/l)	Phosphate (mg/l)
(1)	(2)	(3)	(4)	(5)	(6)	(7)	(8)	(9)
Sen Nursing Home	Inlet	7.8	152	115	324	22.0	1.9	9.6
	Outlet	7.6	14	19	44	2.4	1.5	1.1
Delhi Gate STP	Inlet	7.7	144	180	596	26.4	2.0	4.3
	Outlet	7.9	16	20	56	2.0	0.15	2.7
Kondli STP (Ph- I (20))	Inlet	7.8	112	130	324	20.4	6.7	11.3
	Outlet	7.9	44	28	96	3.2	4.0	4.2
Kondli STP (Ph- II (25))	Inlet	7.8	152	150	348	24.8	5.2	11.3
	Outlet	7.7	20	26	100	2.4	2.4	2.6
Kondli STP (Ph- III (20))	Inlet	7.8	152	150	348	24.8	5.2	11.3
	Outlet	7.8	**72**	23	76	4.4	2.0	**5.1**
Coronation Pillar STP (Phase-I,II(20))	Inlet	7.6	316	100	324	32.4	2.0	11.3
	Outlet	8.0	44	30	124	2.8	0.4	**7.2**
Coronation Pillar STP (Phase-III(10))	Inlet	7.5	504	150	372	36.0	0.9	11.0
	Outlet	8.1	26	26	92	2.4	0.1	1.8
Coronation Pillar STP* (Old Clarifier(10))	Inlet	-	-	-	-	-	-	-
	Outlet	-	-	-	-	-	-	-
Oxidation Pond (Nehru Vihar) STP#	Inlet	-	-	-	-	-	-	-
	Outlet	-	-	-	-	-	-	-
Narela STP#(10)	Inlet	-	-	-	-	-	-	-
	Outlet	-	-	-	-	-	-	-
Okhla STP Plant-I(12)	Inlet	7.8	128	110	320	24.4	2.3	11.3
	Outlet	8.0	20	21	72	3.2	0.5	3.0
Okhla STP Plant-II(30)	Inlet	7.8	128	110	320	24.4	2.3	11.3
	Outlet	8.0	44	29	104	2.4	1.6	1.3
Okhla STP Plant-III(37)	Inlet	7.8	128	110	320	24.4	2.3	11.3
	Outlet	8.0	40	30	124	2.8	0.2	2.3
Okhla STP Plant-IV(45)	Inlet	7.8	128	110	320	24.4	2.3	11.3
	Outlet	7.8	30	25	92	2.4	0.5	4.0
Okhla STP Plant-V(16)	Inlet	7.8	128	110	320	24.4	2.3	11.3
	Outlet	8.1	16	28	116	2.0	0.4	0.8
Vasant Kunj STP) Plant-I(2.2)	Inlet	7.4	1016	160	440	36.8	3.3	11.3
	Outlet	8.4	42	21	64	4.0	2.2	1.4
Vasant Kunj STP) Plant-II(3.0)	Inlet	7.7	200	135	264	24.8	0.5	11.3
	Outlet	8.0	50	30	104	3.2	0.1	1.3
Mehrauli STP	Inlet	7.8	208	215	484	24.8	0.8	11.0
	Outlet	7.0	42	28	64	3.6	0.3	1.1

(Table Contd...)

(1)	(2)	(3)	(4)	(5)	(6)	(7)	(8)	(9)
Yamuna Vihar STP Plant-I(10)	Inlet	7.5	168	110	320	25.2	0.8	11.3
	Outlet	7.9	18	27	96	3.6	0.1	3.3
Yamuna Vihar STP* Plant-II(10)	Inlet	-	-	-	-	-	-	-
	Outlet	-	-	-	-	-	-	-
Rithala STP Plant-I(40)	Inlet	7.7	108	105	264	25.6	1.3	4.9
	Outlet	7.6	14	24	88	2.0	0.2	4.7
Rithala STP Plant-II (40)	Inlet	7.7	108	105	264	25.6	1.3	4.9
	Outlet	7.7	22	22	56	2.8	1.0	4.0
Keshopur STP# Plant-I(12)	Inlet	-	-	-	-	-	-	-
	Outlet	-	-	-	-	-	-	-
Keshopur STP# Plant-II(40)	Inlet	-	-	-	-	-	-	-
	Outlet	-	-	-	-	-	-	-
Nilothi STP	Inlet	7.6	148	145	416	22.4	2.2	3.7
	Outlet	8.5	22	26	104	2.0	1.4	0.5
Pappankala STP	Inlet	7.6	596	205	492	28.4	1.6	9.5
	Outlet	8.0	44	23	72	4.0	1.2	4.5
Najafgarh STP	Inlet	7.7	156	140	396	20.4	1.5	11.3
	Outlet	7.6	28	27	96	2.8	0.1	1.4
Rohini STP#	Inlet	-	-	-	-	-	-	-
	Outlet	-	-	-	-	-	-	-
STP standard		5.5-9.0	50	30	250	10	50	5

* Plant was not operational

Data not provided

Source: Delhi Pollution Control Committee

Table 6.23: Performance Evaluation of Sewage Treatment Plant in Delhi (Month-December, 2011)

Name of STP		pH	TSS (mg/l)	BOD (mg/l)	COD (mg/l)	Oil and grease (mg/l)	Ammonical Nitrogen (mg/l)	Phosphate (mg/l)
(1)	(2)	(3)	(4)	(5)	(6)	(7)	(8)	(9)
Sen Nursing Home	Inlet	7.4	392	145	424	22.0	1.34	3.0
	Outlet	7.3	22	08	40	4.4	0.73	2.78
Delhi Gate STP	Inlet	7.1	424	110	196	26.4	1.92	2.64
	Outlet	7.2	28	10	48	2.4	0.92	2.14
Kondli STP (Ph- I (20))	Inlet	7.2	192	170	316	18.4	5.0	3.15
	Outlet	7.3	44	27	92	4.0	4.5	1.85
Kondli STP (Ph- II (25))	Inlet	7.2	284	165	284	24.8	4.4	11.34
	Outlet	7.4	22	30	96	3.2	3.5	2.7
Kondli STP (Ph- III (20))	Inlet	7.2	284	165	284	24.8	4.4	11.34
	Outlet	7.5	36	28	88	3.6	2.1	3.2

(Table Contd...)

(1)	(2)	(3)	(4)	(5)	(6)	(7)	(8)	(9)
Coronation Pillar STP (Phase-I,II(20))	Inlet	7.9	188	170	324	16.0	2.28	6.1
	Outlet	8.0	20	26	116	2.0	0.55	2.13
Coronation Pillar STP (Phase-III(10))	Inlet	7.7	348	150	272	20.4	0.72	11.34
	Outlet	7.6	**54**	30	104	4.4	0.54	1.95
Coronation Pillar STP* (Old Clarifier(10))	Inlet	-	-	-	-	-	-	-
	Outlet	-	-	-	-	-	-	-
Oxidation Pond (Nehru Vihar) STP#	Inlet	-	-	-	-	-	-	-
	Outlet	-	-	-	-	-	-	-
Narela STP(10)	Inlet	7.8	660	215	464	36.8	5.22	11.34
	Outlet	8.8	46	22	60	5.2	3.11	0.77
Okhla STP Plant-I(12)	Inlet	7.4	324	155	304	22.0	3.52	11.34
	Outlet	7.4	18	28	68	2.8	0.11	3.16
Okhla STP Plant-II(30)	Inlet	7.4	324	155	304	22.0	3.52	11.34
	Outlet	7.4	28	26	60	3.2	0.28	2.31
Okhla STP Plant-III(37)	Inlet	7.4	324	155	304	22.0	3.52	11.34
	Outlet	7.3	30	21	56	2.4	1.14	2.1
Okhla STP Plant-IV(45)	Inlet	7.4	324	155	304	22.0	3.52	11.34
	Outlet	7.4	34	**31**	88	3.2	0.32	2.3
Okhla STP Plant-V(16)	Inlet	7.4	324	155	304	22.0	3.52	11.34
	Outlet	7.6	24	30	116	4.0	0.44	**5.5**
Vasant Kunj STP) Plant-I(2.2)	Inlet	7.9	300	165	276	23.2	4.58	8.78
	Outlet	7.6	28	18	44	4.8	3.11	0.85
Vasant Kunj STP) Plant-II(3.0)	Inlet	7.4	268	135	232	24.4	0.62	6.83
	Outlet	7.8	26	25	92	3.6	0.57	1.1
Mehrauli STP	Inlet	7.6	484	160	248	12.4	0.88	11.34
	Outlet	7.8	46	28	88	2.8	0.56	2.34
Yamuna Vihar STP Plant-I(10)	Inlet	7.8	188	195	364	26.4	1.13	9.13
	Outlet	7.5	20	16	92	1.2	1.1	2.4
Yamuna Vihar STP Plant-II(10)	Inlet	7.8	280	180	336	18.4	3.4	8.78
	Outlet	7.6	16	23	100	1.6	2.3	1.29
Rithala STP Plant-I(40)	Inlet	7.7	284	120	212	25.6	1.1	3.22
	Outlet	7.6	40	29	88	3.2	0.34	3.0
Rithala STP Plant-II (40)	Inlet	7.7	284	120	212	25.6	1.1	3.22
	Outlet	7.4	38	26	76	4.0	0.36	0.94
Keshopur STP* Plant-I(12)	Inlet	-	-	-	-	-	-	-
	Outlet	-	-	-	-	-	-	-
Keshopur STP* Plant-II(40)	Inlet	-	-	-	-	-	-	-
	Outlet	-	-	-	-	-	-	-
Nilothi STP	Inlet	7.5	146	110	124	24.4	9.21	14.01
	Outlet	7.6	20	25	64	3.2	7.20	**8.15**

(Table Contd...)

(1)	(2)	(3)	(4)	(5)	(6)	(7)	(8)	(9)
Pappankala STP	Inlet	7.9	132	170	324	8.0	1.61	5.93
	Outlet	7.7	44	29	96	3.2	1.1	3.62
Najafgarh STP	Inlet	7.4	228	100	224	22.0	1.13	7.26
	Outlet	7.3	16	29	84	2.8	0.34	3.55
Rohini STP*	Inlet	-	-	-	-	-	-	-
	Outlet	-	-	-	-	-	-	-
STP standard		5.5-9.0	50	30	250	10	50	5

* Plant was not operational

Data not provided

Source: Delhi Pollution Control Committee

Table 6.24: Performance Evaluation of Sewage Treatment Plant in Delhi (Month-January, 2012)

Name of STP		pH	TSS (mg/l)	BOD (mg/l)	COD (mg/l)	Oil and grease (mg/l)	Ammonical Nitrogen (mg/l)	Phosphate (mg/l)
(1)	(2)	(3)	(4)	(5)	(6)	(7)	(8)	(9)
Sen Nursing Home	Inlet	8.0	244	165	368	22.0	1.5	11.3
	Outlet	8.3	14	22	88	2.8	0.5	0.6
Delhi Gate STP	Inlet	7.9	228	185	324	16.4	3.1	11.0
	Outlet	8.0	18	28	72	2.8	0.06	0.5
Kondli STP (Ph- I (20))	Inlet	7.6	204	160	368	18.8	1.1	11.3
	Outlet	7.9	32	29	104	3.2	0.8	6.4
Kondli STP (Ph- II (25))	Inlet	7.7	296	130	308	25.6	1.1	11.0
	Outlet	7.7	28	25	64	3.6	0.8	3.0
Kondli STP (Ph- III (20))	Inlet	7.7	296	130	308	25.6	1.1	11.0
	Outlet	7.8	50	27	72	2.8	0.7	2.7
Coronation Pillar STP (Phase-I,II(20))	Inlet	8.1	208	210	560	24.8	2.1	5.7
	Outlet	8.0	24	18	64	4.4	2.0	2.3
Coronation Pillar STP (Phase-III(10))	Inlet	7.9	192	215	564	23.2	4.0	11.3
	Outlet	8.0	28	26	88	4.0	0.3	4.8
Coronation Pillar STP* (Old Clarifier(10))	Inlet	-	-	-	-	-	-	-
	Outlet	-	-	-	-	-	-	-
Oxidation Pond (Nehru Vihar) STP	Inlet	8.1	88	155	392	15.2	0.2	5.0
	Outlet	8.0	10	21	64	2.0	ND	3.3
Narela STP(10)	Inlet	7.9	160	115	272	32.0	2.7	11.3
	Outlet	8.2	34	20	52	4.4	2.2	4.0
Okhla STP Plant-I(12)	Inlet	8.0	212	100	324	25.2	1.7	6.7
	Outlet	8.0	14	28	60	3.6	0.6	1.6
Okhla STP Plant-II(30)	Inlet	8.0	212	100	324	25.2	1.7	6.7
	Outlet	8.2	24	30	88	4.4	0.1	2.9

(Table Contd...)

(1)	(2)	(3)	(4)	(5)	(6)	(7)	(8)	(9)
Okhla STP Plant-III(37)	Inlet	8.0	212	100	324	25.2	1.7	6.7
	Outlet	8.4	18	25	92	4.0	1.0	3.0
Okhla STP Plant-IV(45)	Inlet	8.0	212	100	324	25.2	1.7	6.7
	Outlet	8.1	38	21	88	2.4	0.4	5.0
Okhla STP Plant-V(16)	Inlet	8.0	212	100	324	25.2	1.7	6.7
	Outlet	8.4	30	23	72	4.0	0.3	2.5
Vasant Kunj STP) Plant-I(2.2)	Inlet	8.0	120	95	328	26.8	1.5	3.6
	Outlet	8.3	30	24	80	3.6	1.0	1.6
Vasant Kunj STP) Plant-II(3.0)	Inlet	8.2	248	110	252	25.2	1.2	5.7
	Outlet	8.1	30	26	72	4.0	0.06	3.0
Mehrauli STP	Inlet	8.2	376	165	304	15.6	2.2	6.8
	Outlet	8.0	34	30	96	4.4	1.3	1.0
Yamuna Vihar STP Plant-I(10)	Inlet	7.7	284	270	616	16.0	1.7	7.8
	Outlet	7.6	34	24	64	2.8	1.1	3.1
Yamuna Vihar STP Plant-II(10)	Inlet	7.2	440	200	416	18.8	2.5	9.1
	Outlet	7.6	44	30	76	4.8	1.4	2.5
Rithala STP Plant-I(40)	Inlet	8.0	216	160	364	23.2	1.0	5.3
	Outlet	7.6	40	27	72	3.2	0.5	1.6
Rithala STP Plant-II (40)	Inlet	8.0	216	160	364	23.2	1.0	5.3
	Outlet	8.3	38	19	52	2.8	0.02	0.6
Keshopur STP* Plant-I(12)	Inlet	-	-	-	-	-	-	-
	Outlet	-	-	-	-	-	-	-
Keshopur STP* Plant-II(40)	Inlet	-	-	-	-	-	-	-
	Outlet	-	-	-	-	-	-	-
Nilothi STP	Inlet	8.0	308	200	424	23.2	0.9	5.1
	Outlet	7.7	14	24	68	3.6	0.6	2.2
Pappankala STP	Inlet	7.6	76	130	304	24.4	1.6	11.3
	Outlet	7.7	30	23	88	2.8	0.3	2.1
Najafgarh STP	Inlet	8.2	152	115	264	16.0	1.2	6.5
	Outlet	7.9	36	22	88	2.4	0.1	5.0
Rohini STP*	Inlet	-	-	-	-	-	-	-
	Outlet	-	-	-	-	-	-	-
STP standard		5.5-9.0	50	30	250	10	50	5

* Plant was not operational

Source: Delhi Pollution Control Committee

Table 6.25: Performance Evaluation of Sewage Treatment Plant in Delhi (Month-February, 2012)

Name of STP		pH	TSS (mg/l)	BOD (mg/l)	COD (mg/l)	Oil and grease (mg/l)	Ammonical Nitrogen (mg/l)	Phosphate (mg/l)
(1)	(2)	(3)	(4)	(5)	(6)	(7)	(8)	(9)
Sen Nursing Home	Inlet	7.3	76	110	316	26.8	3.0	8.3
	Outlet	7.4	16	78	72	3.6	0.06	0.5
Delhi Gate STP	Inlet	7.5	176	120	308	23.2	3.0	7.0
	Outlet	7.7	26	14	68	4.0	0.24	1.4
Kondli STP (Ph- I (20))	Inlet	7.2	96	140	364	16.4	4.7	3.2
	Outlet	7.2	32	22	64	4.8	3.7	1.8
Kondli STP (Ph- II (25))	Inlet	7.1	124	210	544	20.4	5.4	3.5
	Outlet	7.2	32	28	72	3.2	1.9	1.0
Kondli STP (Ph- III (20))	Inlet	7.1	124	210	544	20.4	5.4	3.5
	Outlet	7.3	48	30	124	3.6	2.2	1.4
Coronation Pillar STP (Phase-I,II(20))	Inlet	7.2	224	155	480	15.2	4.8	6.5
	Outlet	7.6	34	21	64	3.6	0.3	3.2
Coronation Pillar STP (Phase-III(10))	Inlet	6.8	496	210	784	24.8	8.5	11.4
	Outlet	6.9	32	30	152	2.8	6.7	3.0
Coronation Pillar STP* (Old Clarifier(10))	Inlet	-	-	-	-	-	-	-
	Outlet	-	-	-	-	-	-	-
Oxidation Pond (Nehru Vihar) STP*	Inlet	-	-	-	-	-	-	-
	Outlet	-	-	-	-	-	-	-
Narela STP(10)	Inlet	7.5	60	110	328	8.0	2.3	0.9
	Outlet	7.4	18	27	96	2.4	1.2	0.7
Okhla STP Plant-I(12)	Inlet	8.1	272	130	324	23.6	1.43	5.5
	Outlet	8.0	36	28	72	2.8	0.8	1.9
Okhla STP Plant-II(30)	Inlet	8.1	272	130	324	23.6	1.43	5.5
	Outlet	8.3	40	34	104	3.6	0.5	2.5
Okhla STP Plant-III(37)	Inlet	8.1	272	130	324	23.6	1.43	5.5
	Outlet	8.1	44	32	96	4.4	1.7	2.9
Okhla STP Plant-IV(45)	Inlet	8.1	272	130	324	23.6	1.43	5.5
	Outlet	8.2	24	30	88	3.2	0.9	4.3
Okhla STP Plant-V(16)	Inlet	8.1	272	130	324	23.6	1.43	5.5
	Outlet	8.2	32	14	44	4.0	0.5	2.0
Vasant Kunj STP) Plant-I(2.2)	Inlet	7.2	124	245	520	24.8	4.3	4.8
	Outlet	7.3	36	29	84	4.0	0.1	0.8
Vasant Kunj STP) Plant-II(3.0)	Inlet	6.7	136	160	324	28.4	4.9	3.7
	Outlet	6.9	24	21	64	4.0	0.1	2.1
Mehrauli STP	Inlet	7.0	104	115	236	12.4	3.8	4.1
	Outlet	7.2	28	29	72	2.8	1.5	2.7

(Table Contd...)

(1)	(2)	(3)	(4)	(5)	(6)	(7)	(8)	(9)
Yamuna Vihar STP Plant-I(10)	Inlet	7.3	116	115	336	16.0	6.7	3.7
	Outlet	7.2	**66**	28	116	3.6	5.8	0.8
Yamuna Vihar STP Plant-II(10)	Inlet	7.1	320	215	580	20.4	6.2	3.6
	Outlet	7.1	42	29	88	3.2	1.3	0.7
Rithala STP Plant-I(40)	Inlet	8.0	164	135	392	16.4	5.0	3.8
	Outlet	7.8	32	25	112	4.0	3.5	2.9
Rithala STP Plant-II (40)	Inlet	8.0	164	135	392	16.4	5.0	3.8
	Outlet	7.9	34	29	132	3.2	2.1	2.7
Keshopur STP* Plant-I(12)	Inlet	-	-	-	-	-	-	-
	Outlet	-	-	-	-	-	-	-
Keshopur STP* Plant-II(40)	Inlet	-	-	-	-	-	-	-
	Outlet	-	-	-	-	-	-	-
Nilothi STP	Inlet	7.5	116	240	688	20.4	3.2	2.7
	Outlet	7.3	40	23	88	5.6	2.3	0.5
Pappankala STP	Inlet	7.0	216	180	496	32.0	4.9	3.3
	Outlet	7.2	34	30	120	2.8	0.2	0.9
Najafgarh STP	Inlet	7.1	224	115	324	28.4	6.8	4.3
	Outlet	7.1	28	28	132	4.4	1.8	2.1
Rohini STP*	Inlet	-	-	-	-	-	-	-
	Outlet	-	-	-	-	-	-	-
STP standard		5.5-9.0	50	30	250	10	50	5

* Plant was not operational

Source: Delhi Pollution Control Committee

Table 6.26: Performance Evaluation of Sewage Treatment Plant in Delhi (Month-March, 2012)

Name of STP		pH	TSS (mg/l)	BOD (mg/l)	COD (mg/l)	Oil and grease (mg/l)	Ammonical Nitrogen (mg/l)	Phosphate (mg/l)
(1)	(2)	(3)	(4)	(5)	(6)	(7)	(8)	(9)
Sen Nursing Home	Inlet	7.8	584	255	676	8.0	2.7	11.3
	Outlet	7.9	14	10	52	3.2	0.2	1.1
Delhi Gate STP	Inlet	7.9	260	180	368	10.4	1.7	8.5
	Outlet	7.9	18	14	60	2.8	0.2	1.4
Kondli STP (Ph- I (20))	Inlet	7.9	188	125	284	24.0	2.5	7.5
	Outlet	8.5	**66**	**35**	132	6.4	1.8	**5.4**
Kondli STP (Ph- II (25))	Inlet	8.4	256	160	616	28.0	1.9	11.3
	Outlet	8.0	50	24	78	4.4	0.2	3.4
Kondli STP* (Ph- III (20))	Inlet	-	-	-	-	-	-	-
	Outlet	-	-	-	-	-	-	-
Coronation Pillar STP (Phase-I,II(20))	Inlet	7.9	148	140	420	12.4	1.3	9.9
	Outlet	7.8	20	27	100	4.8	0.3	4.6

(Table Contd...)

(1)	(2)	(3)	(4)	(5)	(6)	(7)	(8)	(9)
Coronation Pillar STP (Phase-III(10))	Inlet	7.7	160	130	400	16.4	0.9	7.3
	Outlet	7.6	40	30	144	4.0	0.1	2.3
Coronation Pillar STP* (Old Clarifier(10))	Inlet	-	-	-	-	-	-	-
	Outlet	-	-	-	-	-	-	-
Oxidation Pond (Nehru Vihar) STP*	Inlet	-	-	-	-	-	-	-
	Outlet	-	-	-	-	-	-	-
Narela STP(10)	Inlet	7.3	312	130	456	25.2	3.2	11.3
	Outlet	7.2	12	33	104	1.6	1.2	3.4
Okhla STP* Plant-I(12)	Inlet	-	-	-	-	-	-	-
	Outlet	-	-	-	-	-	-	-
Okhla STP Plant-II(30)	Inlet	7.9	220	130	460	24.4	1.1	4.0
	Outlet	7.6	26	18	64	3.2	0.7	1.2
Okhla STP Plant-III(37)	Inlet	7.9	220	130	460	24.4	1.1	4.0
	Outlet	7.7	32	23	84	2.8	0.4	2.8
Okhla STP Plant-IV(45)	Inlet	7.9	220	130	460	24.4	1.1	4.0
	Outlet	7.8	36	20	60	2.8	0.9	2.7
Okhla STP Plant-V(16)	Inlet	7.9	220	130	460	24.4	1.1	4.0
	Outlet	7.7	32	24	64	3.6	0.6	0.2
Vasant Kunj STP) Plant-I(2.2)	Inlet	7.8	304	145	388	16.4	4.1	11.3
	Outlet	8.0	20	12	48	2.4	0.2	5.0
Vasant Kunj STP) Plant-II(3.0)	Inlet	8.1	144	180	412	18.4	0.6	11.3
	Outlet	7.6	42	14	52	1.6	0.2	4.5
Mehrauli STP	Inlet	7.2	152	190	560	20.4	2.5	11.3
	Outlet	7.3	34	28	136	4.0	1.2	4.0
Yamuna Vihar STP Plant-I(10)	Inlet	7.4	288	135	396	20.4	2.2	11.3
	Outlet	7.4	20	18	64	2.4	1.1	2.3
Yamuna Vihar STP Plant-II(10)	Inlet	7.6	428	210	596	32.0	2.4	11.3
	Outlet	7.5	40	28	88	4.0	0.7	0.7
Rithala STP Plant-I(40)	Inlet	7.8	264	180	412	32.0	1.0	11.3
	Outlet	7.8	20	24	80	4.0	0.2	3.5
Rithala STP Plant-II (40)	Inlet	7.8	264	180	412	32.0	1.0	11.3
	Outlet	7.0	12	18	64	1.6	0.05	2.0
Keshopur STP Plant-I(12)	Inlet	7.7	404	115	348	32.0	5.5	11.3
	Outlet	7.5	32	20	100	3.2	3.1	5.4
Keshopur STP* Plant-II(40)	Inlet	-	-	-	-	-	-	-
	Outlet	-	-	-	-	-	-	-
Nilothi STP	Inlet	7.4	332	115	352	28.4	3.1	6.0
	Outlet	7.5	30	27	112	2.8	2.0	2.6
Pappankala STP	Inlet	7.5	348	150	384	24.8	10.4	11.0
	Outlet	7.4	48	27	96	2.4	1.3	3.0
Najafgarh STP	Inlet	7.0	140	165	392	16.0	3.2	3.0
	Outlet	7.1	42	23	88	2.0	1.9	2.6
Rohini STP*	Inlet	-	-	-	-	-	-	-
	Outlet	-	-	-	-	-	-	-
STP standard		5.5-9.0	50	30	250	10	50	5

* Plant was not operational

Source: Delhi Pollution Control Committee

Table 6.27: Performance Evaluation of Sewage Treatment Plant in Delhi (Month-April, 2012)

Name of STP		pH	TSS (mg/l)	BOD (mg/l)	COD (mg/l)	Oil and grease (mg/l)	Ammonical Nitrogen (mg/l)	Phosphate (mg/l)
(1)	(2)	(3)	(4)	(5)	(6)	(7)	(8)	(9)
Sen Nursing Home	Inlet	7.6	244	145	340	22	1.7	8.8
	Outlet	7.5	18	9	36	1.2	0.44	2.7
Delhi Gate STP	Inlet	7.4	160	250	312	18	1.1	8.8
	Outlet	7.3	16	10	32	1.6	0.36	1.38
Kondli STP (Ph- I (20))	Inlet	7.4	104	265	576	16	5.43	7.11
	Outlet	7.3	38	28	100	1.2	3.42	4.8
Kondli STP (Ph- II (25))	Inlet	7.8	200	200	520	20.4	8.72	6.8
	Outlet	7.8	42	30	128	4	3.16	2.1
Kondli STP (Ph- III (20))	Inlet	7.8	200	200	520	20.4	8.72	6.8
	Outlet	7.7	44	29	120	4.8	3.05	2.0
Coronation Pillar STP (Phase-I,II(20))	Inlet	7.8	156	155	396	16.4	3.48	9.13
	Outlet	7.9	58	30	164	4.0	0.36	0.57
Coronation Pillar STP (Phase-III(10)*)	Inlet	-	-	-	-	-	-	-
	Outlet	-	-	-	-	-	-	-
Coronation Pillar STP (Old Clarifier(10)) *	Inlet	-	-	-	-	-	-	-
	Outlet	-	-	-	-	-	-	-
Oxidation Pond (Nehru Vihar) STP *	Inlet	-	-	-	-	-	-	-
	Outlet	-	-	-	-	-	-	-
Narela STP(10)	Inlet	7.6	140	145	340	12.8	6.4	8.5
	Outlet	7.7	32	14	32	4.4	2.4	3.3
Okhla STP Plant-I(12)	Inlet	7.4	156	175	404	6.4	3.7	8.73
	Outlet	7.1	12	28	136	1.2	1.0	2.5
Okhla STP Plant-II(30)	Inlet	7.4	156	175	404	6.4	3.7	8.73
	Outlet	7.2	18	26	104	3.6	3.2	1.1
Okhla STP Plant-III(37)	Inlet	7.4	156	175	404	6.4	3.7	8.73
	Outlet	7.3	24	23	96	2.8	2.7	2.9
Okhla STP Plant-IV(45)	Inlet	7.4	156	175	404	6.4	3.7	8.73
	Outlet	7.4	34	30	112	2.0	2.8	3.4
Okhla STP Plant-V(16)	Inlet	7.4	156	175	404	6.4	3.7	8.73
	Outlet	7.2	20	17	40	3.2	2.7	1.0
Vasant Kunj STP) Plant-I(2.2)	Inlet	7.9	92	160	340	7.6	5.6	4.7
	Outlet	7.9	34	26	80	4.4	3.2	3.7
Vasant Kunj STP) Plant-II(3.0)	Inlet	7.8	236	125	288	28.0	4.7	8.7
	Outlet	7.9	12	27	88	1.6	1.1	4.7
Mehrauli STP	Inlet	7.8	64	135	324	3.2	2.1	4.2
	Outlet	7.9	22	21	72	2.8	1.9	3.1

(Table Contd...)

(1)	(2)	(3)	(4)	(5)	(6)	(7)	(8)	(9)
Yamuna Vihar STP Plant-I(10)	Inlet	7.7	492	285	684	32	7.9	5.5
	Outlet	7.6	34	27	104	3.2	3.6	2.1
Yamuna Vihar STP Plant-II(10)	Inlet	7.4	532	250	624	36.4	6.5	7.6
	Outlet	7.4	44	25	96	4.4	2.8	4.3
Rithala STP Plant-I(40)	Inlet	8.0	108	130	284	12.4	4.3	1.6
	Outlet	7.9	48	25	120	3.6	2.7	0.9
Rithala STP Plant-II (40)	Inlet	7.9	136	145	364	20.0	7.2	9.1
	Outlet	7.9	32	28	132	2.4	0.04	1.7
Keshopur STP Plant-I(12)	Inlet	7.8	256	225	552	16.4	6.8	5.0
	Outlet	7.9	46	28	108	3.6	4.2	3.2
Keshopur STP Plant-II(40)*	Inlet	-	-	-	-	-	-	-
	Outlet	-	-	-	-	-	-	-
Keshopur STP Plant-III(12)*	Inlet	-	-	-	-	-	-	-
	Outlet	-	-	-	-	-	-	-
Nilothi STP	Inlet	8.1	112	155	356	12.0	1.4	7.0
	Outlet	7.9	10	27	140	1.2	1.1	4.0
Pappankala STP	Inlet	7.0	188	140	324	12.4	1.23	5.5
	Outlet	6.9	22	25	124	2.4	0.05	1.4
Najafgarh STP	Inlet	7.1	292	145	336	24.4	0.7	5.5
	Outlet	7.1	32	30	152	2.4	0.07	2.7
Rohini STP *	Inlet	-	-	-	-	-	-	-
	Outlet	-	-	-	-	-	-	-
STP standard		5.5-9.0	50	30	250	10	50	5

* Plant was not operational

Source: Delhi Pollution Control Committee

TREATED WASTE WATER DISPOSAL AND RECYCLING

Disposal of Wastewater

Proper collection, treatment and discharge of waste water, and correct disposal or re-use of the resulting sludge help to protect and improve water quality in Delhi. Satisfactory disposal of wastewater, whether by surface, subsurface methods or dilution, is dependent on its treatment prior to disposal to safe aquatic life and eco-system.

Disposal Methods

There are three methods by which final disposal of wastewater can be accomplished.

Table 6.28: Annual performance and abnormal characteristics of outlet sample from all Sewage Treatment Plant in Delhi (April 2011 to April 2012)

STP (MGD)	Apr. 11	May 11	June 11	July 11	Aug. 11	Sept. 11	Oct. 11	Nov. 11	Dec. 11	Jan. 12	Feb. 12	Mar. 12	Apr. 12
(1)	(2)	(3)	(4)	(5)	(6)	(7)	(8)	(9)	(10)	(11)	(12)	(13)	(14)
Sen Nursing Home (2.2)					PO_4 (11.0)								
Delhi Gate STP (2.2)					PO_4 (14.3)								
Kondli STP (Ph- I (20))			PO_4 (6.0)		PO_4 (6.4)					PO_4 (6.4)		TSS(66), BOD(35) PO_4(6.4)	
Kondli STP (Ph- II (25))			PO_4 (7.0)	TSS(54)	TSS(74), PO_4 (7.4)	TSS(76)							
Kondli STP* (Ph- III (20))		BOD(34)						TSS(72), PO_4 (5.1)					
Coronation Pillar STP (Phase-I,II(20))					BOD(43) PO_4(11.3)			PO_4 (7.2)					TSS(58)
Coronation Pillar STP (Phase-III(10))			PO_4(9.0)		PO_4(11.0)				TSS(54)				
Coronation Pillar STP* (Old Clarifier(10))													
Oxidation Pond (Nehru Vihar) STP* (6)													
Narela STP(10)			PO_4(7.7)		TSS(164)								
Okhla STP* Plant-I(12)							TSS(52), BOD(32)						
Okhla STP Plant-II(30)					TSS(66)		TSS(84)				BOD(34)		
Okhla STP Plant-III(37)			BOD(42)	TSS(56)		TSS(62)					BOD(32)		
Okhla STP Plant-IV(45)					TSS(62)		TSS(76)		BOD(31)				
Okhla STP Plant-V(16)		BOD(36)					PO_4(7.39)		PO_4(5.5)				
Vasant Kunj STP) Plant-I(2.2)					PO_4(11.6)								
Vasant Kunj STP) Plant-II(3.0)		BOD(33)			TSS(64)								
Mehrauli STP (5)													

(Table Contd…)

(1)	(2)	(3)	(4)	(5)	(6)	(7)	(8)	(9)	(10)	(11)	(12)	(13)	(14)
Yamuna Vihar STP Plant-I(10)						PO_4(7.3)					TSS(66)		
Yamuna Vihar STP Plant-II(10)			PO_4(8.4)										
Rithala STP Plant-I(40)					TSS(112) PO_4(12.0)								
Rithala STP Plant-II (40)					PO_4(13.9)								
Keshopur STP Plant-I(12)												PO_4(5.4)	
Keshopur STP* Plant-II(40)													
Nilothi STP (40)					PO_4(8.2)				PO_4(8.15)				
Pappankala STP (20)					TSS(54), PO_4(12.8)		TSS(54)						
Najafgarh STP (5)													
Rohini STP (15)													

Surface Disposal

The method in which raw sewage or partly treated sewage is evenly spread on the surface of land is called land treatment. This method is quite suitable when no dilution projects are possible. In this method water of sewage percolates in the ground and suspended solids remains at the surface of the ground. These suspended organic solids are partly oxidized by exposure to atmospheric action of light, air and heat and partly acted upon by the bacteria. This is a very good method of sewage disposal in a country like where lands are available at cheap rates and there is lots of sunshine which helps biological activity. Generally this is disposal by irrigation. This involves spreading the wastewater over the surface of the ground, generally by irrigation ditches. There is some evaporation, but most of the wastewater soaks into the ground and supplies moisture with small amounts of fertilizing ingredients for plant life. This method is largely restricted to small volumes of wastewater from a relatively small population where land area is available and where nuisance problems will not be created. It has its best use in arid or semi-arid areas where the moisture added to the soil is of special value. If crops are cultivated on the disposal area, the growth of vegetation often must be excluded from wastewater. Because untreated wastewater will also contain pathogenic organisms, the production of foods for human consumption which may be eaten without cooking is not desirable.

Subsurface Disposal

By this method wastewater is introduced into the ground below its surface through pits or tile fields. It is commonly used for disposal of settled wastewater from residences or institutions where there is only a limited volume of wastewater.

Disposal by Dilution

Disposal by dilution is the simple method of discharging wastewater into surface water such as a river, lake, ocean, estuaries or wetlands. This results in the pollution of the receiving water. This method is possible only when the natural water is available in large quantity near the town. Proper care should be taken while discharging sewage in water so that sewage may not pollute natural water and make it unfit for any other purposes like bathing, drinking, irrigation, etc. The degree of pollution depends on the dilution, volume and composition of the wastewater as compared to the volume and quality of the water with which it is mixed. When the volume and organic content of the wastewater is small, compared with the volume of the receiving water, the dissolved oxygen present in the receiving water is adequate to provide for aerobic decomposition of the organic solids in the wastewater so that nuisance conditions do not develop. However, in spite of the continued aerobic status of the receiving water, microbial pollution remains a health menace and floating solids in the wastewater, if not previously removed, is visible evidence of the pollution.

Where the dissolved oxygen in the receiving water is inadequate to maintain aerobic decomposition, anaerobic decomposition takes place and putrefaction with objectionable conditions results. It is not so much the volume of wastewater that is the critical factor as the amount of readily decomposable organic matter in the wastewater. Thus a volume of wastewater that has been treated to remove or reduce this organic matter can be discharged to a natural surface water without creating objectionable conditions while the same volume of raw or untreated wastewater might produce a nuisance. The dissolved oxygen in the receiving water is the determining factor.

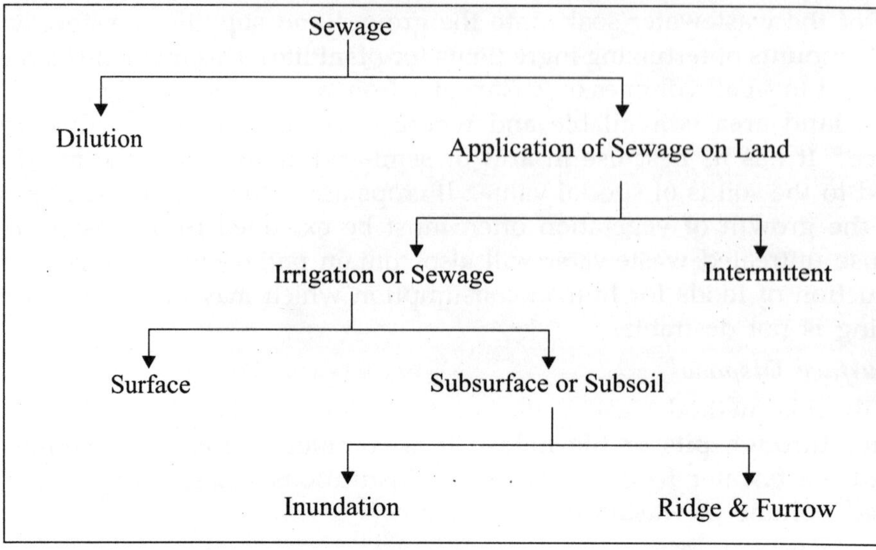

Fig. 6.8: Types of Sewage disposal techniques

Status of Disposal of Treated Sewage

Out of 328 MGD treated sewage, it is estimated that 275 MGD treated sewage is being dispose back to the open drain ultimately find access to the River Yamuna/Agra canal. Out of 30 STPs, only two sewage treatment plants using treated sewage for irrigation i.e. Coronation pillar & Okhla. Coronation pillar STPs using around 7.9 MGD treated sewage for irrigation purpose and Okhla STP using around 20 MGD for horticulture purpose in NDMS areas. The remaining treated sewage is being discharged from Okhla STP goes to old Agara canal and finally to new Agra canal for irrigation purpose. Vasant Kunj Oxidation pond ultimately discharges treated sewage to Kushak-Barapulla drain. The Keshopur STPs authority claim that the whole treated sewage is being diverted to minor irrigation department and they use as and when required otherwise ultimately disposed into Najafgarh drain.

The effluent from Shadara STPs (Yamuna Vihar and Kondali) finds its way into the Shadara Drain. Other two STPs Dr. Sen Nursing home and Delhi gate used treated sewage for cooling purpose in power plant. It is estimated that 7.9 MGD from coronation pillar is being used for irrigation purpose and may not put back to the river Yamuna and 4.5 MGD from Dr. Sen nursing home and Delhi gate STP are being used for cooling purpose by Pragati Power Plant near ITO and possible of used water from Pragati Power corporation limited to the river Yamuna cannot be ruled out, whereas all other STP finally discharge into Najafgarh drain or Shadara drain either directly or through various sub drains. It is further estimated that out of 275 MGD treated sewage joining to the receiving water bodies. Out of 275 MGD, 171 MGD is being discharged into the river Yamuna & 104 MGD joining to the Agra canal. Thus, out of 328 MGD treated effluent or treated sewage, only 177 MGD is being used for irrigation and horticulture purpose (including New Agra canal carrying 104 MGD treated sewage from Okhla treatment plant approaches to Agra city for irrigation purpose) and 4.5 MGD for cooling purpose and remaining 167 MGD to join to the river Yamuna without any secondary treatment. A detailed account of treated sewage disposal in Delhi is presented in table 6.29.

Table 6.29: Status of disposal of treated waste water (Source: DJB, 2012)

S.N.	Name of STP	Design capacity (MGD)	Actual Treated (MGD)	Ultimate Disposal
(1)	(2)	(3)	(4)	(5)
1.	Okhla	170	128.57	It is claimed by DJB that about 20 MGD is being given to NDMC for horticulture purpose and rest goes in to new Agra canal through old Agra canal at near Jasola Village/Sarita Vihar bridge
2.	Rithala	80	46.39	Rohini/Nangloi drain to supplementary drain and finally to Yamuna River d/s Wazirabad Barrage
3.	Keshopur	72	45.39	It is claimed by DJB that whole treated effluent goes to MID, but observed that maximum treated water flows to Najafgarh drain to Yamuna river
4.	Kondli	90	41.08	Shahdara drain to Yamuna River
5.	C. Pillar with oxidation Pond	40	11.33	7.9 MGD for irrigation purpose & rest goes to Najafgarh drain to Yamuna river
6.	Nilothi	40	12.50	Najafgarh drain to Yamuna River
7.	Yamuna Vihar	20	11.63	Shahdara Drain to Yamuna River
8.	Pappankalan	20	18.20	Najafgarh drain to Yamuna River
9.	Rohini	15	-	Supplementary drain to Najafgarch drain to Yamuna
10.	Narela	10	1.08	Najafgarh Drain to Yamuna river

(Table Contd...)

(1)	(2)	(3)	(4)	(5)
11.	Najafgach	5	0.90	Najafgarh Drain to Yamuna river
12.	Vasant Kunj	5	3.99	Partly to Sanjay van to open drain (Kushak drain) to Barapulla drain to Yamuna river
13.	Mehrauli	5	2.33	Yamuna river through open drain
14.	Ghitorni	5	-	Yamuna river through open drain
15.	Delhi Gate	2.2	2.38	2.2 MGD utilize for cooling purpose at Pragati Power Corporation and finally to Yamuna river through open drain
16.	Dr Sen N H	2.2	2.40	2.2 MGD utilize for cooling purpose at Pragati Power Corporation and finally to Yamuna river through open drain

In Delhi, it is estimated that at the point of discharge into receiving water bodies the total sewage generation (treated and untreated) is 866 MGD, out of which 104+7.9+20.2 MGD treated sewage is being used for irrigation/horticulture purpose through Agra canal and other area while 4.5 MGD is used for cooling purpose which again put back to the river Yamuna, Remaining 705 MGD should also be used for irrigation purpose to restore and maintain the wholesomeness of the river Yamuna.

Table 6.30: Quality of discharged waste water (Source: DJB)

S.N.	Name of Drain	pH	TSS (mg/l)	COD (mg/l)	BOD (mg/l)
(1)	(2)	(3)	(4)	(5)	(6)
	General Standard	5.5- 9.0	100	250	30
1.	Najafgarh Drain	8.1	204	220	65
2.	Metcalf House Drain	7.9	54	120	31
3.	Khyber Pass Drain	8.4	22	40	10
4.	Sweeper Colony Drain	7.7	26	100	22
5.	Magazine Road Drain	8.0	316	364	115
6.	ISBT Drain	8.0	40	180	50
7.	Tonga Stand Drain	8.0	304	360	110
8.	Moat Drain	No Flow	No Flow	No Flow	No Flow
9.	Civil Mill Drain	7.6	368	472	160
10.	Power House Drain	7.8	144	304	85
11.	Sen Nursing Home Drain	7.9	576	340	95
12.	Drain No. 12A	No Flow	No Flow	No Flow	No Flow
13.	Drain No. 14	8.4	34	72	16

(Table Contd...)

(1)	(2)	(3)	(4)	(5)	(6)
14.	Barapulla Drain	7.5	208	260	80
15.	Maharani Bagh Drain	7.9	276	376	105
16.	Kalkaji Drain	7.9	26	36	4
17.	SaritaVihar Drain (Mathura Road)	7.4	484	596	165
18.	Tehkhand Drain	7.9	512	584	230
19.	Tuglakabad Drain	8.0	352	200	80
20.	Drain Near LPG Bottling Plant	8.0	106	200	85
21.	Drain Near Sarita Vihar Bridge	8.2	78	152	56
22.	Shahdara Drain	8.2	504	272	62
23.	Sahibabad Drain	7.8	608	624	250
24.	Indrapuri Drain	8.1	280	456	155

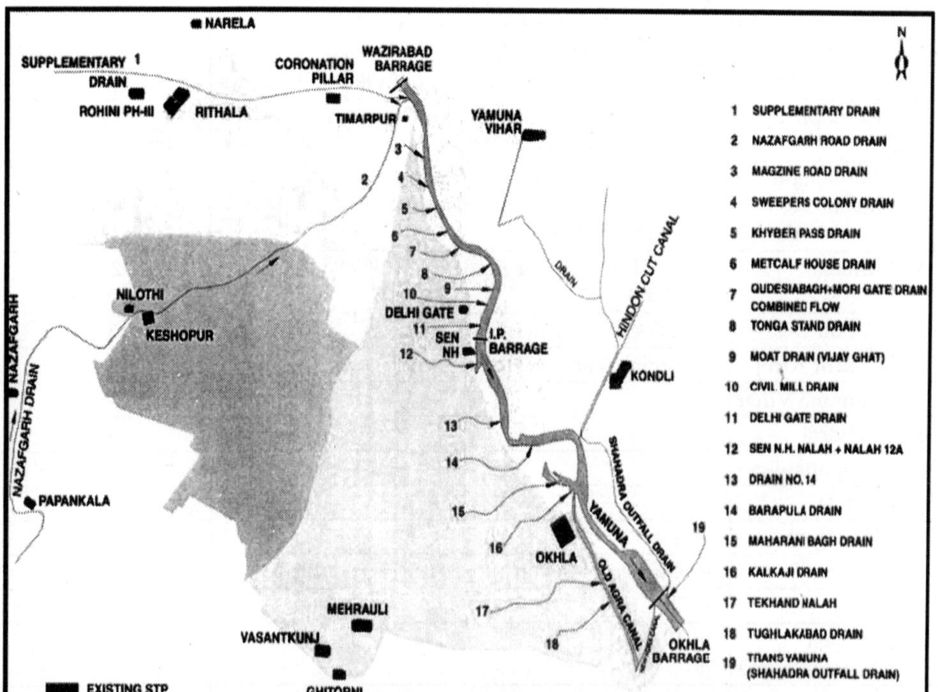

Fig. 6.9: Locations of STPs and drains at Delhi

Recycling and Reuse of Wastewater

In almost all major urban cities, there is a serious problem of adequate water supply while the sources of water are very few. In addition to the storm water harvesting, recycling is an important measure of conservation of water resource. It is estimated that around 80% of water consumed by a house hold is let of to the drain of sewer as waste water. Management of the scare resource would be incomplete without adequate measure in the reuse of the waste water after primary treatment for non portable purpose. There is substantial scope for segregation use of the water for appropriate used and recycling of the water for further use for gardening, industrial cooling, street cleaning, vehicular washing, fire fighting, irrigation, yard cleaning, fountains, recreational lakes etc. Though methods are available to improve the quality of recycled water to potable grade, the lack of social acceptance and prohibitive costs may prevent the adaptation of these techniques.

Table 6.31: Recycling/reuse of waste water in Delhi (Source: DJB, 2012)

S.N.	Plant	Present utilization of treated Wastewater	Quantity (MGD)
(1)	(2)	(3)	(4)
1.	Okhla	➢ CPWD for Horticulture ➢ Jaitpur Village for irrigation ➢ CRRI for Horticulture ➢ Internal Horticultural use of Okhla SDW	20 10 2 5
2.	Keshopur	➢ Flood control & Irigation Department (FCID) Delhi Govt. for irrigation	12
3.	Coronation pillar	➢ DDA Golf course at Bhalaswa Lake ➢ Gammon India for Casting Yard ➢ MIDC at Palla	0.8 0.1 7
4.	Rithala	➢ PPCL for Power Plant ➢ NDPL	25 2
5.	Kondli	➢ DDA for Horticulture	1
6.	Vasant Kunj	➢ Sanjay Van for Horticulture	4.13
7.	Yamuna Vihar	-	-
8.	Ghitorni	-	-
9.	Pappankalan	-	-
10.	Narela	-	-
11.	Najafgarh	-	-
12.	Mehrauli	➢ Garden of Seven Senses for Horticulture	2.49
13.	Delhi gate	➢ PPCL	2.37
14.	Dr. Sen Nursing home	➢ PPCL	2.39
15.	Rohini	-	-
16.	Nilothi	➢ FCID	12.5

(Table Contd...)

(1)	(2)	(3)	(4)
17.	CWG Village/ Akshardham	➢ CWG Village complex for Horticulture	0.1
18.	Oxidation pond Timarpur	-	-
19.	Kapashera	-	-
20.	Molar Bandh	-	-
21.	Bakkarwala	-	-
	Total		**109**

CONCLUSION AND RECOMMENDATIONS

- Delhi has a population of over 16.7 million. It has grown by more than five times since 1961 and expected to increase 19 million by 2021.
- Domestic water requirement in Delhi is rising with the rate of 30-40% per decade.
- Waste water generation is increasing with the rate of 25-35% per decade in Delhi.
- The existing capacity of all STPs is 594.72 MGD but actual treatment is 328.91 MGD which is around 60% of total capacity.
- The maximum treatments plants are under utilize condition. Out of 19 STPs 2 STPs are under maintenance.
- Two STPs namely Delhi Gate Nala and Dr Sen Nursing Home Nala are working beyond their installed capacities.
- The discharged treated water from all STPs are within the prescribed limit of CPCB standards except few STP in few months, where the value of few parameters like TSS, BOD, PO_4 is higher than the prescribed limit.
- During the month of august 2011, maximum STPs performance was worst as TSS, BOD & PO_4 were exceeding the standards.
- Value of wastewater parameters are crossing the limits many times especially in Kondli I, Kondli II, Kondli III, Coronation Pillar I,II, Okhla II, Okhla III, Okhla IV, Okhla V and Pappankala STPs.
- Performance of few STPs like Dr. Sen Nursing Home, Delhi gate, Narela, Vasant Kunj, Yamuna Vihar, Rithala, Keshopur & Nilothi is medium, as parameters hardly exceed the limits.
- Performance of Najafgarh, Oxidation Pond (Nehru Vihar) was found to be excellent because all the parameters of wastewater were within the limits throughout the year.
- The policy should be formulated for development of technical skills, training in plant operation and staff motivation.

- The technical supervisory staff of urban local bodies should have the requisite technical expertise to manage the operational and maintenance of the STP for their optimum utilization
- Incorporate well defined norms (viz. CPHEEO norms) prescribed for staffing at various level vis-a-vis size of the plant and treatment flow sheet.
- Enhance the manpower for proper attention for critical activities of STP
- Most of the STPs are not utilized at their installed capacity. Only 60% capacity is being utilized in current practice
- Increase the utilization of treated from STP water such as gardening, industrial cooling, street cleaning, vehicular washing, fire fighting, irrigation, yard cleaning, fountains, recreational lakes etc
- Utilization of rain water for domestic purposes (Rain Water Harvesting)
- Performance evaluation of all STPs plants should be conducted regularly for every essential parameter as per ISO specification
- Water loses through transportation should be evaluated to justify the water budget.
- Development of a sustainability model for water management in Delhi

REFERENCES

CPCB (2004): Status of Sewerage and Sewage Treatment Plants in Delhi, Control of Urban Pollution Series: CUPS/57/2003-2004, *Central Pollution Control Board, Delhi, Parivesh Bhawan*, East Arjun Nagar, Delhi-110032, pp: 112.

CPCB (2008): Status of Groundwater Quality In India -Part-II, Groundwater Quality Series: GWQS/ 10/2007-2008, Central Pollution Control Board (Ministry of Environment and Forests), Delhi, pp: 367.

CPCB (2009): Status of water supply, wastewater generation and treatment in class-I cities and class-II towns of India, Control of Urban Pollution Series: CUPS/70/2009-2010, *Central Pollution Control Board, Delhi, Parivesh Bhawan*, East Arjun Nagar, Delhi-110032, pp: 88.

Lal, D. and Upadhyay, A.K. (2011) Water Supply and Wastewater engineering, *S.K. Kataria and Sons Publisher, New Delhi*, pp: 410.

Robbins, R.J. (2000): Mechanization of underground mining: a quick look backward and forward, *IJRM*, 37: 413-421.

http://www.water.me.vccs.edu

http://www.ielrc.org/content/e7402.pdf

http://www.dpcc.delhigovt.nic.in/indexdup.php

http://www.delhi.gov.in/wps/wcm/connect/doit_djb/DJB/Home/

http://urbanindia.nic.in/theministry/ministry_page.htm

http://www.cpcb.nic.in/

http://water.me.vccs.edu/courses/ENV149/methods.htm

Pages: 133-157

Water and Waste Water: ***Issues and Management***
Edited by: **Dr. Pawan Kumar 'Bharti'**
ISBN: 978-93-88854-15-3
Edition: **2019**
Published by: **Discovery Publishing House Pvt. Ltd., New Delhi (India)**

7

Synthesis of K_3 [Fe $(C_2O_4)_3$]-Kaolin Nanocomposite and Degradation of Leachate by K_3 [Fe $(C_2O_4)_3$] - Kaolin Nanocomposite

Okeacha Ezinne Grace
*Osu Charles I.
Iwuoha, G.N.

ABSTRACT

K_3[Fe $(C_2O_4)_3$]-Kaolin Nano composite was synthesized by impregnating or intercalation ofK_3[Fe$(C_2O_4)_3$] into kaolin. The Nano composite was used to degrade landfill leachate by oxidation/reduction of organic and inorganic substances present in the landfill leachate.Landfill leachate 1 and 3 had the highest concentration of characteristics of contaminants (COD, BOD_5, TDS, TSS, Organic - N, NH_3 - N, Cr, Pb and Cd) than landfill leachate 2. In landfill 1, the percentage reduction of Cd, Pb, COD, NH_3-N, Cr using kaolin were 88.69, 76.32, 65.6, 46.7, and 35.56 respectively which were less than the values obtained when K_3[Fe$(C_2O_4)_3$]-KaolinNano compositewas used for the degradation of Cd, Pb, COD, NH_3-N, and Cr with values 92.4, 83.5, 91.5, 92.4, and 81.00 respectively. In landfill 2 and 3, K_3[Fe $(C_2O_4)_3$]-Kaolin Nano compositedemonstrated higher percentage reduction than that of the unmodified kaolin. These results showed that increasing the pH and the temperature of the solution (leachate), increased the percentage reduction of the contaminants such that the optimum temperature for the reduction of the various characteristics was at 100° C while that of pH was at 10.5 beyond this value no further significance reduction was observed therefore, at the point the reaction was said to be completed. The change in enthalpy (ΔH) value of the reaction processes were all positives which denoted that the reaction process was endothermic that is, heat was absorbed into the

Department of Pure and Industrial Chemistry, University of Port Harcourt, Nigeria surrounding. The correlation factor, R^2 for the three leachate samples showed less proximity and high remoteness from unity which also confirmed that the reduction process of COD, Pb and Cd using kaolin impregnated with ferrioxalate was temperature dependent reaction (Walter and Geoffrey, 1992). The change in entropy of the reaction (ΔS) is highly temperature dependent too because it is positive. The values of ΔG for the three landfill leachate samples were positives.

Keywords: Nano compound, Thermodynamics, oxidation, kaolin, ferrioxalate

INTRODUCTION

A common and accessible route through which water bodies (rivers, lake, oceans, delta, sea) or ground water could be polluted is by water percolation through dumped wastes in a landfill and ground water seepage, generally regarded as Landfill leachate, (Ali *et al.*, 2004). A conversant way of this leachate formation is rainfall. As the rainfall percolates through the dumped wastes, the amountof all suspended and dissolved components present in it increases due to several chemical and physical reactions occurring during the leachate migration processes of decomposed wastes. Generation of Landfill leachates can also occur through other medium such as; the inflow of groundwater, biologicaldecomposition, surface moisture and the liquid form of the degradable wastes (Reinhart & Townsend, 1998). The amount of leachate available within the waste is basically a function of chemical changes and microbialactions underwaywithin the cell of dumped wastes, percolation of rainwater through the wastes materials and the extent of wastes compactions. Leachate generation will be high if the extent of wastes compaction are low because the filtration rate will be reduced or minimized as more wastes are being compacted (Lema, Mendez & Blazquez., 1988). Leachates at different landfill locations comprise of different compositions and varying components which is precisely a function of the type of wastes, composition of the wastes, the life span or age of the landfills and seasonal weather changes. A leachate is termed old if it is above five years,while it is regarded as medium the wastes are within 1 - 5 years but considered to be young if it is less than a year. (Baig, Coulomb, Courant & Liechti 1999; Silva, Dezotti & Santanna, 2003). Hence to minimize pollution in the environment, leachates should be remediated prior to their disposal to other water bodies probably by using any suitable natural adsorbent and oxidants (calcium hypochlorite, potassium ferrate, chlorine dioxide, and ferrioxalate. Ferrioxalate impregnated with hydrogen peroxide produces hydroxyl radicals that could attack and remove contaminants in wastes water (landfill leachates). Oxidants are water additives added to wastes water to reduce contaminants by a chemical process known as oxidation. Oxidation reaction basically depends on pH value, which proves the importance of pH during oxidation reaction process.

Kaolin minerals are often seenin sedimentary deposits alongside with some subsidiary compositions including feldspar, mica, bentonite, rutile, hydrated iron oxide, anatase and quartz. Kaolin also known as hydrated aluminum silicate with chemical formula $Al_2Si_2O_5(OH)_4$ is deemed as a crucial clay mineral which possesses both high economic and great industrial value. Kaolin has been regarded as a handy, nifty and a multipurpose mineral considering its non-toxic effect, unreactive nature, tiny and thin particle sizes, platy structure, whiteness and its extreme brightness. In Nigeria, kaolin is found across the 36 states but Anambra state has the greatest deposit in Ozubulu, Ihiala local government area. Elements such as Magnesium, Calcium, Sodium, Phosphorus are always seen in kaolin, although in minute quantities (Badmus and Olatinsu, 2009). This research investigates the efficiency and effectiveness of kaolin and K_3[Fe $(C_2O_4)_3$]-Kaolin Nano composite for landfill leachates remediation.

SAMPLE COLLECTION AND LOCATIONS

To ascertain landfill leachate quality, four liters of labeled plastics containers were employed for sampling of the landfill leachates. Before these samples were collected the containers were first cleaned using nitric acid (HNO_3) thereafter, rinsed in distilled water. These sample containers were also rinsed more than once with the leachate samples before collection at every sampling location. Samplings were observed at three different landfill locations which were; Obehie in Ukwa-West Local Government Area, Ubakala in Umuahia South Local Government Area both are in Abia State. The third sampling was at a landfill along Owerri-Onitsha road, in Onitsha Anambra state. The collection of landfill Leachates were achieved randomly at the bottom corner of the designated landfills as the leachate drains under gravity from ground level (low lying) land in the heap of solid waste dump at each landfill locations. The samples pHs at every sampling location were determined in-situ using Mettler Toledo pH meter. Sampling were achieved in July, 2017, and were filtered using transparent (glass micro-filter, 0.47 mm) thereafter, were stored at 4° C in research laboratory until further analysis. The kaolin sample used during this research analysis was acquired from profile at Ohiya in Umuahia South Local Government Area of Abia state.

SAMPLE PREPARATION AND METHOD FOR THE ANALYSIS

Adsorbent Preparation

The kaolin specimen was mashed using porcelain mortar and thereafter sieved to obtain particle size of 75 µm. A 2.0 M sulpuric acid solution was added to 25 g of the kaolin sample into the 250 ml conical flask, hence heat was supplied to the product of the mixture under refluxing with hot plate coupled with a magnetic stirrer at 100° C for 2 hours 30 minutes (150 minutes).

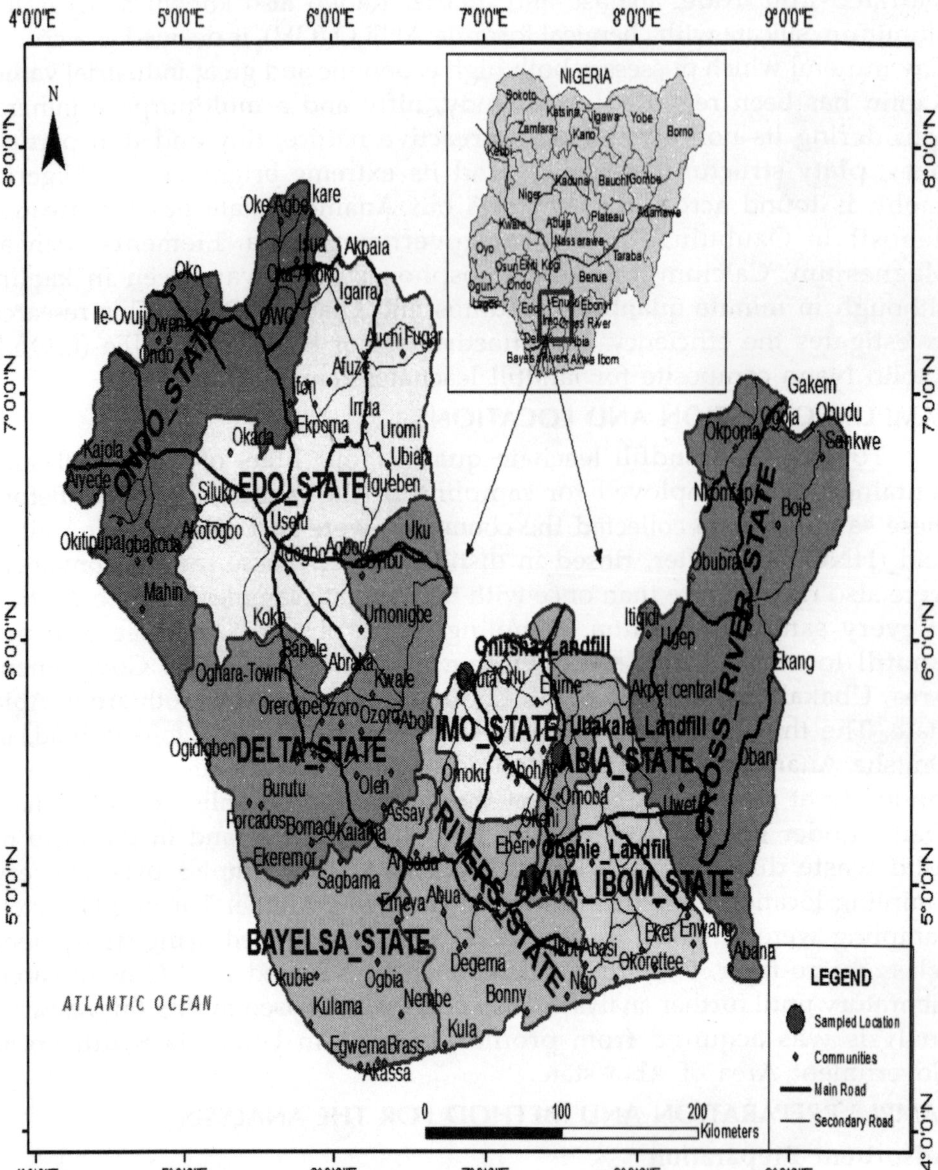

Fig. 7.1: Map showing sampling locations (Abia state, Anambra state)

When the experimental period has come to an end, the reaction process was quenched using distilled water and the slurry formed was filtered using whatmann filter papers. The residual kaolin cake obtained was cleaned (washed) severely with the aid of distilled water till a pH of 6.0 - 7.0 was obtained. The outcome (product) obtained was then oven-dried for 12 hours at 80° C. The product gotten (dried samples) were again mashed and sieved with 60 μm mesh. The product yielded was persevered inside air-tight sample bottle and labeled (Onu *et al.*, 2015)

Synthesis of $K_3[Fe(C_2O_4)_3]$ - nanocomposite

The nanocomposite of kaolin was synthesized by impregnating/ intercalation of Potassium Ferrioxalate reagent into the kaolin in hydrogen peroxide environment (H_2O_2) (Meshram *et al.*, 2011). Initially, 2 g Potassium Ferrioxalate was dissolved into 250 ml DMF (Dimethyl Formamide), thereafter, 10g purified kaolin was added., the mixture was sonicated for 3 hours to obtain homogeneous suspension. Then, 100 ml 0.1M of NaOH reagent was added into the homogenous suspension formed maintaining continuous stirring within a period of 60 minutes. The composite was obtained after successive centrifugation and was dried under vacuum and calcinated at 200° C for 3 hours (Sonawane *et al.*, 2017, Meshram *et al.*, 2011)

Analysis for the Effect of pH

50.0 ml of leachate solutions pH were adjusted to these values; 3.5, 4.5, 6.5, 7.0, 8.5, 9.5, 10.5 and 11.5 using 0.1 M HCl and 0.1 M NaO Hreagent. Then 1g of eachunmodifykaolin and K_3[Fe $(C_2O_4)_3$]-Kaolin Nano composite in the presence of hydrogen peroxidewas introduced, then thoroughly shaken (agitated) in a shaker for 1 hour over 29° C. The outcome suspensions produced were filtered using filter paper (whatman). Then the filtrate was divided into portions. One portion was analyzed for metal ions concentrations using air-acetylene atomic absorption spectrophotometer (model no. UNICAM SOLARR: 32) and the other portion was used for the determination of COD using open Reflux method accompanied by Ferrous-Ammonium Sulfate (FAS) titration.

Analysis for the Effect of Temperature

The leachate samples were divided into portions using different labeled sample containers. 1g of each of unmodify kaolin and K_3[Fe $(C_2O_4)_3$]-Kaolin Nano composite was introduced into conical flasks containing 100 ml of the leachate each resulting into a suspension. The suspensions were adjusted to pH 5.0 using 0.1 M HCl. These samples were then shaken at a constant speed 100xgin a shaking water bath at these various temperatures; 30° C, 50° C, 80° C, 100° C respectively for 45 minutes; the resulting suspensions were filtered using filter paper (whatman:42). The various filtrates were divided into portions and analyzed for metal ions content using Flame Atomic Absorption Spectrophotometer (model: 55B SPECTRAR) with appropriate hollow cathode lamp and resonance wavelength for metals (D3110: Standard method). The second part of the sample was analysed for the concentration of COD using reflux Method followed by titration with Ferrous Ammonium Sulfate (FAS) and Ferrion indicator.

Chemical Oxygen Demand, Ammonia-Nitrogen, Biological Oxygen Demand (BOD) and Dissolve Oxygenwere determined Using Open Reflux Method 508, Powder Pillows Method 8155, Method 5220-B and Wrinkler Method respectively.

RESULTS AND DISCUSSION

Results

The results for characteristics of landfill leachate (LFL) before treatment and after treatment using kaolin and $K_3[Fe\ (C_2O_4)_3]$-Kaolin Nano composite were presented in figures 7.2, 7.3 and 7.4 respectively. Similarly, results of influence of pH on COD, Pb and Cd reduction using both kaolin and $K_3[Fe\ (C_2O_4)_3]$-Kaolin Nano compositewere presented in figures 7.5 to 7.10. Also the results for influence of temperature on the reduction of COD, Pb, Cd using kaolin and $K_3[Fe\ (C_2O_4)_3]$-Kaolin Nano composite were presented in figures 7.11 to 7.16. The various van't Hoff graphs (plots) for COD, Pb and Cd reduction were presented in figures 7.17 to 7.22 and finally the thermodynamics parameters calculated from Van't Hoff plots were presented in tables 7.1 to 7.6 for all the samples respectively.

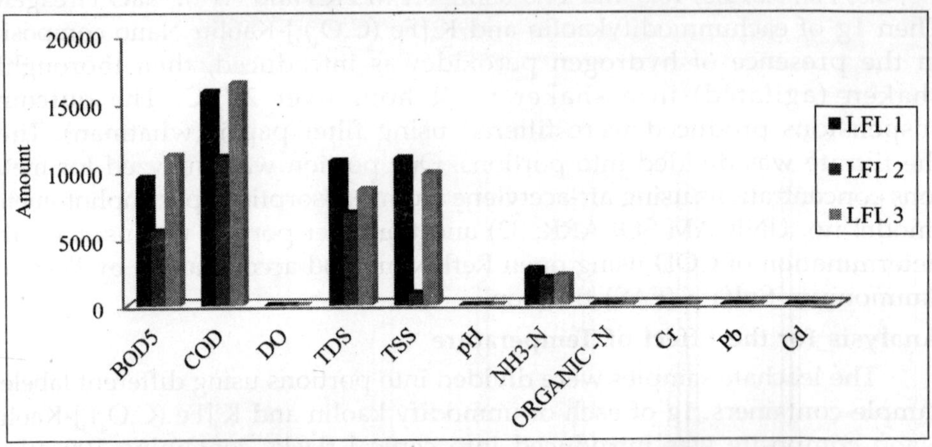

Fig. 7.2: Concentration of characteristics of LFL before treatment

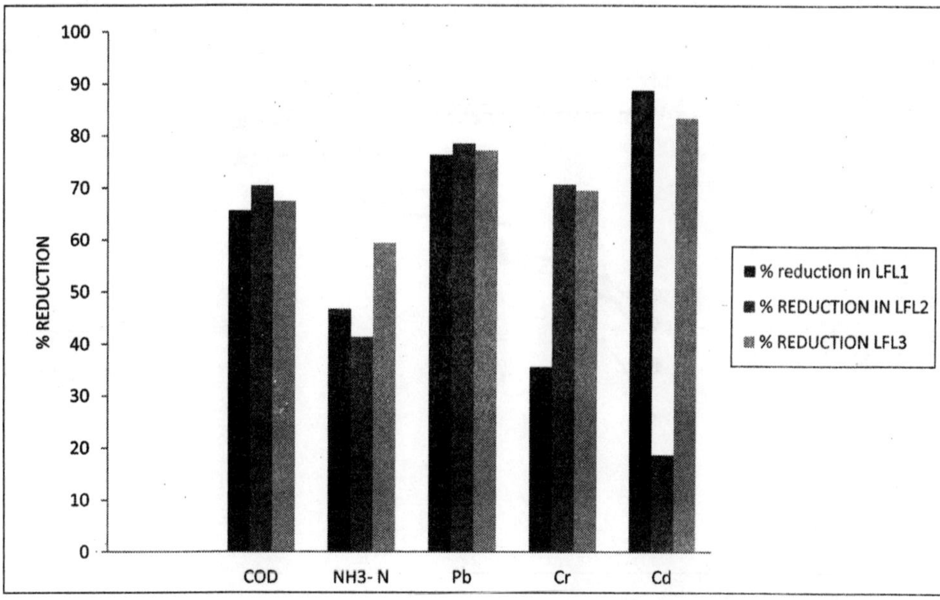

Fig. 7.3: Percentage reductions of characteristics ofLFL using kaolin

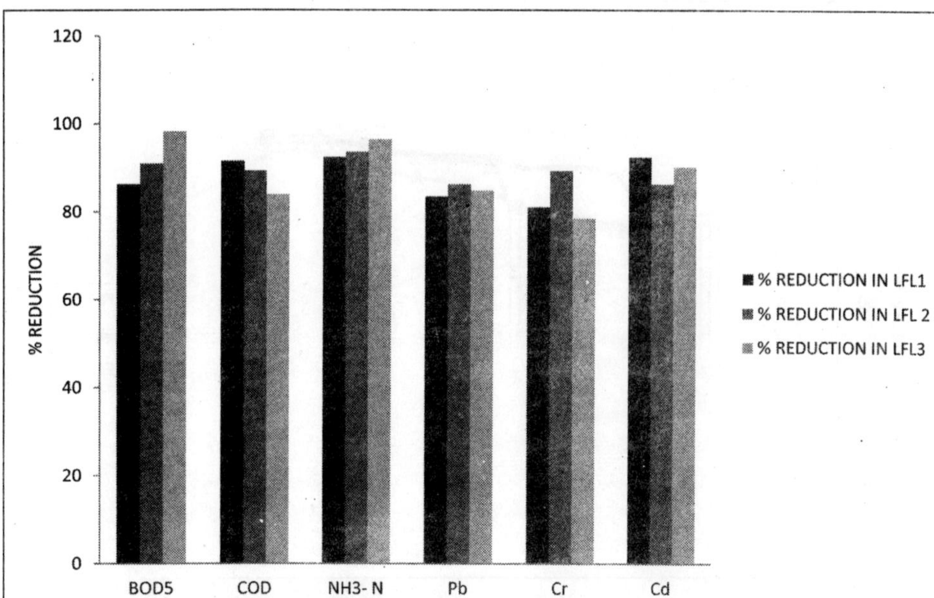

Fig. 7.4: Percentage reductions of characteristics of LFL using K_3[Fe $(C_2O_4)_3$]-Kaolin Nano composite

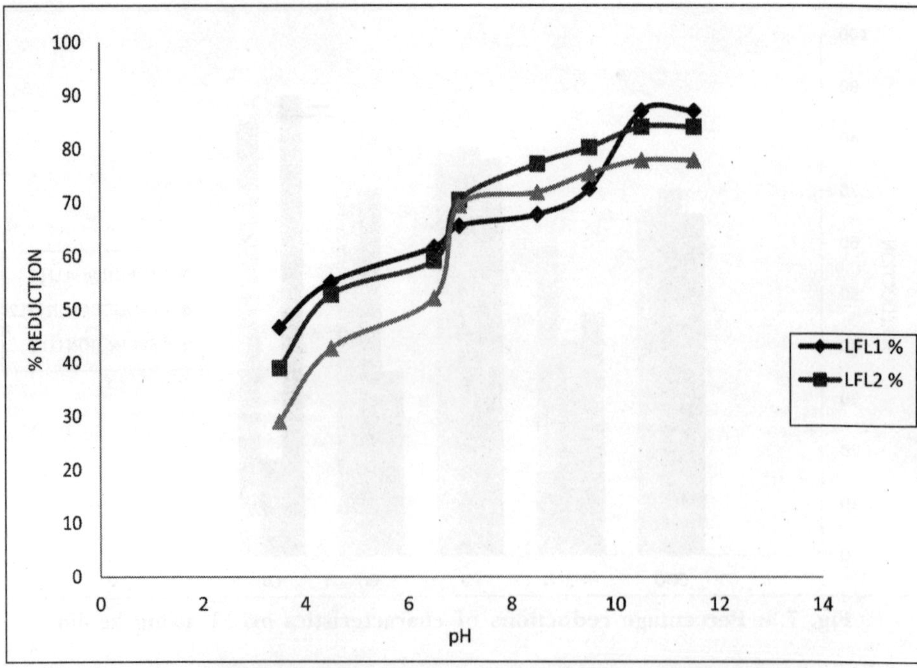

Fig. 7.5: Effect of pH on the reduction of COD in leachate using kaolin

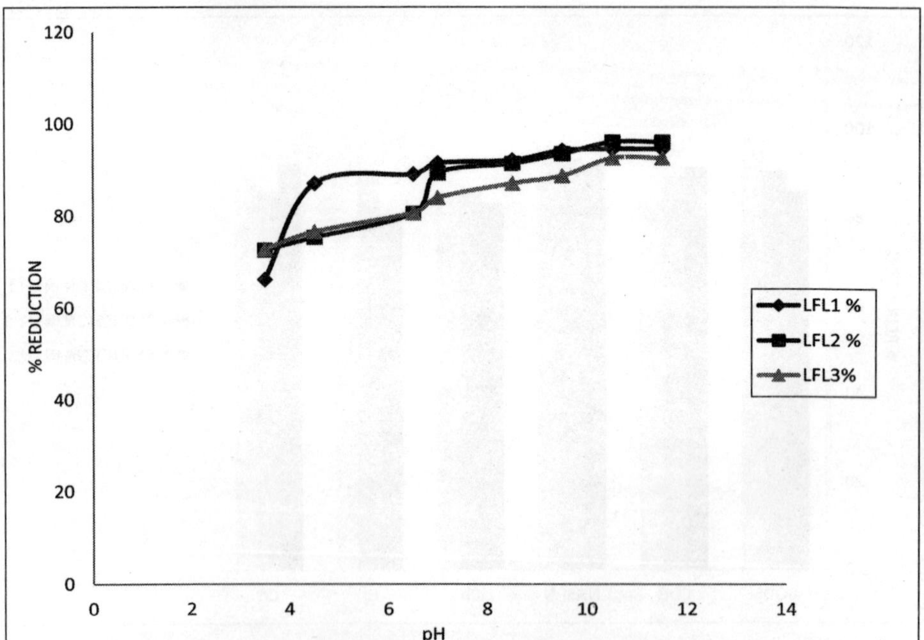

Fig. 7.6: Effect of pH on the reduction of COD in leachate using $K_3[Fe(C_2O_4)_3]$-Kaolin Nano composite

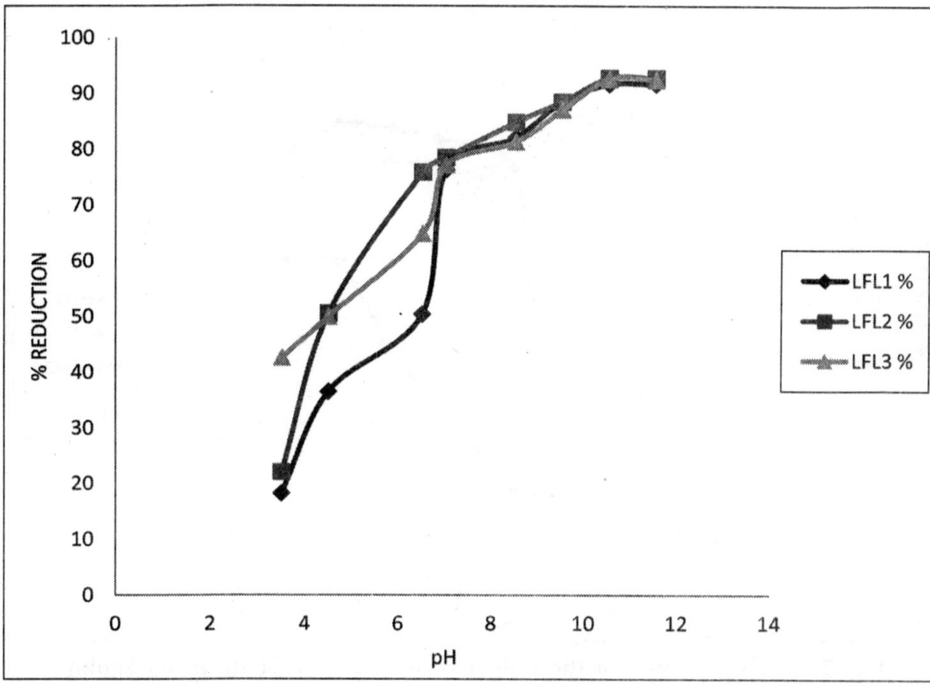

Fig. 7.7: Effect of pH on the reduction of Pb in leachate using kaolin

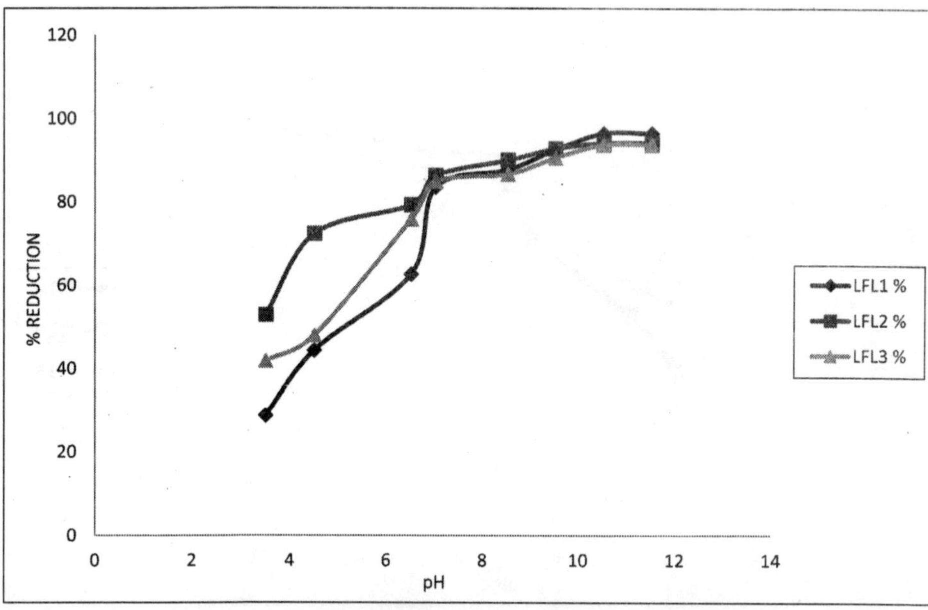

Fig. 7.8: Effect of pH on the reduction of Pb in leachate using K_3[Fe (C_2O_4)$_3$]-Kaolin Nano composite

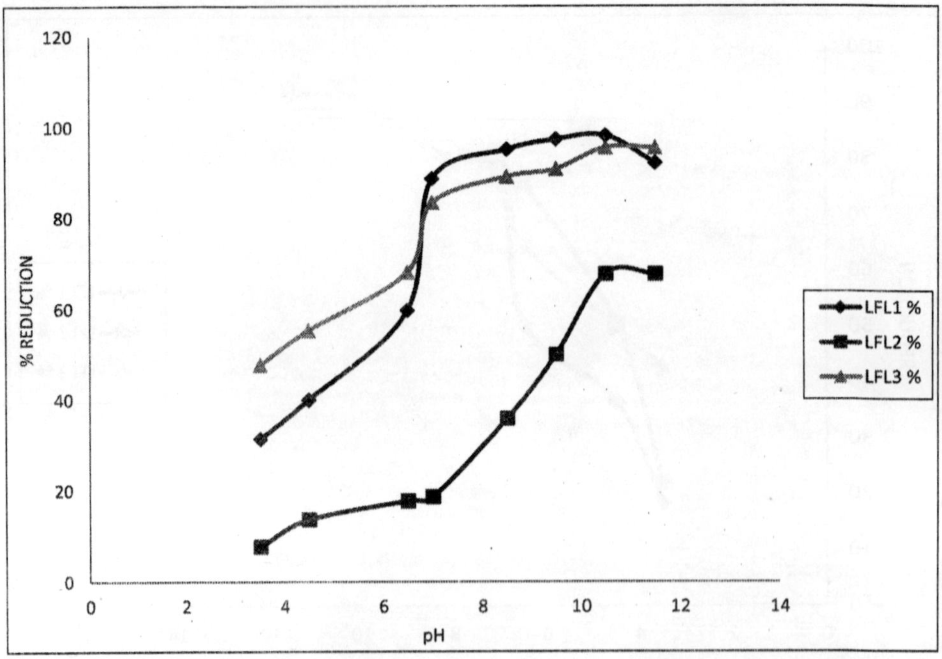

Fig. 7.9: Effect of pH on the reduction of Cd in leachate using kaolin

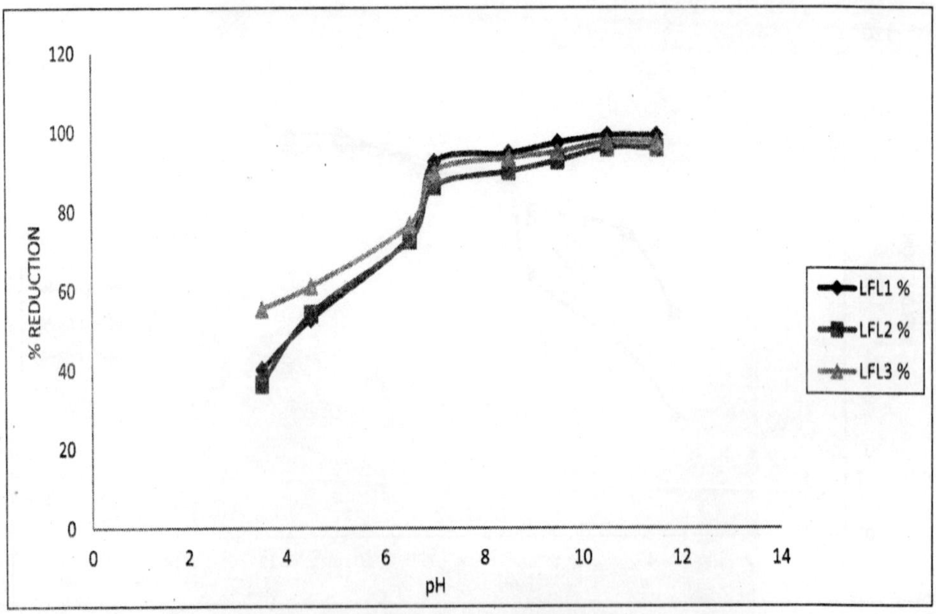

Fig. 7.10: Effect of pH on the reduction of Cd in leachate using $K_3[Fe\ (C_2O_4)_3]$-Kaolin Nano composite

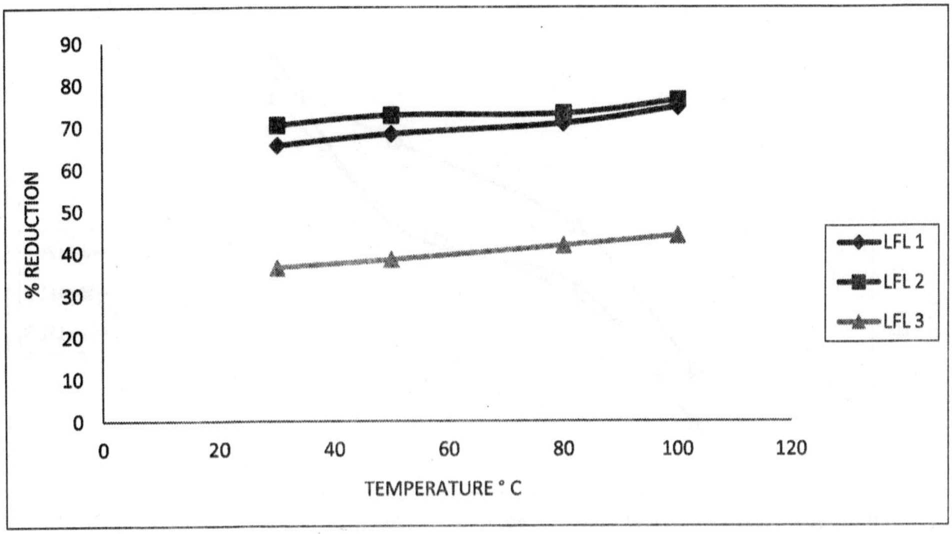

Fig. 7.11: Effect of Temperature on the reduction of COD using Kaolin

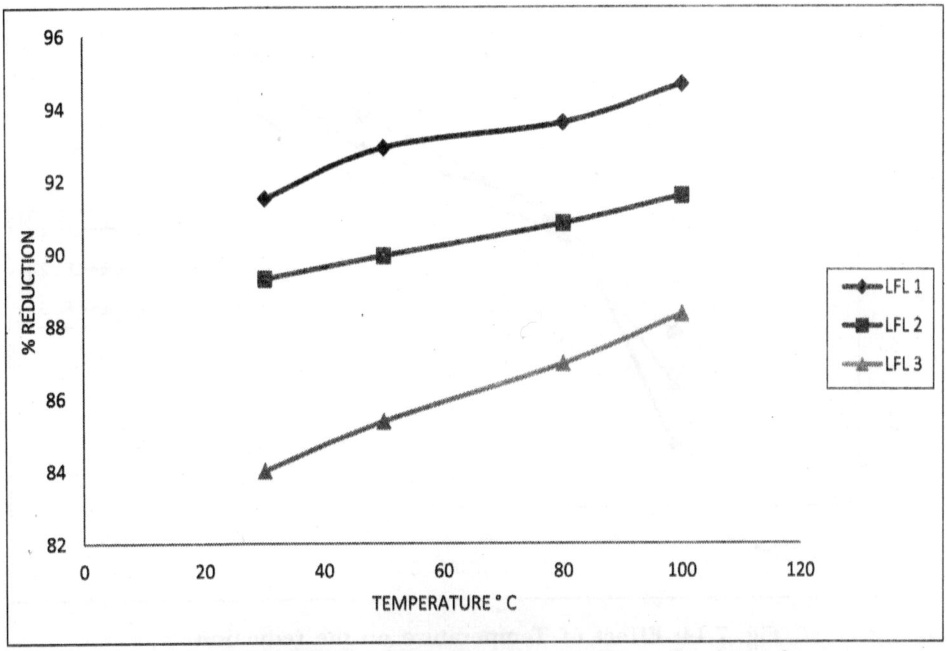

Fig. 7.12: Effect of Temperature on the reduction of COD using K_3[Fe $(C_2O_4)_3$]-Kaolin Nano composite

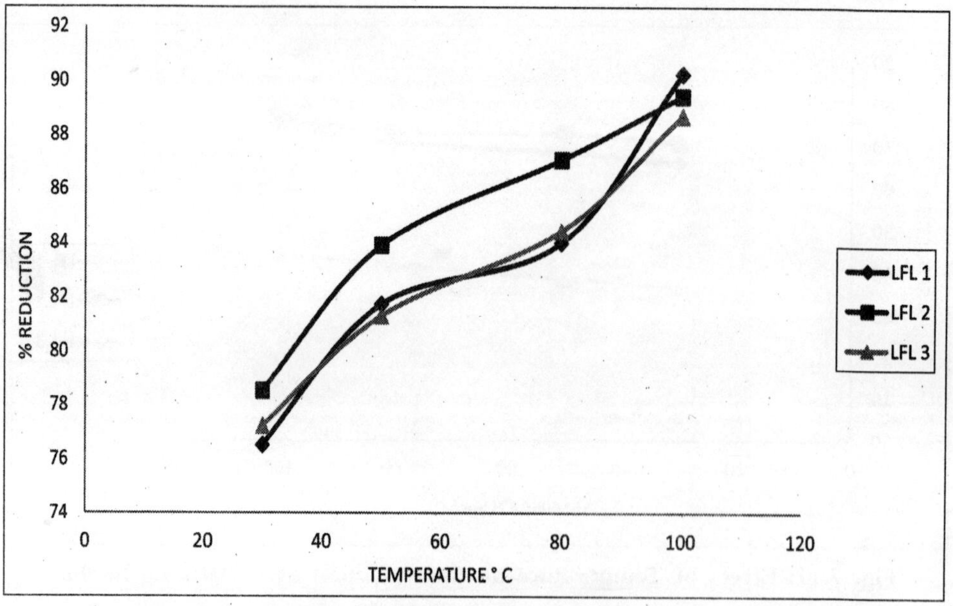

Fig. 7.13: Effect of Temperature on the reduction of Pb using kaolin

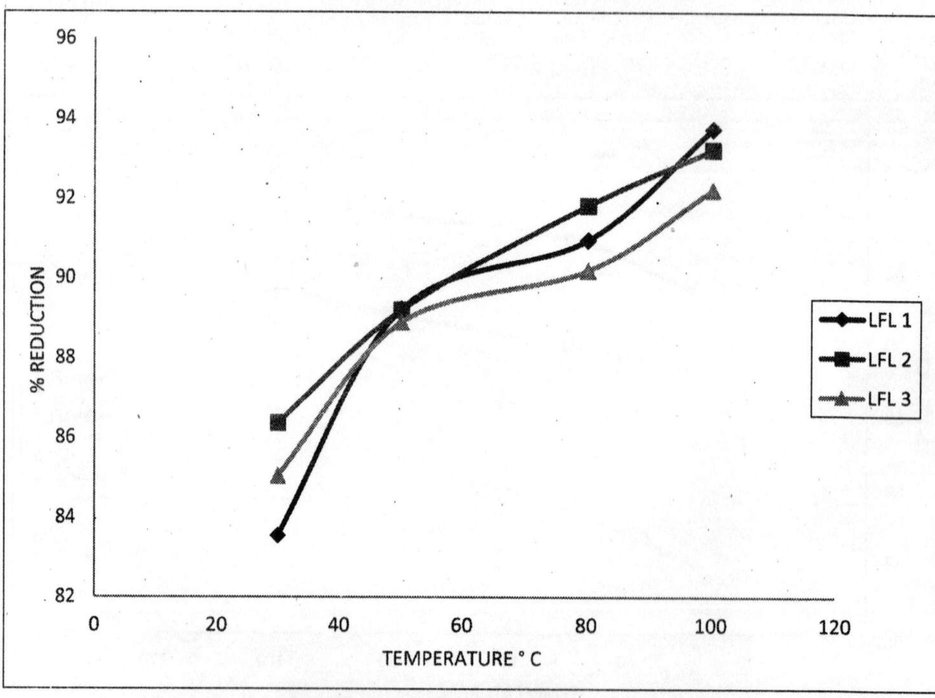

Fig. 7.14: Effect of Temperature on the reduction of Pb using$K_3[Fe(C_2O_4)_3]$-Kaolin Nano composite

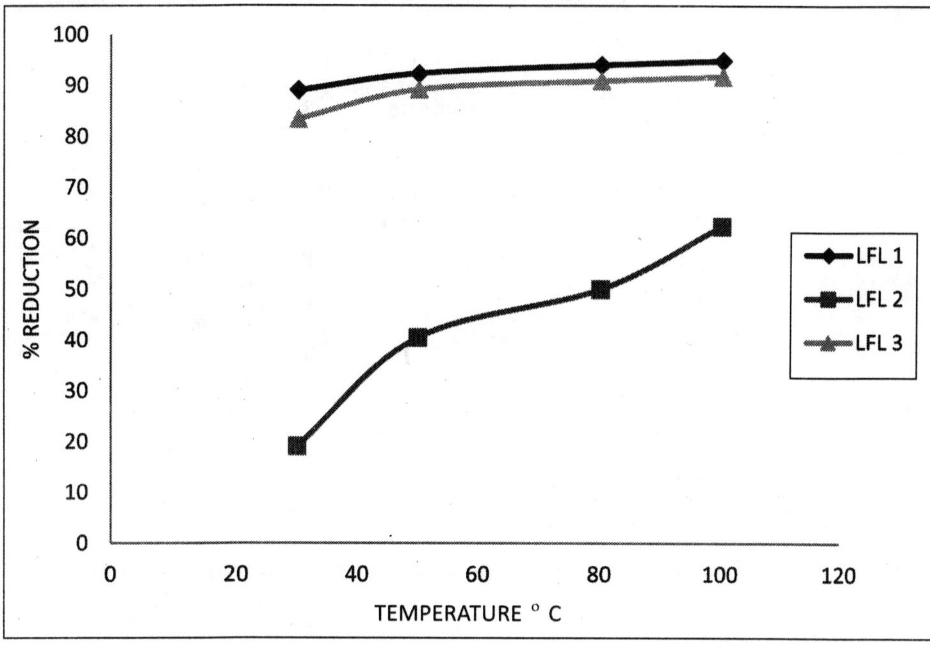

Fig. 7.15: Effect of Temperature on the reduction Cd using Kaolin

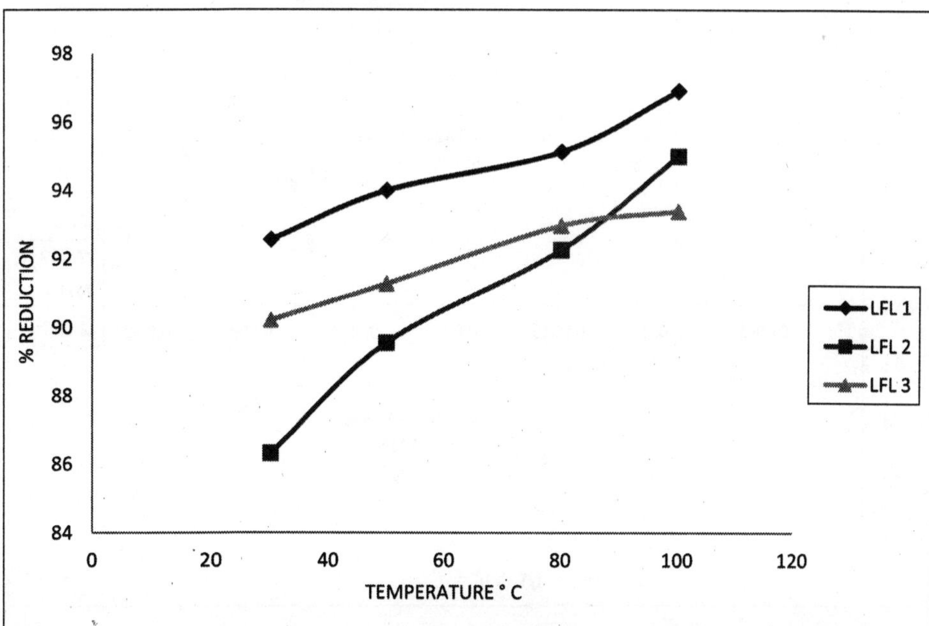

Fig. 7.16: Effect of Temperature on the reduction of Cd using K_3[Fe (C_2O_4)$_3$]-Kaolin Nano composite

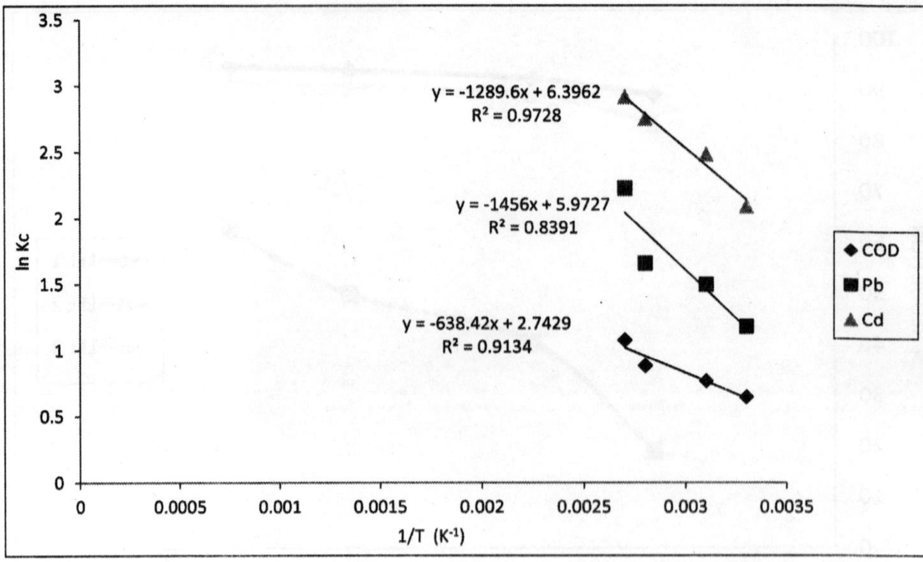

Fig. 7.17: Van't Hoff Plot on the reduction of COD, Pb, Cd from LFL 1

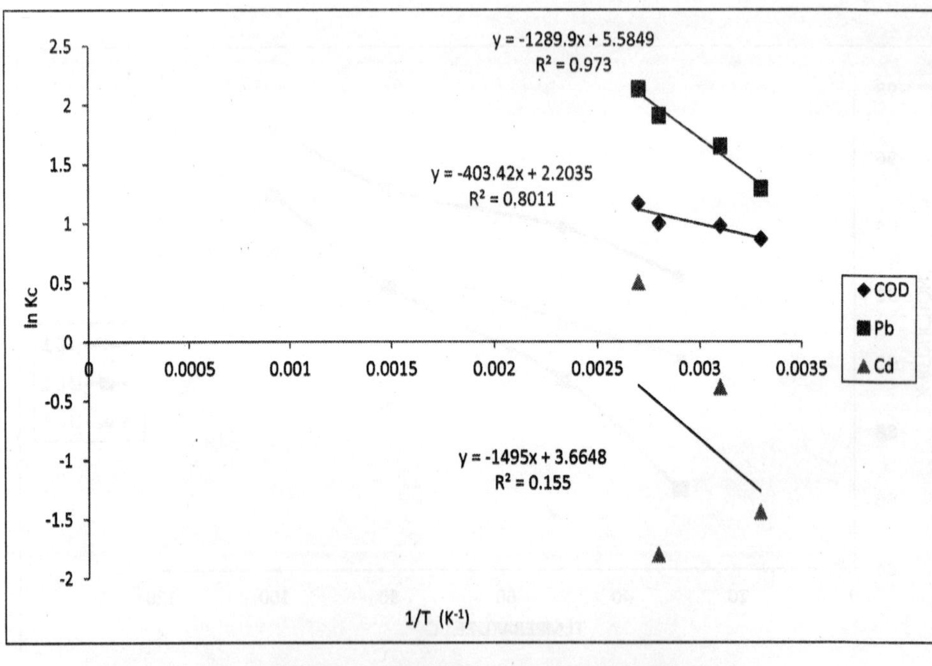

Fig. 7.18: Van't Hoff Plot on the reduction of COD, Pb, Cd from LFL 2 using Kaolin

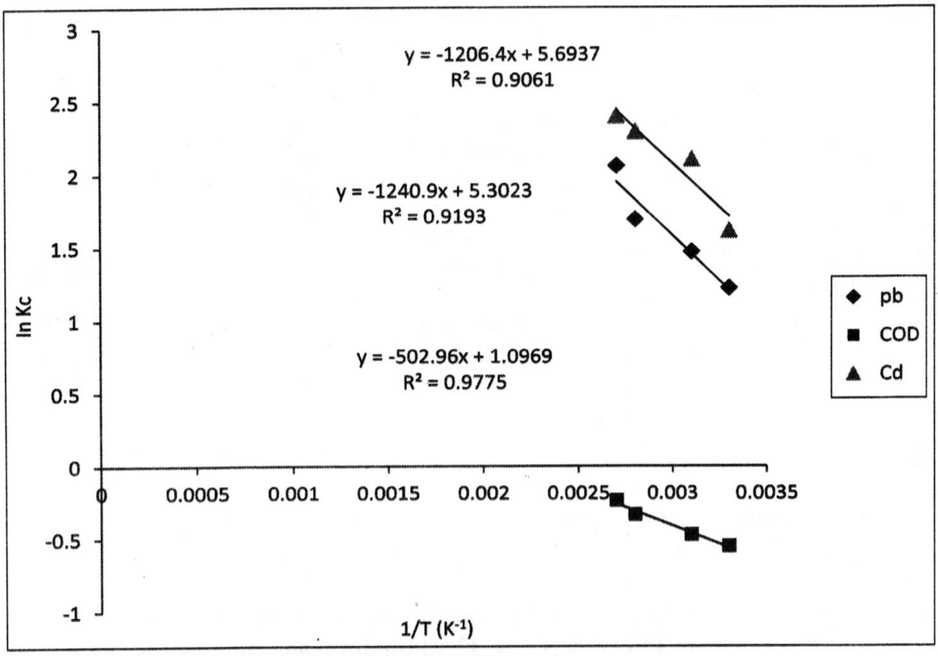

Fig. 7.19: Van't Hoff Plot on the reduction of COD, Pb, Cd from LFL 3 using Kaolin

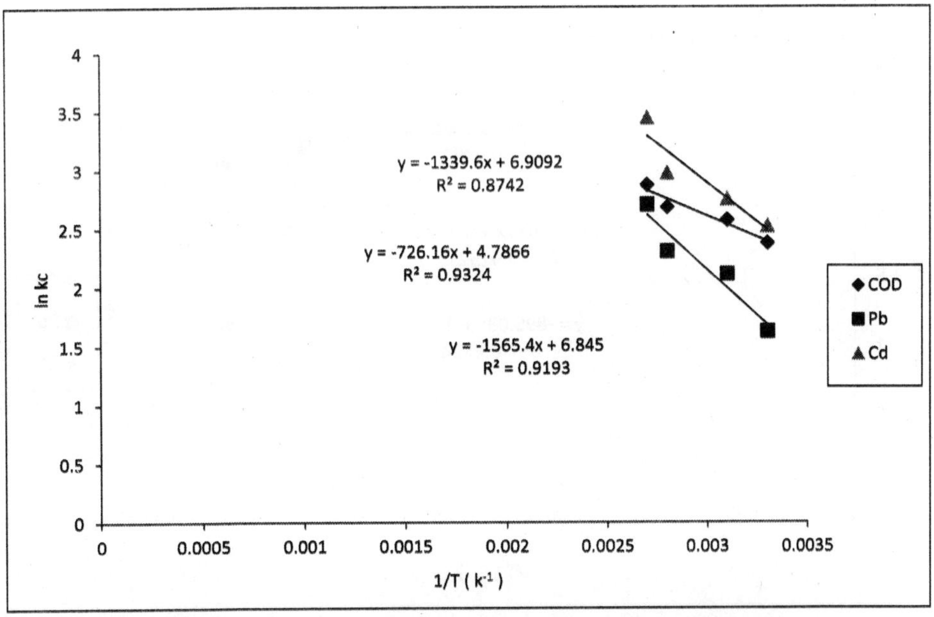

Fig. 7.20: Van't Hoff Plot on the reduction of COD, Pb, Cd from LFL 1 usingK_3[Fe $(C_2O_4)_3$]-Kaolin Nano composite

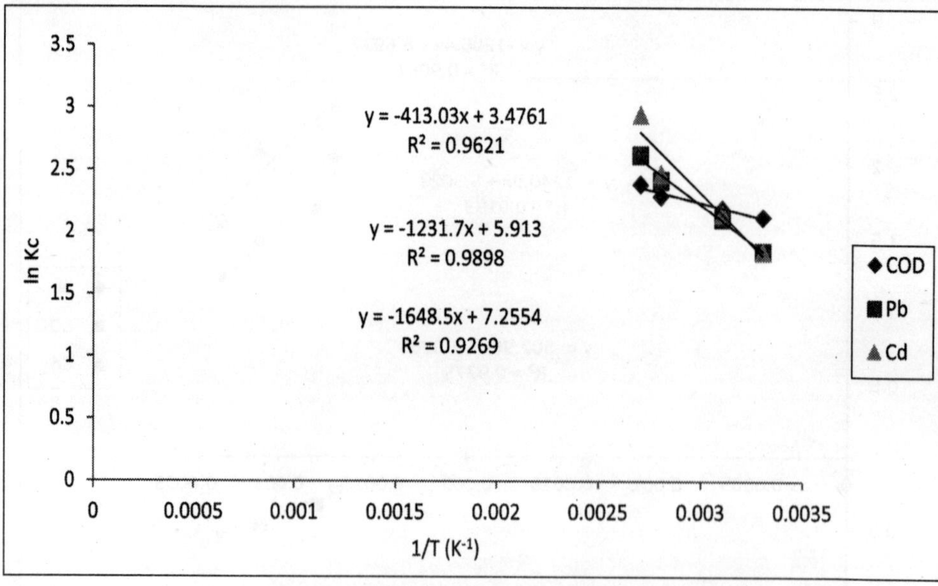

Fig. 7.21: Van't Hoff Plot on the reduction of COD, Pb, Cd from LFL 2 $K_3[Fe(C_2O_4)_3]$-Kaolin Nano composite

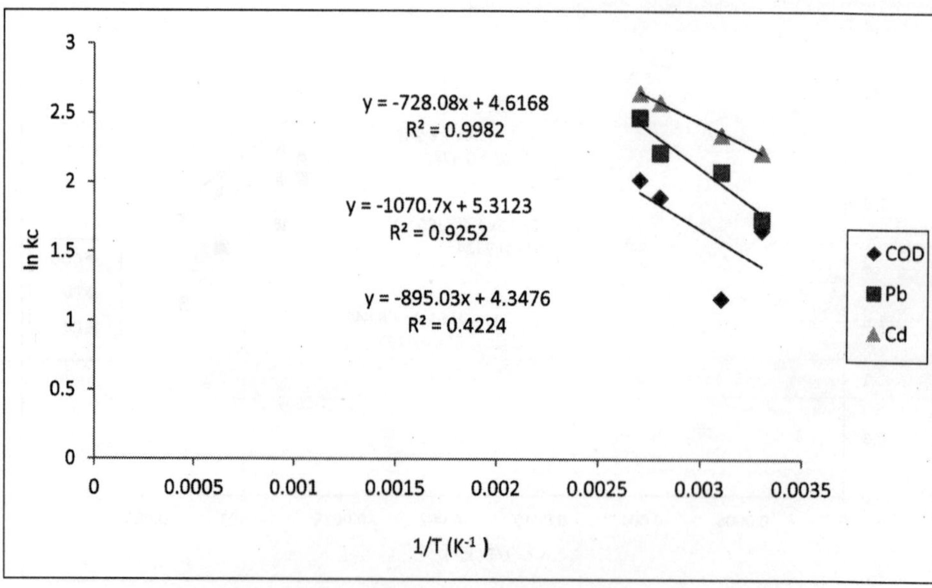

Fig. 7.22: Van't Hoff Plot on the reduction of COD, Pb, Cd from LFL 3 using $K_3[Fe(C_2O_4)_3]$-Kaolin Nano composite

Table 7.1: Thermodynamic parameters for LFL 1 on the reduction of COD, Pb,Cd using Kaolin

Parameters	ΔH°Kj/mol	ΔS°J/mol	ΔG°Kj/mol	R^2
COD	5.3078	22.8045	- 2.4001	0.9134
Pb	12.1052	49.6570	- 4.6789	0.8391
Cd	10.7217	53.1780	- 7.2525	0.9728

Table 7.2: Thermodynamic parameters for LFL 2 on the reduction of COD, Pb, Cd using Kaolin

Parameters	ΔH°KJ/mol	ΔS°J/mol	ΔG°KJ/mol	R^2
COD	3.3540	18.3199	- 2.8381	0.8011
Pb	10.7242	46.4329	- 4.9701	0.973
Cd	12.4294	30.4691	2.1308	0.155

Table 7.3: Thermodynamic parameters for LFL 3 on the reduction of COD, Pb, Cd using Kaolin

Parameters	ΔH°KJ/mol	ΔS°J/mol	ΔG°KJ/mol	R^2
COD	4.1816	9.1196	1.0992	0.9775
Pb	10.3168	44.0833	- 4.5834	0.9193
Cd	10.0300	47.3374	- 5.9700	0.9061

Table 7.4: Thermodynamic parameters for LFL 1 on the reduction of COD, Pb,CdK_3[Fe (C_2O_4)$_3$]-Kaolin Nano composite

Parameters	ΔH°KJ/mol	ΔS°J/mol	ΔG°KJ/mol	R^2
COD	6.0373	39.7958	- 7.4137	0.9324
Pb	13.0147	56.9093	- 6.2206	0.9193
Cd	11.1374	57.4431	- 8.2784	0.8742

Table 7.5: Thermodynamic parameters for LFL 2on the reduction of COD, Pb,Cd usingK_3[Fe (C_2O_4)$_3$]-Kaolin Nano composite

Parameters	ΔH°KJmol	ΔS°J/mol	ΔG°KJ/mol	R^2
COD	3.4339	28.9003	- 6.3344	0.9621
Pb	10.2404	49.1607	- 6.3759	0.9898
Cd	13.7056	60.3214	- 6.6830	0.9269

Table 7.6: Thermodynamic parameters for LFL 3 on the reduction of COD, Pb,Cd kaolin-ferrioxalatenanocomposite

Parameters	ΔH°KJ/mol	ΔS°J/mol	ΔG°KJ/mol	R^2
COD	7.4413	36.1459	- 4.7760	0.4224
Pb	8.9018	44.1665	- 6.0265	0.9252
Cd	6.0533	38.3841	- 6.9205	0.9982

DISCUSSION

Concentration of Charateristics of Landfill Leachate (LFL) Before Treatment

The various concentrations of characteristics of Landfill leachates in three landfills (LFL 1, LFL 2 and LFL 3) were shown in figure 7.2. The various characteristics determined in the landfill leachate samples were BOD_5, COD, DO, TDS,TSS, Ammonia - nitrogen compound (NH_3 - N), organic - nitrogen compound (organic - N) and heavy metals such as Cr, Pb, Cd. LFL 1 and LFL 3 were observed to have the highest quantities (concentrations) of these characteristics with BOD_5 value of 9460.00 mg/L for LFL 1, 11120.30 mg/L for LFL 3 and COD value of 15800.10 mg/L for LFL 1 and 16400.00 mg/L for LFL 3 respectively. while LFL 2 has low quantities (concentrations) of these characteristics with BOD_5 value of 5500.80 mg/L and COD value of 11000.40 mg/L as compared with that of LFL 1 and LFL 3 respectively. BOD_5, COD, TDS,TSS occurred most for the assessed three landfills than other parameters that were determined, with values of $BOD_5$and COD as seen above and TDS as 10670.00, 6800.00, 8540.30 mg/L for LFL 1,2,3 respectively while TSS as 10870.60, 870.60, 9706.90 mg/L for LFL 1,2,3 respectively.

Percentage Reduction of the Characteristics of Landfill Leachate Using Kaolin

The reductions of the various landfill leachate (LFL) characteristics using kaolin were shown in figure 7.3. In LFL 1, the reduction of Cd from the leachate sample was more pronounced compared to other parameters present in the leachate sample while Chromium was the least reduced. The order of the characteristics reduction of the parameters in the leachate samples for LFL 1 were Cd(88.69) >Pb(76.32) > COD(65.6) > NH_3 - N(46.7) > Cr(35.56). In LFL 2, Pb showed highest percentage reduction while Cd showed the least percentage reduced. Hence, the trend (order) of percentage reduction were; Pb(78.49) > Cr(70.63) > COD(70.4) > NH_3-N(41.3) > Cd(18.64). In LFL 3, Cd showed the highest percentage reduction, while NH_3 - N was the least reduced from the leachate sample. The order of reduction were given as Cd(83.4) >Pb(77.2) > Cr (69.48) > COD (67.4) > NH_3-N(59.3).This result demonstrated that kaolin could be employed and exploited for Cd,Pb and Cr adsorption thus reducing their various concentrations in leachate samples and also was efficient for organic and inorganic contaminants reduction in the leachate. The positive influence observed on this adsorbent (Kaolin) to reduce these contaminants from leachate could be related to the accessibility of vacant site on the surface of the adsorbent (kaolin). Thus kaolin would facilitate the reduction processes for these pollutants owing to its pore nature and its maximum surface area.

Percentage Reduction of the Characteristics of Landfill Leachate Using K_3[Fe ($C_2O_4)_3$]-Kaolin Nano composite

K_3[Fe ($C_2O_4)_3$]-Kaolin Nano composite was utilized for remediation of three different landfill leachates. The percentage reduction of each of the landfill characteristics was shown in figure 7.4. This result demonstrated that percentage reduction of each of the characteristics were above 78%. In LFL 1, Cd and NH_3 - N had greatest reduction of 92.4%, while chromium showed least reduction of about 81.0 % thus, the order of reduction for LFL 1 is Cd(92.4), NH_3 - N(92.4) > COD (91.5) > BOD_5(86.30) >Pb(83.5) > Cr(81.00). In LFL 2, NH_3 - N showed the highest reduction (93.6%), while Pb showed least reduction (86.3%), the order of reduction in percentage is; NH_3 - N (93.6) > BOD_5(91.00) >COD(89.3), Cr (89.3) > Cd(86.32) >Pb (86.30). In LFL 3, BOD_5 has the highest percentage reduction (98.3%), while chromium has the least percentage reduction (78.43%) their order of percentage reduction are BOD_5 (98.3) > NH_3-N (96.4) > Cd (90.19)>Pb (84.91) > COD (84.00) >Cr(78.43). However, K_3[Fe ($C_2O_4)_3$]-Kaolin Nano composite showed more effectiveness on the various landfill leachate characteristics reduction than unmodified kaolin as shown in figure 7.3 and 7.4. Thus Ferrioxalate in the presence of hydrogen peroxide is an effective oxidant with positive influence on contaminants reduction from landfill leachate samples. It could be inferred that adsorbent modification using Ferrioxalatein the presence of hydrogen peroxide demonstrated its proficient, prowess capabilities and could be a best method employed for landfill leachates remediation.

Effect of pH on the Reduction COD Using Kaolin

The influence observed on pH for COD reduction in three landfill leachates using kaolin is presented in figure 7.4. The result showed that the percentage reduction of COD increased from 46.64% to 72.52%, 39% to 80.27% then from 28.96% to 75.4% for LFL 1, LFL 2 and LFL 3 respectively the pH of leachate sample was increased from 3.5 to 9.5, further increased to 10.5, a minor influence was observed then at of pH 11.5 no significant difference was observed compared to pH of 10.5. This was a clear indication that the optimum pH for COD reduction from landfill leachate was 10.5. Thus, the percentage reduction of COD on the three leachate samples followed this order; LFL 1 > LFL 2 > LFL 3. The result portrayed that COD reduction was slightly favoured at low acidity rate (acidic medium) of the leachate sample but highly favoured at a slightly basic or alkaline condition. Hence assessment pH of the leachate sample was a paramount factor that must not be overlooked during landfill leachates remediationt. The result corresponded with that obtained by Shabiimam & Dikshit, 2012.

Effect of pH on COD Reduction Using$K_3[Fe(C_2O_4)_3]$-Kaolin Nano composite

The reduction of COD using $K_3[Fe(C_2O_4)_3]$-Kaolin Nano composite was higher than the reduction of COD using unmodified kaolin as shown in figure 7.6. From the result, the percentage reduction of COD increased from 66.16% to 94.25%, 72.78% to 93.51% and from 72.78% to 88.74% for LFL 1, LFL 2 and LFL 3 respectively as pH of the aliquot (leachate) sample was increased from 3.5 to 9.5. Increasing the pH further to 10.5 only showed a little difference on the reduction of COD. Hence, further increase of pH to 11.5 showed no difference with that of 10.5. This indicated that the optimum pH for COD reduction using $K_3[Fe(C_2O_4)_3]$-Kaolin Nano composite was 10.5. Hence, $K_3[Fe(C_2O_4)_3]$-Kaolin Nano composite showed better effectiveness on COD reduction from the leachate sample at a diminutive acidic condition (less preferable) and lower alkaline condition (more preferable). This result is in good agreement with result obtained by Shabiimam and Dikshit, 2012.

Effect of pH on Pb Reduction using Kaolin

The influence imparted by pH for Pb reduction using kaolin as adsorbent is presented in figure 7.6. The result showed that the percentage reduction of Pb increased from 18.26% to 91.65%, 22.1% to 92.5 % and 42.59 to 92.59% in LFL1, LFL 2 and LFL 3 respectively as the pH was increased from 3.5 to 10.5. At pH 11.5, the percentage reduction of Pb showed no difference compared to pH 10.5. This clearly indicates that the maximum and optimum pH preferred for the uptake of Pb using a suitable and a porous adsorbent (kaolin) is 10.5, which implies that the reduction of Pb from a leachate sample is highly and greatly favoured by an alkaline condition, imperceptibly and moderately favoured at a lower acidic condition but unremarkably favoured at a highly acidic condition. The order of Pbreduction in the three landfill leachate is given as LFL 2 > LFL 3 > LFL 1. Hence, kaolin is a suitable and an apt adsorbent that ought to be exploited in the treatment of leachate for heavy metal reduction due to its adsorptivity to clays or sediments at higher pH. The above statement has been proven by Stansley *et al.*, (1992). According to his study on mobility of heavy metals (Pb) in solution, he reviewed that Pb has lower or no mobility effect in solution at a pH close to neutral or alkalinity consequently, it is easily adsorbed by adsorbents in solution of such higher pH and are desorbed at a lower pH. Hence, at acidic conditions (low pH) the effectiveness of clays (kaolin) as adsorbents for Pb adsorption shows very little effect than at neutral or alkaline conditions as reported by Scrudata and Estes, (1975).

Effect of pH on Pb Reduction Using$K_3[Fe(C_2O_4)_3]$-Kaolin Nano composite

The effect of pH onPb reduction using $K_3[Fe(C_2O_4)_3]$-Kaolin Nano composite was presented in figure 7.8. The percentage reduction of Pb increased from 52.87% to 93.7%, 41.85% to 93.7% and from 28.7% to 96.43% for LFL 2, LFL 3 and LFL 1 respectively as the pH increased from 3.5 to 10.5. The maximum pH forPb adsorption from a landfill leachate sample using both unmodified adsorbent (kaolin) and K_3[Fe $(C_2O_4)_3$]-Kaolin Nano composite was 10.5. This showed that at alkaline medium the leachate sample showed greater heavy metal adsorption hence their reduction in leachate samples. However modified adsorbent showed higher effectiveness in Pb reduction from landfill leachate samples than unmodified adsorbent because the ferrioxalate in the presence of hydrogen peroxide helped to enhance, promote and provide better adsorption surface area of adsorbent and its porosity at higher pH as reported by Korte *et al.*, (1976).

Effect of pH on Cd Reduction Using Kaolin

The effect of pH on percentage reduction of Cd using kaolin is presented in figure 7.9. This shows that the reduction of Cd increases with increase in pH of the leachate sample. As the pH was increased from 3.5 to 10.5, the percentage reduction of Cd increased from 31.43% to 98.2%, 7.73% to 67.73% and from 47.66% to 95.53% for LFL 1, LFL 2 and LFL 3 respectively. The maximum percentage reduction was observed at pH of 10.5. Beyond pH of 10.5 there was not any significant increase in percentage reduction of Cd for LFL 2 and LFL 3, but that of LFL 1 apparently dropped from 98.2% to 92.2%. This demonstrated that Cd reduction from leachate samples depends highly and largely on its pH which was best achieved at pH of 10.5. This confirmed that kaolin was an apt and suitable adsorbent for Cd removal from landfill leachate. Hence effect of pH on Cd reduction was and reported by Balkaya & Cesur, (2008).

Effect of pH on Cd Reduction Using K_3[Fe $(C_2O_4)_3$]-Kaolin Nano Composite

The effect of pH on the reduction of Cd using kaolin impregnated with Ferrioxalate is presented in figure 7.10. From the result there is a visible increment in the percentage reduction of Cd as the pH increases. The percentage reduction increased from 40% to 99.14%, 36.36% to 95.91% and from 53.32% to 97.47% for LFL 1, LFL 2 and LFL 3 respectively as the pH increased from 3.5 to 10.5. Increasing the pH value to 11.5 showed no difference with that of pH of 10.5. This demonstrated that the maximum pH for Cd reduction in landfill leachate was 10.5. However, it could be inferred that K_3[Fe $(C_2O_4)_3$]-Kaolin Nano composite has greater efficiency in Cd reduction than unmodified Kaolin. Also Cd reduction from landfill leachate sample was pH dependent as studied by Balkaya and Cesur, 2008.

Effect of Temperature on COD Reduction Using Kaolin

The effect of temperature on COD reduction from Landfill leachate using kaolin is shown in figure 7.11. Increasing the temperature of the landfill leachate increases the percentage reduction of COD. As the temperatures was increased from 30° C - 100° C the percentage reduction of COD increased from 65.61 to 74.62, 70.40 to 76.27 and 36.54 to 44.08 for LFL 1, LFL 2 and LFL 3 respectively. The optimum temperature for the reduction of COD from landfill leachate samples occurred at 100° C. Hence, the descending order of percentage reduction in the three landfills are LFL 2 > LFL 1 > LFL 3. This showed that at elevated temperatures more COD are removed from leachate samples than at lower temperatures using kaolin adsorbent.

Effect of Temperature on COD Reduction Using$K_3[Fe(C_2O_4)_3]$-Kaolin Nano Composite

The effect of temperature on COD reduction using $K_3[Fe(C_2O_4)_3]$-Kaolin Nano composite is shown in figure 7.12. The result showed that COD reduction increases with increased temperature. The result showed that percentage reduction increased from 91.51 to 94.65, 89.3 to 91.58 and 84.0 to 88.31 in LFL 1, LFL 2 and LFL 3 respectively as the temperature increased from 30° C to 100° C. The highest percentage reduction for the three landfills occurred at 100° C which is the optimum temperature for COD removal from leachate in this research. The decreasing order of COD percentage reduction in the leachate samples is LFL 1 > LFL 2 > LFL 3. This result demonstrated that COD could be effectively reduced if not completely removed at a higher temperature (specifically at 100° C) than at lower temperatures for this study. However, there was a greater percentage reduction when kaolin impregnated with Ferrioxalate was used than using unmodified kaolin. This effectiveness was because the oxidant (Ferrioxalate) in the presences of hydrogen peroxide was able to breakdown the recalcitrant organic compounds into mineralization.

Effect of Temperature on the Reduction of Pb and Cd Using Kaolin

The effect of temperature on the percentage reduction of Pb and Cd using kaolin are shown in figures 7.14 and 7.15 respectively. The percentage reduction of Pb greatly increased as the leachate sample temperature from the three landfills was increased. The percentage reduction of Cd as shown in figure 7.15 increased greatly and apparently only in LFL 2 as the temperature was increased, while the percentage reduction of Cd in LFL 1 and LFL 3 showed a slight increase with increased of temperature. The percentage reduction of Pb in LFL 1, LFL 2 and LFL 3 increased from 76.52 to 90.26, 78.52 to 88.7 and from 77.22 to 88.7 respectively. While the percentage reduction of Cd in LFL 1, LFL 2 and LFL 3 increased from 89 to 94.86, 19.0 to 62.27 and 83.4 to 91.7 respectively. The results revealed that the heavy metals (Pb and Cd) reduction from landfill leachates using Kaolin adsorbent were favoured at higher temperatures. Hence, increasing the reaction temperature, made the adsorbent (kaolin) sorption capacity to be greatly enhanced thus giving rise to maximum reduction of heavy metals in landfill leachates. Thus the reduction rates of Cd supersede that of Pb, because the sorption capacity of Cd was greater than that of Pb in the leachate sample. This result was in good agreement with the result obtained by Saikia and Kojima, 2011.

Effect of Temperature on the Reduction of Pb and Cd UsingK_3[Fe (C_2O_4)$_3$]-Kaolin Nano Composite

The effect of temperature on the reduction of Pb and Cd are shown in figures 7.14 and 7.16. The results proved that Pb reduction increased from 83.54 % to 93.74%, 86.36 to 93.22% and from 85.04% to 92.22% for LFL 1, LFL 2 and LFL 3 respectively. While that of Cd increased from 92.57% to 96.91%, 86.32% to 95.0 and from 90.21% to 93.4% as the temperature increased from 30°C to 100° C for LFL 1, LFL 2 and LFL 3 respectively. These results connote that K_3[Fe (C_2O_4)$_3$]-Kaolin Nano composite has more efficiency in heavy metals reduction than unmodified kaolin (adsorbent) for the three (3) different landfills because the Ferrioxalate in the presence of hydrogen peroxide enhances the adsorption sites on adsorbent's surface. This result was in good agreement with result obtained by Saikia and Kojima, 2011.

Van't Hoff Plot for COD, Pb and Cd Reduction Using Kaolin

The Van't Hoff plots for COD, Pb and Cd reduction in LFL 1, LFL 2 and LFL 3 using kaolin are shown in figures 7.17 to 7.19. The various Van't Hoff parameters (ΔH, ΔS, ΔG and R^2) were calculated from the plots and were shown in tables 7.1, 7.2 and 7.3 respectively. The result showed that ΔH (change-in-enthalpy) for the three (3) landfill leachate samples were positive. This connotes that using kaolin for landfill leachate treatment gave an endothermic reaction because heat was absorbed into the environment as the reaction temperature was increased. The above statement was in line with Van't Hoff principle, which asserts that, during chemical reactions all equilibrium positions are shifted at elevated temperatures in favour of reactions involving heat absorption (Van't, 1898). The correlation coefficients (R^2) for COD, Pb and Cd reduction for the three landfill leachate samples obtained from Van't Hoff plots showed less proximity and high remoteness to unity (value of 1) this indicated that the reaction processes were temperature dependent hence, entropy of the reaction is temperature dependent too. The order of the degree of disorderliness is; COD >Pb> Cd. This denotes that the higher the values of ΔS the greater the degree of disorderliness for LFL 1 and LFL 3. Also the negative values of ΔG for LFL 1, LFL 3 and the positive values of ΔG for COD in LFL 3 and Cd seen in LFL 2 implied that the reaction processes were energicallyunfavoured, entropicallyfavoured and spontaneous at elevated temperatures. Hence, the more negative the values of ΔG°, the greater the values of K, implying that the reaction is thermodynamicallyfavoured. This result corresponds with result obtained by Walter and Geoffrey, 1992.

Van't Hoff Plot for COD, Pb and Cd Reduction Using $K_3[Fe (C_2O_4)_3]$-Kaolin Nano composite

The Van't Hoff plots for the reduction of COD, Pb and Cd from three landfill leachate samples using $K_3[Fe (C_2O_4)_3]$-Kaolin Nano composite were presented in figures 7.20, 7.21 and 7.22 respectively. The various Van't Hoff parameters (ΔH, ΔS, ΔG and R^2) were equally presented in tables 7.4, 7.5 and 7.6. The change in enthalpy (ΔH) value of the reaction processes were all positives which denoted that the reaction process was endothermic that is, heat was absorbed into the surrounding. The correlation factor, R^2 for the three leachate samples showed less proximity and high remoteness from unity just like that of kaolin which also confirmed that the reduction process of COD, Pb and Cd using $K_3[Fe (C_2O_4)_3]$-Kaolin Nano composite was temperature dependent reaction (Walter and Geoffrey, 1992). The change in entropy of the reaction (ΔS) is highly temperature dependent too because it is positive. The values of ΔG for the three landfill leachate samples were positives. This showed that the reaction processes were energically unfavoured, entropically favoured and spontaneous at elevated temperatures. This result corresponded with the result obtained by Walter & Geoffrey, 1992.

CONCLUSION

The inorganic (heavy metals) and organic pollutants (COD, NH_3 - N, BOD) were successfully reduced from the leachate solution at a reasonable amount using both kaolin (which is more economical) and $K_3[Fe (C_2O_4)_3]$-Kaolin Nano composite. $K_3[Fe (C_2O_4)_3]$-Kaolin Nano compositeshowed higher percentage reduction (> 78%) than unmodified kaolin. Ferrioxalate in the adsorbent (kaolin) improved the surface area of the kaolin and its adsorptivity power. Thus, the oxidant aided the surface modification of the adsorbent (kaolin) and improved its efficiency. The result demonstrated that elevating the pH and the temperature of the landfill leachate solution also influenced greatly an increase in the percentage reduction of the contaminants. Hence, this research has demonstrated that Kaolin (unmodified adsorbent) and $K_3[Fe (C_2O_4)_3]$-Kaolin Nano composite could be employed for effective reduction of organic and inorganic contaminants from landfill leachate.

REFERENCES

Ali, M.A.B., Rakib, M., Laborie, S., Viers, P. H. & Durand, G. (2004). Coupling of Bipolar Membrane Electrodialysis and Ammonia Stripping for Direct Treatment of Wastewater Containing Ammonium Nitrate. *Journal of Member Science*, 244, 89-96.

Badmus, B. S. & Olatinsu, O.B. (2009). Geophysical Evaluation and Chemical Analysis of Kaolin Clay Deposit of Lakiri Village, Southwestern Nigeria.*International Journal of Physical Sciences*, 4(10), 592-606.

Baig, S., Coulomb, I., Courant, P. & Liechti, P. (1999) Treatment of Landfill Leachates: Lapeyrouse and Satrod Case Studies.*Ozone Science and Engineering*, 21(1), 1-22.

Balkaya, N. & Cesur, H. (2008). Adsorption of Cadmium from Aqueous Solution by Phosphogypsum. *Journal of Chemical Engineering Elsevier*, 140(1-3), 247-254.

Korte, P.E., J. Skopp, W.H. Fuller, E.E. Niebla, and B.A. Aleshi. (1976). Trace Element Movement in Soils, Influence of Soil Physical and Chemical Properties. *Journal of Soil Science*. 22 (6): 350-359.

Lema, J.M., Mendez, R. & Blazquez, R. (1988). Characteristic of Landfill Leachates and Alternatives for their Treatment: A Review. *Water Air Soil Pollution*., 40: 223-250.

Meshram, S. Limaye, R., Ghodke, S., Nigam, S., Sonawane, S., & Chikate, R. (2011). Methodology of Adsorbent Modifications.*Chemical Engineering Journal*, 172: 1008-1015.

Onu, M.A., Joseph, O. Okafor, Abdusalami, S., Kovo & Yahaya, S. Mohammed (2015). Development of Optimum Conditions for Modification of Kpautagi Clay for Application in Peteroleum Refinery Waste Water Treatment. *Leonardo Electronic Journal of Practices and Technologies*, 27: 131-137.

Reinhart, D.R. & Townsend, T.G. (1998) Landfill Bioreactor Design and Operation. Ist Edition. Lewis Publisher, Boca Raton, Florida, pp. 189.

Saikia, N. & Kojima, T. (2011). Behaviours of $MeCl_2$(Me: Pb and Cd) during Thermal Treatment of Kaolin-lime Mixture. *African Journal of Environmental Science and Technology*. 5(10), 778-785.

Scrudata, R. J., and Estes. E. L. (1975). Clay-lead sorption Relations. *Environmental Geology*. 1: 167-170.

Shabiimam, M.A. & Dikshit, A.K. (2012). Treatment of Municipal Landfill Leachate by Oxidants.*American Journal of Environmental Engineering*, 2(2): 1-5.

Silva, A.C., Dezotti, M. & Santanna, G.L. (2003) Treatment and Detoxification of a Sanitary Landfill Leachate. *Chemosphere*, 55: 207-214.

Sonawane, G.H., Sandip, P.P., Villas, K.M & Vinod, S.S. (2017). Kinetics of Photocatalytic Degradation of Methylene Blue by ZnO - bentonite Composite. *Iranian Chemical Communication*, 5: 417-428.

Stansley, W., L. Widjeskog, & Roscoe, D.E. (1992). Lead and Mobility in Surface Water at Trap and Skeet Ranges. Bull. *Environmental Contaminants Toxicology*. 49: 640-647.

Van't Hoff, J.H. (1898). Lectures on Theorical and Physical Chemistry, *Edward Arnold, London*.

Walter, E.T. & Geoffrey, P.D. (1992). Effect of Temperature on the Creatine Kinase Equilibrium. *The Journal of Biological Chemistry*, 267(20): 14084-14093.

Pages: 158-184

Water and Waste Water: ***Issues and Management***
Edited by: **Dr. Pawan Kumar 'Bharti'**
ISBN: 978-93-88854-15-3
Edition: **2019**
Published by: **Discovery Publishing House Pvt. Ltd., New Delhi (India)**

8 Waste Management

Sabira Aalia Dkhar*
Muzamil Hassan

Waste are "substance or objects which are disposed of or are intended to be disposed of or are required to be disposed of by the provision of law".

Waste can also be defined as any unwanted or useless material

Any material unused and rejected as worthless or unwanted and "A useless or profile less activity using or expanding or consuming thoughtlessly or carefully".

Types of waste:

- Solid waste
- Chemical waste
- Commercial/business waste
- Bio-medical waste
- Bulky waste
- Liquid waste
- Gaseous waste
- Animal by-products
- Biodegradable waste
- e-waste

REFUSE

It is the solid waste

It consist of the following types

Street refuse - consists of leaves, straw, papers, animal dung and litter of all kinds

Department of Community Medicine, Government Medical College, Kashmir University, Srinagar - 190010 (Jammu and Kashmir) (India)

Market refuse - consists of putrid vegetable and animal matters.

Domestic refuse - consists of ash,

- *rubbish* (pieces of papers, clothes, wood, metal, glass, dust and dirt)
- *garbage* (waste matter arising from the preparation, cooking and consumption of food such as peeling of vegetables,waste food, rotten fruits and vegetables etc.)

Industrial refuse - consist of wide variety of toxic chemicals compounds

Stable litter - consist of mainly animal dung and left over animal feeds from animal stables.

EFFECTS OF SOLID WASTE

A. Health hazard:

- When not collected and allowed to accumulate they create unsanitary condition.
- Nuisance due to unsightly appearance and bad odour.
- Contamination of food and drinks through dust and flies.
- It decomposes and favourable fly breeding space.
- Attracts rodents and vermin.
- Radioactive waste can lead to harmful effects on human being.
- crops and water supply may get contaminated leading to epidemics.
- rodents living on these solid waste transmit disease like plague, salmonellosis, endemic typhus and others.

B. Environmental impact:

- Pollutes water and soil.
- Effect aquatic life
- Burning of solid waste leads to air pollution.
- Reduces the aesthetic value of soil.

WASTE MANAGEMENT CONCEPT

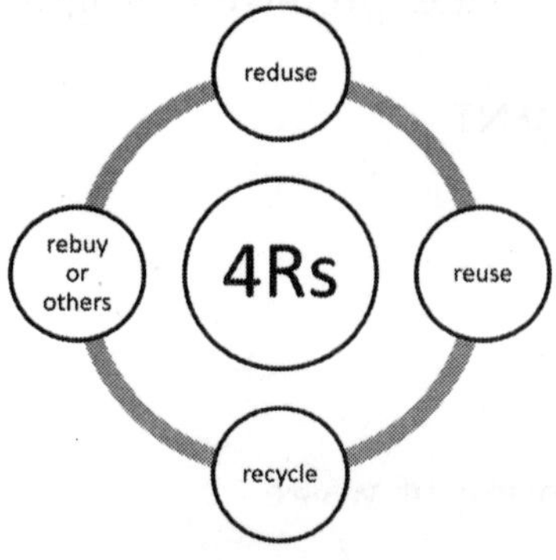

Fig. 8.1: Waste management concept

The 4Rs – reduce, reuse, recycle and rebuy/repair/recover/renewable (depending on type of solid waste) to be followed for waste management.

WASTE MANAGEMENT HIERARCHY

The waste hierarchy refers to the 3Rs "reduce, reuse and recycle "which classify waste management strategies according to their desirability in terms of waste minimization. The waste hierarchy remains the cornerstone of most minimization strategies.

The aim of the waste hierarchy is to extract the maximum practical benefits from by products and to generate the minimum amount of waste.

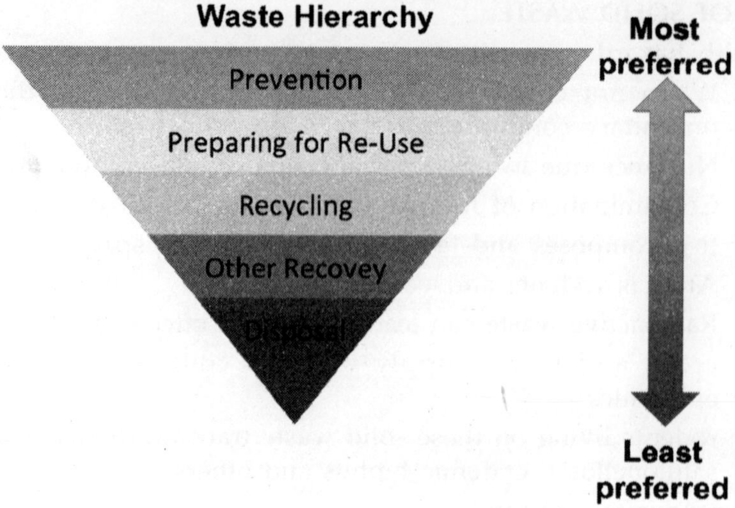

Fig. 8.2: Waste hierarchy

Importance:

- Waste hierarchy is a tool used in the evaluation of processes that protect the environment alongside resource and energy consumption to most favourable to least favourable actions.
- The hierarchy establishes preferred program priorities based on sustainability.

SOLID WASTE MANAGEMENT

It comprises of:

- Storage
- Collection
- Transport and handling
- Recycling
- Disposal and monitoring of waste

STORAGE

- *Galvanized steel dust bins* – with cover/lid people will not open but throw the refuse around.
- Without cover/lid - animals scatter the content thus creating nuisance
- *Paper sack* - developed countries, the dustbin have paper sacks when it is completely filled it is removed and is replaced by a new one
- *Public bins*

When storing hazardous waste and recyclables: the container should be in good condition and not leaking, not affected by weather, compatible with the waste they are storing, closed at all times and opened only while adding waste, clearly marked and labelled.

COLLECTION

- House to house collection-best method
- Open refuse carts
- Scavenging - collection and removal of domestic refuse apart from human excreta by means of manual labour.
- Wheel barrows - small hand pushed carts beneficial for houses around small lanes

All the collection should be done in the early morning hours to reduce nuisance.

Waste collection in India:

- Primarily by city municipalities: dump in city outskirts
- Local raddiwala/kabadiwala (rag pickers): collects bottles, iron, and other recyclable materials.

In case of medical waste it should be collected at point of generation in appropriate colour coded bags.

TRANSPORT AND HANDLING

Waste handling and separation involves activities associated with waste management until the waste is placed in storage containers for collection.

Handling also encompasses the movement of loaded containers to the point of collection. Waste is transferred from a smaller collection vehicle to larger transport equipment.

RECYCLING

Recycling refers to the collection and refuse of waste materials. The materials from which the items are made can be processed into new by-products.

Materials for recycling may be collected separately from general waste using dedicated bins.

Benefits of recycling:

- Reduce environmental degradation
- Generate money out of waste
- Save energy that would have gone into manufacturing and handling eg: making paper from waste saves around 50% of energy.

METHODS OF DISPOSAL

- Dumping
- Controlled tipping and sanitary landfills
- Incineration
- Composting
- Manure pits
- Burial

OBJECTIVES

- Public hygiene and health
- Reuse, recovery and recycle
- Energy generation
- Sustainable development
- Aesthetic

DUMPING

Dumping in low lying areas, mainly for dry refuses. Later the reclaimed land is given for cultivation Eg: – Kolkata disposes by this method. This method is unsanitary method as it is:

- Exposed to flies and rodents
- Nuisance
- Dispersed by wind
- Pollution of surface water

CONTROLLED TIPPING/SANITARY LANDFILL

Dumping and burial of refuse in a sanitary method so as to prevent the health hazard.

The site should be away from human habitation or outside city limits and source of water to prevent leaching. Differs from ordinary dumping in that the material is placed in a trench or other prepared area, adequately compacted, and covered with earth at the end of each working day.

Process of sanitary landfill: dumping followed by a layer of soil on top, thus reducing nuisance due to smell and odour and fly breeding.

'Modified sanitary landfill'- when compaction and covering with soil is done once or twice a week.

There are three methods of sanitary landfill:

- The trench method
- The ramp method
- The area method

The trench method: A trench is preferred in not low lying area. It is about 2-3 metres (6-10 feet) deep and 4-12 metres (12-36 feet) wide; the refused in the trench is later covered by soil. One acre of land per year will be required for 10000 populations.

The ramp method: preferred in terrain where it is sloping. Some excavation is done to secure the covering material.

The area method: here the land is not dug but land depressions like dried ponds, lakes, and clay pits are used for placing the refuse and covering it with soil. Such area is known as *'made up soil'*. The refuse is deposited, packed, and consolidated in uniform layers of 2-2.5 metres (6-8 feet) deep. This soil is suitable for gardening for construction purposes it is utilised after some years.

Once the refuse is buried the temperature starts rising after one week to about 60° C. In next 2-3 weeks, the temperature starts to cool down.

All the organic matter gets decomposed into harmless mass in about 4-6 months.

COMPOSTING

The refuse and the night soil (sewage) are disposed of together. There are two methods:

- Biological (Bangalore/anaerobic/hot fermentation process)
- Mechanical (Aerobic method)

BIOLOGICAL

Away from the city limits the trench is dug measuring 5-10 metres length, 2 metres wide and 1 metres depth.

Alternate layers of refuse and night soil are put in the trench in the thickness of 15cm and 5cm respectively. The first and the last layer comprises of refuse, finally covered by excavated soil marking the end of the trench.

By the end of 2-3 weeks decomposition due to high temperature takes place killing all the pathogens and parasite. The decomposed matter is acted upon by fungi and anaerobic bacteria,resulting in harmless, odourless, harmless humus mass, called *'Compost'* which has high manurial value. It is sold as organic manure.

MECHANICAL

This method is more in use in the developed countries. First the refuse is removed/cleared of salvageable material such as rags, bones, piece of metals, woods, glasses etc. and then powdered in a pulveriser to a size of particles less than 2 inches. It is then mixed with human night soil in a rotating machine and incubated for 4 to 6 weeks; the entire process of composting is completed by action of moisture, temperature, ph. and aerobic bacteria.

MANURE PITS

More preferred in rural areas and is simple and effective method and does not require collection and disposal of waste like in urban areas. In this method the individual household should have a 'manure pit' where daily domestic refuse (garbage, animal dung, leaves and straw) is dumped and later covered with soil.

When one pit is completely filled, other pit is made. After 4-6 months the compost is formed and is used as manure.

BURIAL

Made for small camps, where refuse alone is dumped and covered by soil. When one trench is filled other pit should be dug out. After 4-6 months the compost can be used for gardening.

A trench of 1.5 metres and 2 metres deep is excavated and at the end of each day the refuse is covered with 20-30 cm of earth. If the trench of is 1 metre in length for every 200 persons, it is filled within one week.

INCINERATION

Process of complete and control combustion, for burning solid waste. It leads to energy recovery and destruction of toxic wastes.

Mostly for hospital waste being dangerous is discarded with this method.

The incinerators consist of:

- A furnace/combustion chamber- lined with firebricks.
- A platform for tipping the refuse.
- Stoker to bring the refuse together for burning completely.
- A baffle plate to drive of all the fumes
- By burning the refuse is reduced to one-fourth of its original weight and the organic matter is transformed into harmless vapours-carbon dioxide and nitrogen. The residue left after combustion is a mass of hard material called *'clinker'* utilised for making roads as well as cement by powdering it and blending it with lime.

Advantages:

- Most feasible method for cities where daily considerable quantity of refuse is produced and sanitary landfill areas are not available.
- Mostly used sanitary method where the solid waste is burned.
- Waste to energy method
- Produce less carbon emission compared to fossil fuel plants

- Volume of solid waste reduced by 90%.
- The heat produces steam that can be used for electricity
- Hygienic method of disposal
- Suitable for hazardous material

Disadvantages:

- Ash production
- More expensive method compared to other
- Most of the incinerators do not have sufficient draught, hence give offensive smell creating nuisance. To reduce this temperature inside should be more than 1250° F, the chimney tall and the draught sufficient.

RECYCLING OF REFUSE

All reusable materials should be segregated from the refuse like plastic is sorted out and can be used in the manufacturing of plastic buckets, pots, mugs etc. paper used for paper production. Discarded tube lights used for manufacture of glassware. Animal excreta separated and used for biogas.

DISPOSAL OF EXCRETA

Hazards of improper excreta disposal

- Soil pollution
- Water pollution
- Contamination of foods
- Propagation of flies
- Endemicity of water borne and soil borne disease
- Nuisance by sight and smell

SANITATION BARRIER

Transmission of most of the water borne and soil borne disease can be reduced by preventing the contamination of soil, water, and food. This is achieved by a *'sanitation barrier'*. This involves construction and use of sanitary latrines, which prevents the access of the pathogens from *faeces (F)* through 6 F's such as:

- Fluid (water and milk)
- food, fruits and vegetables
- fomites (utensils)
- flies (vectors)
- fingers

To the mouth of the susceptible persons.

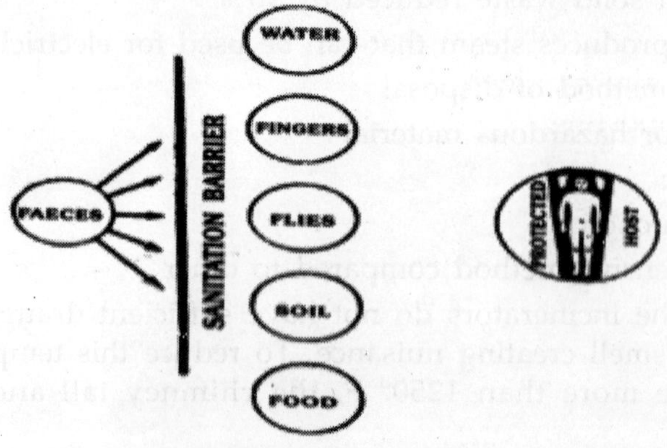

Fig. 8.3: Sanitary barrier

Sanitary latrines are supplemented by the following procedures like chlorination of water, pasteurization of milk, hand-washing, adoption of food hygiene practices, disinfection of fruits and vegetables, utensils, control of flies etc.

CRITERIA FOR SANITARY LATRINES

The following criteria should be met to be called sanitary latrines:

- Excreta should not contaminate the ground and surface water.
- Excreta should not pollute the soil.
- Excreta should not be accessible to lies, rodents, and animals.
- Excreta should not create a nuisance due to odour or unsightly appearance.
- It should be cheap, easy to construct and acceptable to the people.

METHODS OF DISPOSAL OF EXCRETA

The following types will depend on the sewage system/sewer line (underground sewage system)

A. Unsewered areas- disposal is in situ
  - Bore hole latrine
  - Dug well (pit) latrine
  - Waterseal latrine –PRAI type
    - RCA type
    - VIP latrines
    - Sulabh shauchalaya
  - Septic tank latrines
  - Aqua privy
  - Sanitary latrines for fairs, mela, camps etc.-shallow trench latrine
    - deep trench latrine

- pit latrines
- bore hole latrine
- Biogas plant

- Composting

B. Sewered areas- transported by water carriage system to the point of disposal.

'Service type' or the 'conservancy system'- the collection and removal of excreta from the bucket by a human, this was not consistent with human dignity and is no longer pardonable. Hence the Environmental Hygiene Committee (1949) had recommended that in unsewered areas the service system would be replaced by sanitary latrines where the excreta would be disposed of *in situ*.

'Direct type' latrine –the pit is directly below the squatting plate. Eg. Bore hole and dug well.

'Indirect type' latrine – the pit is away from the squatting plate. Eg. VIP latrine

BORE HOLE LATRINE (SOIL PIT DEEP LATRINE)

In 1930'S Rockefeller foundation introduced bore hole latrine with the aim to control hookworm infestation.

Dimensions: 30-40cm diameters, depth of 6 metres. Such bore hole serves for a family of 6 members for a year.

Lined by bamboo matting to prevent caving in of the soil. Squatting plate with a central opening and two foot rest. Superstructure for privacy was also put up. When the content reached a level of within 50cm of the ground level. The squatting plate and the foot rest removed and the pit is covered with soil and a new hole /pit is constructed. The night soil is converted into harmless humus by anaerobic digestion.

Advantages:

- Pit being dark is not suitable for fly breeding.
- 15 metres away from the source of water supply.
- More feasible in rural areas.
- Cheap to construct.
- Disposal in situ.

Disadvantages:

- Fills up rapidly because of small capacity.
- *'Auger'* may not be available readily.
- Difficult to construct if soil is loose.
- Now they have become out-dated due betterment in literacy level, living conditions, health consciousness and innovation of better latrines.

DUG WELL/PIT LATRINE

First made in *Singur, West Bengal (1949)*

Diameter: bigger than bore hole (75cm wide and 3 metres deep) serves for about 5 years for a family of 5 members.

Advantages:

- No *'auger'* required.
- Easy to construct.
- Larger than bore hole.

WATERSEAL TYPES OF LATRINE

The working of these latrines relies on the availability of water without water these latrines fail to operate. The water flushes out the excreta from the bowl, which consist of waterseal. Characteristic features of waterseal latrines-*'TRAP' i.e. bend pipe below the squatting plate; this allows some water holding thus providing 'waterseal'.* TRAP-Bent pipe of 7.5 diameters, the vertical portion being connected to lower part of the water closet and the bent portion being connected to connecting pipes. It is called trap. Traps certain amount of water –water seal. Depending upon the direction of the outlet outwards it is named as 'P- trap', "S-trap', 'Q-trap', 'Floor tap', 'intercepting trap', and 'gully trap'. A trap is self-cleaning with every flush of water. With no angles, corners, cracks or projections inside.

Caution:

- It should not be liable to 'silt' and it should have an opening for cleaning purpose s in the drainage system.
- The trap may fail to perform its function when there is evaporation of water seal.
- Being blocked with deposit of solid matter due to inefficient flushing.

Waterseal is the distance between the level of water in the trap and the lowest point on the concave upper part of the trap. It is about 2 cm.

Advantage:

- Waterseal prevents the access of flies.
- Prevents the escape of foul smell from drainage pipe into the house.

The types of waterseal latrines are:

- PRAI type- planning research and action institute, Lucknow (Uttar Pradesh)
- ICMR type- Indian Council of Medical Research.
- RCA type- research cum action project in environment sanitation, under the Ministry of Health, GOI.
- VIP type: indirect type as the pit is away from the squatting plate and the superstructure is permanent.

Characteristic of RCA type:

- Location: 15 metres away from a source of water supply.
- Squatting plate: impervious, cement and concrete material thus making it easy to wash and keep it clean.
- Dimensions of squatting plate: 90cm square, 5cm thick with a slope of ½ inch towards the pan, as to drain the ablution water or water used for cleaning purpose.
- Water closet (pan): smooth finish, sloping from front to back, fitted just below the squatting plate.
- Trap
- Connecting pipes: linking the trap and the pit by 7.5 cm diameter and 1 metre length.
- Dug well: pit of 75 cm diameter and 3 metres deep, lined by bamboo matting to prevent soil craving in. Direction of connecting pipe is changed to a new pit when the first gets filled.
- Superstructure: permanent and provides privacy plus shelter maintained for cleanliness.

VIP LATRINE

'Ventilated improved pit' latrine designed to overcome the disadvantages of the traditional pit latrines such as foul smell and breeding of flies.

Characteristics: tall vertical vent pipes fitted with a fly screen at the top for the following function

- Eliminates odour
- Prevents fly entry
- Prevents fly escape

PRAI TYPE LATRINES

Developed by the planning research and action institute, Lucknow, wherein the trap below the pan is *turned in* and opens directly into the pit. There is no lead off pipe (connecting pipe) because the pit is directly under the squatting plate

Advantage:

- Cheaper than RCA type
- It is a direct type of latrine
- Simple and sanitary

Disadvantage:

- Difficult to empty or clean the pit.

SULABH SHAUCHALAYA

First invented in Patna. Low cost, water-seal, eco- friendly, pour flush type of community latrine.

Well lighted and well ventilated, maintaining the privacy and cleanliness (through the nominal fee collected by uses).

'Sulabh International' is the investors of such community latrines.

SEPTIC TANK LATRINE

Sanitary waterseal latrines eligible for places with no sewerage system but having piped water supply.

Septic tank is underground, rectangular, cemented, having an inlet, outlet, cover and a vent pipe into which the household sewage is drained.

The tank with a capacity of 2000 litres for a family of about 5-6 members.3-4 times as long as it is broad. Depth of about 2 metres. Out of which about 1.2 metres should be liquid depth. Deepest at the inlet and sloping evenly at the outlet. The airspace above the waterline should be about 30cm.

Characteristics:

- It is covered by a concrete slab and provided with a manhole for cleaning.
- The vent should be covered with screen.
- The inlet and outlet having T fittings with the lower limb immersed in the sewage.
- More than one baffles walls to prevent straight current of sewage from inlet to outlet.
- The content is retained for at least 24 hours its anaerobic decomposition (digestion).
- Therefore, also called the *'Digestion chamber'* of sewage.

REQUIREMENTS TO INSTALL A SEPTIC TANK

- Abundant supply of water, to flush out the excreta.
- No disinfectant or detergent should be used as it can kill the putrefactive bacteria.
- Sufficient space, between the fluid levels and the cover to have space for scum and the gas.
- Ventilator pipe to let off the foul gas.
- *Desludging* - The sludge removed periodically.

Process:

First stage: Once the sewage enters the septic tank, the non-putrescible black semi solid particles settle down at the bottom of the tank- forms *sludge* while the grease, fat and light solid matter floats on the surface to form *scum*. The scum forms an air tight layer thus promoting the *anaerobic digestion*. The final by products of digestion complex protein converted into amines, amino acids, evoluting gasses like methane, carbon dioxide, carbon monoxide, hydrogen sulphide etc.

Second stage: the effluent (liquid from the outlet) contains numerous bacteria, cysts, organic matter. This effluent contains ammonia and gets converted into nitrates and nitrides in the soil (bacteria) by *aerobic digestion.*

Sludge is finally reduced in volume, stable and inoffensive

When the sludge gets filled up to certain level that it interferes with the functioning of the septic tank, then it must get emptied. The sludge and scum is removed by *trench method.* Cleaning is recommended once in 5 years when used by an individual family.

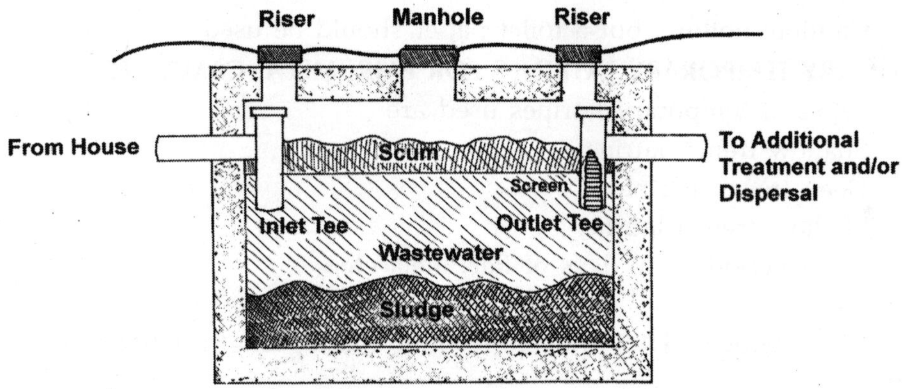

Fig. 8.4: Septic Tank

AQUA PRIVY (AQUA WATER/PRIVY –LATRINE)

It functions like a septic tank. It has a water tight chamber. Anaerobic biological method of disposing the sewage. Funnel shaped pan of the larine seat and a tank underneath filled with water. Drop pipe from latrine pan dips into the water. A vent for escape of foul gases and an outlet for the effluent.

Capacity: 1 cu. meter of aqua privy is recommended for a family of 5-6 members for about 5-6 years.

Process:

The sewage undergoes anaerobic decomposition. The effluent is disposed underground in a trench or soaking pit. The digested sludge is removed periodically from the tank and is disposed in trench.

Disadvantages:

- The scum is disturbed and the gases are released in to the superstructure.
- The scum is visible from the top.
- Insufficient detention time.
- Effluent may have some faecal matter.

CHEMICAL CLOSET

Suitable for isolated homes, boats, aircrafts, motor caravan. Metal tank with disinfectant (caustic soda and phenol and covered with a layer of crude oil), placed underneath the pan of the toilet.

Process:

When the excreta falls into this solution where the alkali disintegrates and dissolves the excreta, phenol kills the bacteria and the oil prevents odour. When the tank gets filled up the content are released into a sump hole

Caution: nothing but a toilet paper should be used.

SANITARY TEMPORARY LATRINES FOR FAIR, MELA, CAMP, ETC.

Two types of temporary latrines used are:

- Shallow trench latrine
- Deep trench latrine

Shallow trench latrine:

For a period of 10 days of fair, mela etc.

Dimensions:

30 cm wide and 1.5 m deep. About 3 metres length if 100 people will use it.

After using the latrine the excreta is covered with excavated soil which is kept on either side. The excreta get decomposed by the aerobic bacteria in the soil. When the trench is filled it is finally covered with soil and a new trench is constructed.

Deep trench latrine:

More suitable for army camps and semi-permanent camps which can last for a longer duration.

Dimensions:

2.5 m deep and 90cm wide and length suitable for about 10 seats with a superstructure. When the level of excreta reaches to about 1 meter below ground level, the trench is covered by soil. After 5-6 months the content can be dug out and the trench can be used again.

BIO-GAS PLANT

Bio-Gas is clean and efficient fuel. It is a mixture of methane, carbon dioxide, hydrogen, hydrogen sulphide. The chief constituent of bio gas is methane around 65%. Bio-gas plant also known as *'gobar gas plant'* in India.

Raw materials required: Here animal dung, human excreta and left over of animal feeds reused.

Construction:

Near the cattle shed, a well of about 3 meters is dug with variable diameter depending the size of livestock. A mixing schamber/digester near the well here blending of dung with water is done. Human urine, excreta and animal urine is also let off in the digester. The well is covered by a metal dome gas holder for holding the gas especial methane gas. The dome rises as the gas is formed, this gas is utilised for lighting and cooking practices. The sludge and scum serve as organic manure.

Advantages:

- Human and animal excreta can be disposed of simultaneously.
- Energy at low cost (economical)
- No smoke or residue produced
- Can be supplied through pipe lines
- Eco friendly (non-polluting)
- Clean fuel
- Organic manure produced.
- Community participation involved.
- Individual or community level installation.

SEWERAGE SYSTEM (WATER CARRIAGE SYSTEM)

'Sewage' means liquid waste containing human excreta, street washing and industrial liquid waste.

'Sullage' waste water of houses excluding human excreta.

Sewer system/sewerage system - liquid waste is carried away through a system of drains and underground pipes (sewers) through the agency of water to its final place of disposal.

Requirements:

- Abundant water supply.
- Good drains and sewers with proper ventilation.
- Proper means of disposal and utilisation of the sewerage.

  The *TWO* types of carriage system
- Combined sewer system: carries both the sewage and the surface water.
- Separate sewer system (more preferred): carries only the sewage.

Components of the water carriage system:

(a) House drainage

(b) Public sewer

(c) Sewer appurtenances

HOUSE DRAINAGE: consist of

(a) Water closet

(b) Soil pipes

(c) House drain

Water closet

Sanitary installation having connection of sewer through soil pipe and house drain, removes the excreta through the agency of water thus prevents nuisance of smell, flies or sight.

It consists of: closer proper (Indian and western) and flushing apparatus.

Closure Proper

Indian type: squatting plate below which is a pan with a trap, opening into the connecting pipe. Western type: bowl with a flushing rim near the surface and a trap below called commode.

Flushing Apparatus

This consist of small cistern or tank, placed about 1 meter above the basin, holding about 15 litres of water and works by siphonic action either by pulling a chain or pedal action and delivers the water pipe to flush out the excreta into connecting pipe keeping the pan clean.

Soil Pipes

These are the pipes laid vertically outside the wall, meant to carry the excreta from closet to house drain on one side and for the escape of foul gas on the other side covered with wire gauze dome. When several closet on different floors discharge into a common soil pipe, the transmission of excreta from upper closet down the soil pipe, the transmission of excreta from upper closet down the soil pipe may cause unsealing of the traps of the lower closet by siphon action. To prevent this, anti-siphonic action is ensured by means of another pipe, fixed on the crown of the trap and carried through the walls and laid on the side of the soil pipe. The soil pipes open directly into the house drain without any intervention of a trap.

House Drain

Underground pipe for draining the discharges from the soil pipe also the waste water from the house or compound to the sewer. Laid on a bed of concrete with a sufficient gradient. If a bend is required then specially designed pipes at acute angle is used with an inspection chamber. It is believes that smaller drains have better flushing.

Requirements:

- Sufficient inclination for good velocity of the flow.
- Water and air tight.
- Flushing arrangement should be proper.
- All branches from main drain should have 'Y' joint to obtain an acute angle.
- Should be laid on a bed of concrete.

GULLY TRAP

Placed in courtyard where rain water and waste water pipes open. About 30 cm away from the wall and the surface opening is protected by a grating. Provision for particles like mud, debris, and other particle to settle at the bottom of the gully trap.

PUBLIC SEWER

Big underground pipes, laid in concrete bed meant for draining of sewage from several houses and other liquid waste of the community. *'Self- cleaning'* velocity due to sufficient gradient to carry for ultimate place of disposal.

SEWER APPURTENANCES

Consist of:

Inspection chamber and intercepting trap.

Inspection chamber (manholes): masonry underground chamber lined with cement as to make water tight and covered with air tight iron lid. Entry inside for inspection, repair and cleaning activities but with precaution for their safety to prevent the risk of gas poisoning and asphyxiation.

Site:

- Where the direction of the sewer is changed.
- Where two or more sewers meet.
- Long straight runs at a distance 100 meters.

Intercepting/disconnecting trap: interposed between the house drain and the sewer designed to remove sand, grit and grease from sewage.

DISPOSAL OF SULLAGE

Sullage: waste water coming from kitchen and bathroom.

Disposed by:

- soaking pit/pervious pits/seepage pit
- non soaking/impervious pit such as septic tank
- surface irrigation such as kitchen garden
- Underground drainage/sewerage system

Soakage Pit

Simplest and the cheapest method of disposal of sullage water, on small scales.

For one single house: 1 and half cubic meter of rectangular shape is dugged, filled from bottom to top with large stones and gravels. Bricks line the pit while keeping the joints open for absorption. Gunny cloth covers the top most layers of sand and gravel to prevent it slipping into the trench and blocking it.

Grease trap: Soiled pot (matka/kerosene tin) filled with straw/hay/grass helps in removing the grease, oil, detergents and solid waste to provide proper functioning of soakage pit.

Periodicity: the grass filled in grease trap needs to be replaced periodically once in 10-15 days.

Requirement: not needed in hot places as the high temperature prevents the solidification of the grease. However, a small grit chamber may be needed between the outlets from the house to the soakage pit.

The connection: house drain leading to a T-shaped pipe connection to the grease trap and then to the soakage pit through the submerged pipes where biological degradation by the aerobic bacteria in the pit, ultimately converting it into harmless inorganic substance. The water further percolates into the ground.

When the pit get sullage sick that is when its pores get clogged, it is dugged up and exposed to air and sun and filled again with fresh stones and gravel. Meanwhile, another pit is constructed by the side and the two pits are made to work alternatively.

DISPOSAL OF SEWAGE

Objectives:

- Prevent water contamination
- Prevent soil pollution
- Protect aquatic life
- Protect food which are eaten raw
- Protect livestock
- Prevent nuisance by smell and site

Nitrates, phosphates, vitamins B12, methane gas for lighting and cooking purposes, grease etc. are the valuable by products obtained from sewage treatment.

Aim:

- To convert or stabilise the organic compound/matter by bacterial action.
- To utilise the harmless by products without any risk to human health.
- To produce effluent this is safe for disposal into land, river or sea.

The quality of the finished by products of sewage treatment is expressed in terms of:

(a) BOD- biological oxygen demand

(b) COD- chemical oxygen demand

(c) Suspended solids

BOD- biological Oxygen Demand

Is the amount of dissolved oxygen needed (i.e. demanded) by aerobic biological organisms to break down organic material present in a given water sample at certain temperature over a specific time period. The BOD value is most commonly expressed in milligrams of oxygen consumed per litre of sample during 5 days of incubation at 20° C and is often used as a surrogate of the degree of organic pollution of water.

Expressed: as mgms/liter of Sewage (i.e. ppm)

Eg. If BOD is 100ppm the sewage is said to be 'weak' and if it300 ppm, the sewage is said to be 'strong. After complete treatment of sewage, the BOD is reduced to nearly 90%.

COD- chemical Oxygen Demand

Is an indicative measure of the amount of oxygen that can be consumed by reactions in a measured solution. It is commonly expressed in mass of oxygen consumed over volume of solution which in SI units is milligrams per litre (mg/L).

A COD test can be used to easily quantify the amount of organics in water.

The most common application of COD is in quantifying the amount of oxidizable pollutants found in surface water (e.g. lakes and rivers) or wastewater.

COD is useful in terms of water quality by providing a metric to determine the effect an effluent will have on the receiving body, much like biochemical oxygen demand (BOD).

NOTE: BOD is similar in function to chemical oxygen demand (COD), in that both measure the amount of organic compounds in water. However, COD is less specific, since it measures everything that can be chemically oxidized, rather than just levels of biodegradable organic matter.

SUSPENDED SOLIDS

If the amount of suspended solids is 100ppm, the sewage is said to be 'weak' and if more than 500 ppm, the sewage is said to be strong.

After treatment of the sewage, it should become weak with reference of BOD and suspended solids.

TREATMENT OF SEWAGE

The treatment is done in two stages: primary and secondary

PRIMARY TREATMENT

In Primary/preliminary treatment, the suspended matters like the floating objects, settle able organic matter and inorganic particles are all removed by employing simple physical methods- screening, grit chamber and primary sedimentation (i.e. anaerobic digestion).

(a) *Screening:* the sewage is allowed to pass through metal screen to hold back the floating objects. Screen may be coarse or fine. Coarse screen consists of metallic bars placed vertically or inclined, set 5 cm apart. The fine screens have meshes. Screening removes leaves, pieces of wood rags, vegetables garbage, waste paper, polythene bags. Dead animals and various other floating objects. The screenings are removed periodically and disposed of by burning or by burial. If not removed, they clog the treatment plant.

(b) *Grit removal:* grit consists sand, gravel, ash, clay etc.
These are removed by allowing the sewage to pass through a 15-20m long, narrow chamber, called Grit chamber or Detritus chamber (after passing through the screens). Where the sewage passes at a velocity of 0.3m per second. This is just sufficient to permit the grit to settle down and the organic matter to pass over. The grit is removed periodically and disposed of by dumping or trenching.

(c) *Primary sedimentation:* after clearing the sewage from the floating objects and gritty matter, it is subjected to sedimentation in a tank for the removal of settle able suspended matter. The rectangular sedimentation tanks provide horizontal flow and circular tanks radial flow, where the sewage is detained for about 6 hours. All the suspended organic matter settles as sludge. The sludge of the primary sedimentation tank is highly organic and offensive. It is removed periodically to control nuisance and to prevent interference in the sedimentation process (i.e. Desludging). Such sludge should not be disposed of directly but transferred to sludge digestion tank for appropriate treatment.

SECONDARY TREATMENT

The effluent is subjected to bacterial action for stabilization (i.e. aerobic oxidation).

Here the final or complete treatment is done by biological action / treatment followed by secondary sedimentation and sludge digestion. Necessary for stabilisation of unsettle able organic matter.

This biological treatment consists of two types:

- Biofiltration
- Bioaeration

Biofiltration

After primary treatment to effluent from the tank is allowed to 'filter' through a medium supporting the aerobic bacteria that carry out the biological treatment.

Three methods for biological treatment:

- Trickling filters

- Intermittent contact beds
- Intermittent sand filters

Trickling filters: these are also called *'percolating filters'* or *'sprinkling filters'* or *'streaming filters'*.

The filters consist of water tight, concrete, enclosure tank, circular in shape, of about 25 meters diameter and 2.5 meters depth, filled with a filter medium consisting of piece of 2 to 10 cm of coarse materials like stones, coke, clinker (hard brick) or cinder (burned coal) etc. arranged loosely to provide oxygen to the aerobic bacteria resting on them. Such a tank is provided with a sewage sprinkling system, which consist of a pipe carried above the tank and fitted with rotatory arms, usually four in number, each arm having a series of spray nozzles, wherefrom the sewage trickles down on the filter medium. This ensures uniform distribution with alternate dosing and resting periods. The sprinkling system is operated by a motor.

As the sewage/effluent passes through the filter, a sling jelly like film called *'zoogleal layer'* is formed over the filtering medium, which will absorb the organic matter and oxidize it with the help of aerobic bacteria. This jelly like layer consists of living flora like algae, protozoa, planktons, diatoms, fungi, aerobic bacteria etc. As the organic matters are oxidized, nitrification takes place. The intermittent application of sewage permits good circulation of air through the bed during the rest period, thus encouraging the growth of aerobic organisms. The oxidized sewage which leaves the trickling filter is passed on to secondary sedimentation tank for further treatment.

These filters can be left as such and need no attention. It is efficient, cheap and requires less space.

Intermittent contact beds:

Watertight containers (rectangular shaped) masonry tanks, filled with granular materials like gravel, crushed stones, brick, etc. up to a depth of about 2 meters.

Drainage pipe is placed at the bottom of the bed, drains the effluent from the septic tank is distributed over the bed and allowed to remain for a fixed period of about 6 hours. During this time the aerobic bacteria convert the nitrogenous matter into nitrates.

A working period of 6 hours is interrupted by a rest period of another 6 hours. This makes the filter bed is loaded twice daily with sewage. During the rest period, the bed is emptied, air comes in and the bed is reaerated done within half an hour.

For intermittent use of beds without causing interruption in the process of sewage treatment a series of contact bed is required.

Disadvantages:

- The effluent from this process is not as good as that from the trickling filters because it contains considerable suspended solids.
- Operator and other such persons are required for proper functioning.

Intermittent sand filter:

Sand bed supported by soil embankments and an under drainage system is also used for the purpose. Intermittently spreading the sewage on the surface of the sand bed by distribution pipes lying inside the soil embarkment. Two loading of sewage, of about 10 cm thickness, are permitted in a 24 hour cycle with intervening rest period, during which the sewage is fed to other beds. As it passes through the sand-bed, there will be nitrification of the sewage by the aerobic bacteria. The effluent is now fit to be discharged into a natural water course. The beds become clogged after several months of use indicating the scrapping off the deposit accumulated over the sand bed and the sand is loosened by racking. The bed becomes fit for use again.

BIOAERATION

Also known as 'ACTIVATED SLUDGE PROCESS'. This is a modern and satisfactory method of purifying the sewage, better than trickling filter method.

The plant has two chambers:

- Blending chamber: sewage coming from preliminary treatment is mixed with 'activated/return sludge' obtained from the secondary sedimentation tank. The ratio is 70:30(%) which leads into the next chamber.
- Aeration chamber: compressed air aeration for a period of 6 hours, from the bottom of the tank. This is continued till all the ammonia of the sewage is oxidised into nitrates, now the aeration is stopped and allowed to settle, called as 'activated/ aerated sludge'. Now this sludge is inoffensive and is an aerobic 'bacterial culture' which is not employed in activated sludge process but also has a high manurial value which makes it different from the sludge of primary sedimentation.

The purification is done in two stages:

1. First stage: organic compounds are broken down and carbon is converted into carbon dioxide and the effluent becomes more or less stable.
2. Second stage: nitrates are formed.

Advantages:

- The effluent now oxidised, clear and free from colloids.
- Rapid method

- Free from smell and flies
- Inoffensive and high manurial value of sludge
- Small area of land required
- Skilled attendant to manage the work

SECONDARY SEDIMENTATION

Once the effluent from the aeration chamber is out it is treated in the secondary sedimentation tank by detaining for about three hours.

The sludge at the bottom of this sedimentation tank is inoffensive. Desludging of the tank is done to avoid any interference with the functioning the tank. When this sludge is dried it becomes very good manure. Part of it is pumped back into the aeration tank for the aerated sludge process, while the rest is let into the sludge digestion tanks for further treatment and disposal (i.e. anaerobic decomposition)

The effluent which is out of the sedimentation tank is stable and shows no putrefactive changes even on long storage.

Its BOD is reduced to minimum and is chlorinated and let into water bodies.

Since most of the rivers are used for drinking purposes, the BOD of the effluent released should be lesser than 30ppm and 5 day BOD should be less than 20ppm, according to royal commission of England.

SLUDGE DIGESTION

The sludge from primary and secondary sedimentation consists of 95 per cent water, thick, black mass with a bad odour which can be a nuisance. This needs further treatment to make it harmless with the help of anaerobic bacteria.

Description of the digester

This digestion is carried out in a concrete tank with a leak proof cover. There is a heating arrangement (hot water circulating coil) and a blending arrangement (propeller pump), gas collecting – floating cover with a central gas dome and a disposal arrangement in the form of liquor and sludge outlets.

The sludge in this tank is incubated at a certain temperature and pH. The sludge undergoes liquefaction (anaerobic auto digestion) and water is removed from it.

The solid product is digested sludge used as fertiliser when dried.

The liquid product is known tank liquor which is removed at various level of the tank via liquor outlets. It is returned to the sludge treatment plant ahead of the primary sedimentation tank.

The gaseous by products:

- 65% methane-which is used for heating and lighting purposes.

- 30% carbon dioxide
- 5% others gases.

The effluent can be used for irrigation purpose.

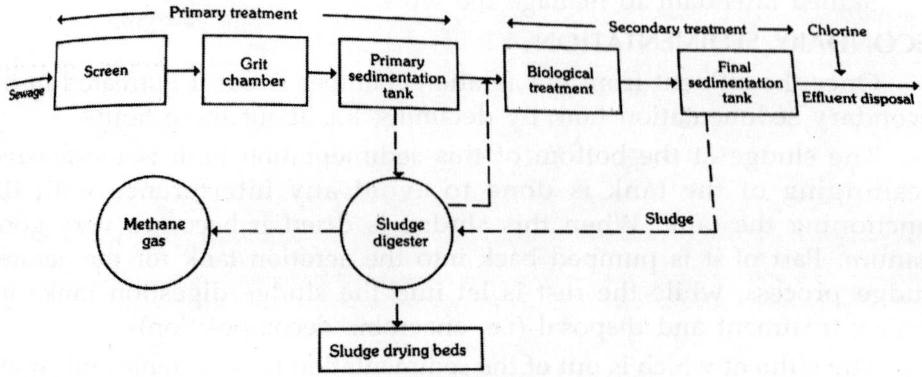

Fig. 8.5: Sewage treatment process

OTHER METHODS OF SEWAGE DISPOSAL

- Sewage dilution
- Sewage lagoon
- Sewage farming

SEWAGE DILUTION

Discharging the sewage into large water bodies such as river (river outfall) or sea (sea outfall).

This is an age old practice still prevalent in many cities located on the bank of large rivers and sea shores this helps in natural purification.

River outfall is hygienically not safe especially discharging the industrial waste.

Sea outfall is good because large water bodies help in dilution and solid oxidization.

Disadvantages:

- Is that the offensive solid matter can be washed back to the shore and create nuisance.
- Affect the aquatic life

To overcome this, the sea outfall is designed to discharge the sewage into deep water at many points.

SEWAGE LAGOON

Also known as *'Oxidation pond or Waste stabilisation pond or Redox pond'*, lagoon which is also called for pond is where the sewage organic matter are oxidised into inorganic substance including carbon dioxide, ammonia, and water and thus the sewage is purified.

The oxidation pond is a shallow pool of about 20 acres area, constructed in open areas, about 1.5 meter deep, having an inlet in the middle of the pond to allow the wind and wave action for the uniform blending and distribution of the sewage and an outlet for the effluent. Better if the sewage is subjected for screening and grit removal and let into lagoons.

Complete inter-independent mechanism involving algae, aerobic bacteria, oxygen and sunlight stabilize the sewage. The name 'Oxidation pond' is due to aerobic bacteria feed on decay organic matter, oxidizing it and converting it into carbon dioxide, ammonia and water.

Photosynthesis is carried out with the help of algae and sunlight, by utilising carbon dioxide, water and inorganic matter and give out oxygen, thus oxygen liberated by photosynthesis and some from the atmosphere is used up by the aerobic bacteria for oxidation.

Sunlight provides the necessary energy required by algae to thrive by carrying out photosynthesis. Therefore, sunlight is an important factor for proper functioning of the oxidation pond. Cloudy weather lowers the efficiency of the process of oxidation pond. The effluent from pond may be let into the land for irrigation purpose or into a water course after treatment.

The lagoon for proper functioning requires servicing; vegetation and other weeds are removed period to avoid breeding mosquitoes. This method is best suited for small communities.

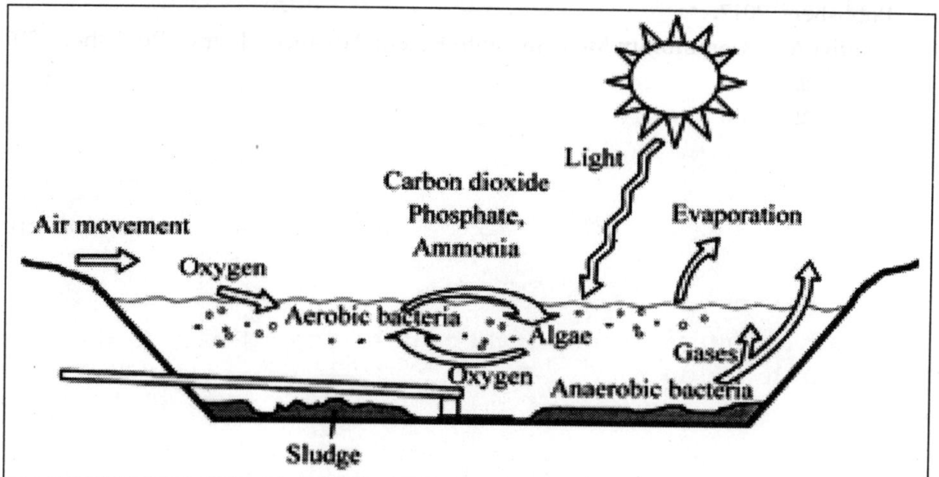

Fig 8.6: Sewage farming

Sewage farming also known as 'Broad irrigation'. It is also old method of sewage treatment, best suited in those areas where porous land is available. Before admitting the sewage into the farm it is subjected to screening and grit removal. Requirement: an acre will suffice the purpose of 300 people.

The land (farming area) is made into ridges and furrows, crops are grown on ridges and the sewage is let into furrows. The selection of crops should be done in such a way that are not eaten raw and which do not come in contact with the sewage like potatoes and fodder grass. Tomatoes, cucumbers, sugar cane, coriander are not to be grown in such farming land.

Advantages: removes 90% of suspended organic matter by the activity of the soil aerobic bacteria.

Disadvantages:

- 'Sewage sickness'; continuous feeding of the land with sewage leads to stinking and soddenness of soil and leads to insufficient aeration of the land.
- Rainy season may not be favourable to operate the farm.

REFERENCES

All you need to know about Recycling [Internet]. [Cited 20 November 2018]. Available from: https://www.recycle-more.co.uk/the-waste-hierarchy.

Gertsakis J, Lewis H. Sustainability and the Waste Management Hierarchy. March 2003. [Cited 15 November 2018]. Available from: http://helenlewisresearch.com.au/wp-content/uploads/2014/05/TZW_-_Sustainability_and_the_Waste_Hierarchy_2003.pdf.

Lal S, Adarsh, Pankaj. Textbook of Community Medicine Preventive and Social Medicine, CBS Publishers and Distributors, 2011.

Park K. Park's Textbook of Preventive and Social Medicine. M/s Banarsidas Bhanot Publishers, 2017.

Suryakantha A H. Community Medicine with Recent Advances. Jaypee Publishers, 2016.

Index

❑❑❑❑❑❑